T0298754

"*Plant-Based Diets for Succulence and Sustainability is the ultimate guide for living a healthy and sustainable lifestyle. Whether you are an educator, a food policy advocate, or looking to improve your own health outcomes, this book has you covered! A wide network of experts cover the many benefits of a plant-based diet for ethical, environmental, and health outcomes. You won't want to miss this comprehensive resource!*"
—Dr. Neal Barnard, Physicians Committee for
Responsible Medicine, USA

"*This is the direction we must go in: creating food systems which promote health and well-being, environmental sustainability, social equity and economic prosperity. It is a huge ask but this book is in the vanguard of showing the change agents of this world (which is all of us) how to turn this enormous challenge into exciting opportunities*".
—Professor Boyd Swinburn, University of
Auckland, New Zealand

"*Beyond paying attention to the strength of the compelling scientific evidence in this book, reading it will reinvigorate your sense of humanity, integrity, and justice. It is abundantly clear that it is both our individual and collective responsibility to choose deliberate actions that are kinder and more sustainable and join with Kevany and her well-assembled team to mobilize and empower people across all sectors of our society to take action*".
—Timaree Hagenburger, Cosumnes
River College, USA

"*This book will ignite imagination to increase health and conscious consumption and reduce preventable suffering and environmental harm. These respected authors shine light on timely findings from disparate, yet interconnected fields, that all point in the direction of plant-based diets for sustainability and sensibility*".
—Dr. Richard Keshen, Cape Breton
University, Canada

"*This book by Kathleen Kevany and the assembled team of authors is exceptionally timely and important. It professionally addresses the major causes of our health, environmental, and food sustainability crises. The whole plant-based foods that make healthy our minds and bodies are the same that make healthy our planet*".
—Dr. T. C. Campbell, Center for Nutrition Studies,
Cornell University, USA

Plant-Based Diets for Succulence and Sustainability

This collection takes an interdisciplinary look at how the transformation towards plant-based diets is becoming more culturally acceptable, economically accessible, technically available, and politically viable. We offer strategies for achieving sustainable food systems without having to forgo succulence, sensuality, and sacredness of food.

Shifting food systems is one of humanity's greatest challenges and opportunities. Adaptable and health-promoting, plant-based diets are explored in this collection which, by their nature, can support nourishing environmental, social, ethical, political, and economic outputs and outcomes. In this book, detailed descriptions are provided of what constitutes a healthy plant-based diet and active lifestyle. Readers are invited to engage with a community of practitioners delving more deeply into strategies for transitioning societies to greater succulence and sustainability. Throughout the first section of the book, environmental challenges and opportunities for reversing climate change are highlighted as our most urgent action. The focus then turns to global food systems and the intersections that are undermining human and animal health. The final section offers preventative approaches and encourages reorienting systems of law, economics, and education to exemplify integrity, coordination, coherence, and compassion.

This book will be of interest to students and academics, as well as policy professionals in all fields engaging with complex issues and systems analyses. It will be of value to those working in health services, policy development, agriculture, economic development, and social change as it provides steps to enhance well-being, pathways to increase jobs in the green economy, and practical ideas to reverse greenhouse gas emissions. It also may be a superb guide for individuals and families looking to become *vibrant eaters and leaders.*

Kathleen May Kevany is Associate Professor, Business and Social Sciences Department, Faculty of Agriculture, and Director of the Rural Research Collaborative at Dalhousie University, Nova Scotia, Canada.

Routledge Studies in Food, Society and the Environment

For further details please visit the series page on the Routledge website:
www.routledge.com/books/series/RSFSE/

Plant-Based Diets for Succulence and Sustainability

Edited by Kathleen May Kevany

Routledge
Taylor & Francis Group
LONDON AND NEW YORK

from Routledge

First published 2020
by Routledge
2 Park Square, Milton Park, Abingdon, Oxon OX14 4RN

and by Routledge
605 Third Avenue, New York, NY 10017

First issued in paperback 2021

Routledge is an imprint of the Taylor & Francis Group, an informa business

British Library Cataloguing-in-Publication Data
A catalogue record for this book is available from the British Library

Library of Congress Cataloging-in-Publication Data
A catalog record for this book has been requested

ISBN 13: 978-0-367-78449-2 (pbk)
ISBN 13: 978-1-138-38540-5 (hbk)

Typeset in Sabon
by Apex CoVantage LLC

This collective effort is dedicated to the renewable energies of sunlight, wind, water, love, and values. To live well on this planet, we are indebted to the life forms that nourish us sustainably and succulently, and we are grateful.

Contents

Contributors

Zeeshan Ali is the Kickstart India programme specialist at the Physicians Committee for Responsible Medicine, a non-profit organization in Washington, DC. He supports work of medical students, physicians, healthcare professionals and researchers at medical schools on the benefits of a plant-based diet for chronic disease prevention. He also writes scientific reviews and articles on non-animal-based research methods and presents at scientific conferences and conventions in the USA and India. He received his doctorate degree from Johann Wolfgang Goethe University, Germany. He held a Marie Curie fellowship from Gabriele D'Annunzio University, Italy, and a postdoctoral fellowship from the University Piemonte Orientale, Italy.

Chinweoke Asagwara is a registered dietitian and certified fitness professional and an award winning athlete, based in Winnipeg, Manitoba, who specializes in women's health and fitness. She promotes healthy eating and active living as a way of life, and empowers her clients with the tools to navigate food choices and physical activity barriers in their daily lives while finding confidence and enjoyment in the process.

Gene Baur is the president of Farm Sanctuary, the first farm animal protection organization. He has published two bestsellers, *Farm Sanctuary: Changing Hearts and Minds About Animals and Food* (Scribner, 2008) and *Living the Farm Sanctuary Life* (Rodale, 2015), which he co-authored with *Forks Over Knives* author Gene Stone. Through his writing and his international speaking, Gene helps change the treatment of animals and our food system. Gene holds a BA in sociology and a master's in agricultural economics from Cornell University. In 2015, Gene was appointed as an adjunct faculty member in the Department of Health, Behavior, and Society at the Johns Hopkins Bloomberg School of Public Health. Gene's work has been covered by the *New York Times*, *Los Angeles Times*, *Chicago Tribune*, and the *Wall Street Journal*.

David A. Cleveland is a research professor in the Environmental Studies Program and the Department of Geography at the University of California,

Santa Barbara. He has done research and project work on sustainable agri-food systems with small-scale farmers and gardeners in Ghana, Mexico, Pakistan, California, and Indian country (Hopi and Zuni). His current research and teaching focuses on food-system localization and diet change to improve health, mitigate anthropogenic climate change and environmental degradation, and promote food and climate justice, including at the University of California, in California, and globally. His latest collaborative book is *Food Gardens for a Changing World. A Resource for Growing Food for Healthy People, Communities, and Ecosystems* (CABI Publishing).

Marcia M. English is an assistant professor, Department of Human Nutrition, StFX University, with expertise in food chemistry, food microbiology, and food product development. Marcia is a board member of Science Atlantic and chair of the Nutrition Committee, as well as a professional member of the Canadian Institute of Food Science and Technology. She heads up the X-Food Research Lab.

Pamela Fergusson is a registered dietitian with a PhD in nutrition and over 15 years of experience. A former lecturer in nutrition at the Liverpool School of Tropical Medicine, UK, and Ryerson University, Canada, Pamela now works in private practice advising patients on a plant-based lifestyle.

Terry Gibbs is a professor of international politics at Cape Breton University. Her fields of expertise include social justice and critical globalization studies. She is the author of several publications, including *Why the Dalai Lama Is a Socialist: Buddhism and the Compassionate Society* (Zed Books, 2017) and co-author with Garry Leech of *The Failure of Global Capitalism: From Cape Breton to Colombia and Beyond* (CBU Press, 2009). Her current research explores the values behind 21st-century global citizenship. She is the co-founder of the Animal Ethics Project and the Sustainability Project and co-coordinator of the ongoing educational series Inspired by Nature.

Roberto Gueli operates Conscious Catering, a whole-food vegetarian catering company and small-scale organic farm. He co-authored *Conscious Cooking*, offers whole-food cooking classes, and is a practising holistic nutritionist with the Canadian School of Natural Nutrition. Roberto and his partner promote "food as medicine" and healthy plant-based meals that are abundant, satisfying, succulent, and sustainable.

Tracey Harris is an assistant professor of sociology at Cape Breton University. She teaches courses in environmental sociology, green criminology, animals and people, and sociology of home. She is the author of *The Tiny House Movement: Challenging Our Consumer Culture* (Lexington Books, 2018) and has recently authored chapters in *Animal Oppression* *and Capitalism: The Oppression of Nonhuman Animals as Sources of Food* (edited by David Nibert, Praeger, 2017) and in *Sociology of Home: Belonging, Community, and Place in the Canadian Context* (edited by Anderson, Moore, and Suski, Canadian Scholars' Press, 2016). She is co-founder of the Animal Ethics Project and the Sustainability Project and co-coordinator of the ongoing educational series Inspired by Nature.

Kathleen May Kevany is an associate professor at Dalhousie University, Faculty of Agriculture, Business and Social Sciences Department. She is known for her work in plant-based, sustainable diets and mindfulness and consumption. She is the director of the Rural Research Collaborative, and member of Canadian Association of Food Studies and Canadian Nutrition Society. Kathleen's research team is investigating the efficacy of plant-based interventions on health, well-being, and ecological footprint. She is the editor of *Plant-Based Diets for Succulence and Sustainability*.

Sara F. L. Kirk is a professor of health promotion and the scientific director of the Healthy Populations Institute at Dalhousie University, Nova Scotia, Canada. She also holds a cross-appointment with Community Health and Epidemiology, an honorary senior scientist position with the Beatrice Hunter Cancer Research Institute, and adjunct faculty status in the Applied Human Nutrition Department at Mount Saint Vincent University. Her programme of research explores the creation of supportive environments for chronic disease prevention. Her research uses a "socio-ecological" approach that considers how individual behaviours are influenced by other broader factors, such as income, education, and societal norms.

Linnea Laestadius is an associate professor of public health policy at the Joseph J. Zilber School of Public Health at the University of Wisconsin–Milwaukee, and holds a PhD and MPP. Her research focuses on the intersections of public health, behaviour, and novel technologies. She has a particular interest in the ethics surrounding novel animal meat alternatives.

Sally Lipsky is a plant-based nutrition author, educator, speaker, and founder of PlantBasedEatingHub.com. She authored *Beyond Cancer: The Powerful Effect of Plant-Based Eating* (Wellness Ink, 2018). She has a PhD and is professor emerita, developmental studies, College of Education and Educational Technology, Indiana University of Pennsylvania, USA and certified in plant-based nutrition from the T. Colin Campbell Center for Nutrition Studies.

Mary McKenna is a professor with University of New Brunswick's Faculty of Kinesiology and previously worked as a health scientist at the Centers for Disease Control and Prevention in Atlanta, Georgia. Mary's specialties are in school nutrition policy and healthy eating in schools.

Tushar Mehta has a B.Arts Sc. from McMaster University, and he obtained his MD from the University of Toronto in family medicine. Tushar has practised addictions medicine and now works as an emergency physician and volunteers in international health in rural India, and more recently in Haiti. Dr. Mehta's strong interest in the medical and nutritional evidence for a plant-based diet and prevention of disease has prompted him to become a frequent presenter at information educational events.

Sarah Pittoello is a counselling therapist, educator, and organic farmer. Sarah has been a vendor at the Wolfville Farmers Market, farmer-in-residence at the Just Us! Centre for Small Farms, and a founding member of the Maritime Small Farm Co-op. She teaches with Acadia University's Community Development Department on Sustainable Food Systems. Sarah was also the assistant to the editor for the book *Plant-Based Diets for Succulence and Sustainability*.

Suchitra Roy is a doctoral student at the Faculty of Interdisciplinary Studies at the University of New Brunswick and trained as a physician in her home country of Bangladesh. Her research focuses on healthy food programmes and positive school food environments in New Brunswick schools.

Chaiti Seth is an environmental educator, organic farmer, and community developer. She has a Master's in Community Development, and her research focuses on factors and processes to facilitate institutional food systems change towards healthy, sustainable, and just food.

Av Singh is an organic and small-scale farming advisor and agronomist. Av is a faculty member at Earth University (Navdanya) and continues to be active in Slow Food Canada, Food Secure Canada, Canadian Organic Growers, and the National Farmers Union.

Gabriela Steier is founder of Food Law International (FLI) and editor of the textbooks *International Food Law* and *Policy and International Farm Animal, Wildlife & Food Safety Law* (both Springer, 2017). She also authored *Advancing Food Integrity: GMO Regulation, Agroecology, and Urban Agriculture* and co-edited *Environmental Resilience and Food Law: Agrobiodiversity and Agroecology* (Taylor and Francis, forthcoming 2019). Gabriela is a US attorney and focuses on food safety, food law and policy, animal welfare, food integrity, agroecology, and genetically engineered food, as well as issues involving sustainable agriculture. She teaches various aspects of food regulation as a Part-Time Lecturer at Northeastern University in Boston. Since 2015, Gabriela has taught at the Duquesne University School of Law as an adjunct professor teaching *Food Law and Policy* and *Climate Change Law*. Steier is also a visiting professor at the University of Perugia, Italy. She holds a BA from Tufts University, a JD from Duquesne University, an LL.M. in food and agriculture law from the Vermont Law School, and a doctorate in comparative law from the University of Cologne in Germany.

Haley Swartz is a research communications specialist at Feeding America. In 2018, she was the Linda Golodner Food and Nutrition Policy Fellow at the National Consumers League. Previously, she was a research programme coordinator for the Global Food Ethics and Policy Program at the Johns Hopkins Berman Institute for Bioethics. She has a passion for food security, sustainable diets, and food ethics. She holds a master's in public policy and a bachelor's of arts, both from the University of Virginia.

Jessica Wall works as a manager of the Tri-Cultural Project within the Co-operative Enterprise Council of New Brunswick. Jessica is a master's of applied health services candidate. She is an active researcher and graduate student, as well as an advocate of active living. She holds a bachelor of community development in Food Hub Management from the University of Vermont.

1 Opportunities and challenges with plant-rich strategies

Kathleen May Kevany

Introduction

What collection of strategies could prompt countries like Canada and the US to not only avert further global warming crises but also reduce the pandemic of growing ill health and address the inequitable distribution of food while also redressing the harm imposed on animals, water, forests, land use, and ecosystems? Researchers from *Project Drawdown* found that reducing food waste and increasing healthy, plant-rich diets are two of the world's most impactful solutions to retain soil carbon, maintain forest integrity, draw down emissions, and reverse climate change (Hawken, 2017). Plant-based diets are also found to reverse the rampant explosion of lifestyle diseases and thus are seen as a prudent approach to curtail escalating health-care costs (Ornish et al., 2008). This collective effort is the first such collection by researchers and practitioners from diverse backgrounds investigating health and well-being, environment, equity, economics, and ethics of plant-based strategies. This book seeks to bridge research and application. Based on cutting-edge research, we argue for consciously and cooperatively feeding a growing world through plant foods, sustainable agriculture, food security, and sovereignty. These efforts will feed into reorienting and recalibrating food systems for succulence, sustainability, prosperity, and equity.

Navigating food systems

What we eat impacts all aspects of human life. Nothing more fully and powerfully influences the daily lives of peoples everywhere than our food, food choices, and food systems, including food environments (Kevany, 2018). Shifting away from unsustainable diets does not mean the end to taste, pleasure, and delight in food.

Sustainability may be viewed as the approach that ensures human needs can be met while also protecting human, animal, and environmental well-being. Sustainability calls for resources not to be used if they cannot be replaced or if their use harms the environment. The term succulent means things that are full of juice, rich in desirable qualities, and afford mental nourishment (*Collins English Dictionary*, 2014). Through highlighting the delights to be harvested through diets that are more plant-rich, this work blends the qualities and goals of succulence, strength, and sustainability. We work to reorient consumers and producers *to focus less on what is given up* and *more on what is gained*. The state of pressing issues facing humanity require new levels of thinking and ways of working together.

Forces driving shifts in food systems

Politics, health, and diet

Correlations between the availability of unhealthy foods, household habits and individual diets, disease, obesity, and food environments are well established (Alvaro et al., 2010; Morland, Wing, Diez Roux, & Poole, 2002). Emphasizing individual dietary habits has proven insufficient. Even with sound science, governments have been criticized for not providing adequate warnings against preventable illnesses and devising policies to address the obesity epidemic (Alvaro et al., 2010; Dodge & Dion, 2011). Meanwhile, more than 60% of Canada's population, like many other nations, is overweight or obese (World Health Organization, 2016). At the same time, the prevalence of child and youth obesity and type 2 diabetes is climbing (Twells, Gregory, Reddigan, & Midodzi, 2014). The available evidence shows that two-thirds of deaths from chronic diseases are associated with modifiable behaviours such as dietary intake and levels of physical activity (Grant, 2012). Such lifestyle diseases and their associated health-care costs are consuming more than 50% of provincial budgets across Canada and are predicted to escalate further (Dodge & Dion, 2011) along with emotional and mental costs for individuals and society.

Strategic efforts are needed to improve the health of citizens through systems changes, including supporting the determinants of health and disease prevention and policy provisions, along with fostering personal well-being and food literacy. Such programmes would educate on the benefits of personal management of wellness, the role of diet and exercise in health, and other programmes to assist in controlling major risk factors (i.e. hypertension, high cholesterol, stroke, smoking cessation, effects of alcohol and drugs). Investing in adequate income for citizens can contribute to reducing the prevalence of largely preventable diseases (Yasin & Helms, 2010). While reforming health care will not be easy, it's not impossible (Yasin & Helms, 2010), and it is not sustainable to leave unchecked the escalating costs from rising illness care (Dodge & Dion, 2011).

Climate change and diet

Canada, like other jurisdictions, is contending with seemingly intractable health, environmental, and equity challenges. Industrial systems of food production and consumption are generating adverse impacts on climate change, water stress, energy pressures, transition to poor nutrition, and societal and environmental issues (Mason & Lang, 2017). While the degree of impact on climate change from animal agriculture varies depending on what and how factors are assessed, based on current North American dietary patterns, food-related greenhouse gas emissions (GHGE) could increase by 51% from 2005/2007 to 2050 (Springmann, Godfray, Rayner, & Scarborough, 2016). The inefficiencies and inequities generated by meat and dairy production are well documented (Cleveland, 2013; Weis, 2015).

The scientific community is largely in agreement around climate change being predominantly human driven and the major threat facing humanity. Plant-rich diets are one of the world's most impactful solutions towards drawing down GHGE through reduced emissions and protecting forests and land use (Hawken, 2017). Emissions could be reduced by as much as 70% through adopting a plant-based diet compared to a standard American diet rich in meat (Poore & Nemecek, 2018). And the reduction in health-care procedures would also make a large contribution to reducing emissions (Hallström, Gee, Scarborough, & Cleveland, 2017).

Equity and ethics

The need to efficiently and ethically feed a growing world population is an additional challenge. Questions of equity and ethics also arise around environmental racism, where disadvantaged communities bear the brunt of the pollution and other adverse effects from industrial agriculture, the confinement and slaughter of animals, and the production and distribution of processed foods that undermine health (Baur & Stone, 2015; Joy, 2011; Weis, 2007). More people could be fed with seven to ten times more food available when not used to feed animals for meat production (Djekic, 2015). We pay too little for animal-based and processed foods, owing to their production benefitting from subsidized ingredients and many of their costs being externalized. It seems prudent to question the justifications behind and implications of feeding global livestock about half of global grain production (Godfray et al., 2010).

Food movements are sparking more citizen-consumers to become conscious and critical of their food choices and food systems and to express concern for their health, illness costs, animal and worker welfare, and the environment (Deckers, 2013; Scrinis, 2007). Food movements are creating change by challenging "the ways we think and talk about food" (Gottlieb, 2001, p. 271), and how we understand, respect, and interact with food (Scrinis, 2007; Tuttle, 2016). More are refusing to participate in the domination of animals, exploitation of the planet, and the dulling of awareness that these require (Gibbs & Leech, 2009).

4   *Kathleen May Kevany*

Industrial agriculture

Food production and consumption practices changed with the advent of industrial agriculture and government subsidies for the "industrial grain-oilseed-livestock complex" (Weis, 2015, p. 298). Consequently, agri-food corporations exercise extensive control over farmers through their control of agricultural inputs and their terms for purchasing farm products (Levkoe, 2011). "In jurisdictions like Canada, government departments take up the role, directly or indirectly, to ensuring that businesses operate 'freely' within the overall government bureaucracy" (Alvaro et al., 2010, p. 96). And in this economic climate, "North Americans pay disproportionally little for their food" (Turner, 2011, p. 37), albeit highly processed, unhealthy food. Such "free-market" orthodoxy includes subsidies to industrial agriculture along with the "privatisation of public resources, the minimisation of labour costs . . . the dismantling of public programmes and the elimination of regulations seen as unfriendly to business" (Levkoe, 2011, p. 690). This can breed working conditions in food processing with low wages, hazardous conditions, and psychological and emotional strain (Campbell, 2015; Kevany, Baur, & Wang, 2018).

It seems rather ironic, or perhaps contradictory, that citizen-consumers concern themselves more with the price of food while they may not hesitate to spend extra money for name-brand products that they wear (Turner, 2011; Walsh, 2009). A 2009 *Time* magazine cover story entitled "The Real Cost of Cheap Food" highlighted the fact that subsidies in food systems make it easy and inexpensive to eat badly (Walsh, 2009). As Gurian-Sherman describes, "The way we farm now is destructive of the soil, the environment and us" (as cited in Walsh, 2009, p. 32).

Countering scientific reductionism

The increasing accessibility of research findings, exposure to social media (i.e. the growing body of food-related documentaries), and greater citizen-consumer consciousness are catalyzing many leaders across all sectors to push for food systems that are less opaque and more transparent. Dr. T. Colin Campbell, widely known as the father of the movement towards plant-based nutrition, points to many signs of inadequate progress, including scientific reductionism as a dysfunctional approach to interconnected problems. He argues for holistic approaches and greater understanding of the evidence behind whole-food, plant-based diets that are found to prevent and reverse disease in ways unmatched by pills and procedures (Campbell & Jacobson, 2013). For decades, many researchers have been pointing to the benefits of plant-based diets. For example, physicians engaged in practising "responsible medicine" studied how adopting a low-fat, plant-based diet, even without prescribing limits on portion size or calories, helped to reduce weight and enhance overall well-being (Barnard, Scialli, Turner-McGrievy,

Lanou, & Glass, 2005). Yet this knowledge is not widely known, and the power of preventative health is overshadowed by the domination and influence of food and pharmaceutical corporations. The practices of reductionism and political short-sightedness undermine the social progress that these times demand. To counter reductionism would involve working across sectors and incorporating insights from disparate fields, such as health, environment, ethics, law, and economics.

Sustainable diets

Plant-based and sustainable diets are largely plant-derived foods that afford humans full nourishment while making a more equitable and efficient use of global resources, and without intentionally harming animals, and when produced with restorative methods, the impact of ecosystems can be minimized. To foster conditions for sustainable diets requires consideration of food policy, governance, production, processing, distribution, consumption, and implications for agriculture, health, environment, culture, society, politics, and economics. In their 2017 book, *Sustainable Diets: How Ecological Nutrition Can Transform Consumption and the Food System*, authors Mason and Lang deliver comprehensive evidence of the need to implement sustainable diets:

> The necessity for the transition to sustainable diets is unlikely to fade . . . the issue of sustainable diets will demand attention. We are heartened that so many scientists, academics, analysts and food campaigners now know this, although politicians lag somewhat. That the scale of the task is immense must not deter us, nor deflect our resolve to help societies to face what needs to be faced.
>
> (Mason & Lang, 2017, p. ix)

The many components that constitute sustainable diets have been well articulated elsewhere (Burlingame & Dernini, 2012; Johnston, Fanzo, & Cogill, 2014; Lang, 2014; Mason & Lang, 2017; Riley & Buttris, 2011).

Plant-based menus are one solution to our interconnected health and environmental and equity issues, as they can simultaneously lighten the load on our bodies, our wallets, and the planet. Plant-based foods are typically less expensive than even the cheapest meats and seafood. A plant-focus is also an opportunity to align menus with seasons and avoid the baggage of animal welfare concerns. Plant foods provide a much higher nutritional return for land, water, and energy used; for example, land produces two to ten times as much protein when planted in cereals than when it is devoted to beef production (Horrigan, Lawrence, & Walker, 2002). Whole-food plant diets can be extremely tasty and nutritious with affordable ingredients that can be easily sourced and do not have to be exotic ingredients, although plant-based foods can be made very fancy.

Thematic chapters

This collection of chapters examines sustainable, plant-based diets and plant-rich living from perspectives in social and health services, agriculture, environment, law, economics, community organizations, policy development, and food movements. We provide theoretical and practical approaches to improve health and well-being, reduce harm, and prevent illness. This work seeks to inspire change by illuminating unexamined practices and assumptions that previously were impenetrable (Meyer & Land, 2005), and by highlighting integral pathways to sustainability and succulence.

The first section of the book illuminates issues impacting the environment through food. Readers may come to realize that this is humanity's biggest challenge and greatest opportunity. In Chapter 2, Marcia M. English explores true cost accounting of food innovation and consumer demand in food systems. Industrial food systems, which include heavy usage of fossil fuel and natural resources to produce meat protein, are unsustainable, inefficient, and extremely wasteful. English considers innovative approaches to develop plant-protein products that are preferred by consumers and not positioned as meat analogues will be a major shift in the food industry.

In Chapter 3, David A. Cleveland answers questions about the potential of plant-based diets (PBDs) and their critical role in avoiding catastrophic climate change. Cleveland elucidates why PBDs could be successful in mitigating climate change and reducing GHGE enough to keep global warming within sustainable limits. Cleveland questions our food choices and food policies and provides examples of success in moving towards more PBDs. Meat-centric diets have proven inefficient and unethical, as they lead to land-use change, with animal agriculture driving extensive biodiversity loss.

In Chapter 4, "Beyond Halos and Technofixes", Haley Swartz and Linnea Laestadius consider meat alternatives and their potential for meaningful food systems change. They discuss the merits and limitations of the influx of new products, such as high-tech meat alternatives that "bleed" and cultured meat grown from animal cells. Cultural shifts underline consumer demand for healthier foods with a smaller footprint, and prudent businesses are seizing opportunities growing in new market segments. The authors offer leading-edge analysis of the health halo effect of plant-based meat alternatives and cultured meat products. They provide readers with environmental impacts of new plant foods as helpful decision-making information for environmentally conscious producers and consumers.

The second section of the book delves into concern for humans, health, and well-being.

Sara F. L. Kirk takes us back to the future, illuminating ways that food production and procurement can be modified to better support health and well-being across the life course and in the context of the health-disrupting environment in which we live. She examines what a health-promoting food system could look like through investigating the overwhelming evidence that our modern food environment, with its reliance on heavily processed convenience foods, is contributing to a range of chronic diseases. Strategies to support the health of populations are shared, along with ways to critically reflect on the factors influencing individual behaviour and beliefs around food intake and approaches to reorienting our broader food systems.

In Chapter 6, one doctor of nutrition and two practising physicians offer their professional advice based on their scouring of the literature for the best recommendations for food consumption. Our food as medicine chapter authors, Tushar Mehta, Pamela Ferguson, and Zeeshan Ali, review the evidence base for whole plant foods in treating, reversing, and preventing chronic diseases and discuss therapeutic strategies used in clinical practices. They advocate for practitioners and patients to take back control of our health.

Public policies and personal practices for succulence and sustainability are investigated by Kathleen Kevany and Chinwe Asagwara in Chapter 7, which emphasizes some lessons learned from plant-rich lifestyles through healthy eating and active living. It recommends policies and practices to foster greater succulence, strength, and sustainability through needed changes to food environments and food practices.

Chapters 8 and 9 offer insights into animal rights and welfare. Practical approaches for fostering compassion and mindfulness in human and animal relations are provided by Gene Baur, the founder of the world's first farm sanctuary, in Chapter 8. This chapter analyzes the ethical, moral, and spiritual perspectives of food production and consumption. It provides perspectives on how citizen-consumers may avoid causing unnecessary harm through compassionate food choices. Baur and Kevany explain how kindness to animals is also good for people. We learn how we have normalized farm animals and animal products as food. Succulent plant-rich living, based on values of compassion and shared responsibility, and practices like mindfulness and conscious consumption are presented as an appealing lifestyle.

Terry Gibbs and Tracey Harris offer a vision for restructuring domination through building compassionate societies and put forward a vegan challenge. In Chapter 9, they examine the animal-industrial complex and ways to reduce captivity, oppression, and domination of non-human animals, in theory and practice. We see the catastrophic consequences of suspending compassion for other animals and the planet. Through examining the structural domination and violence of capitalist production and consumption systems, more intentional and self-reflective citizenship could extend beyond the ethics and rights of human animals to include non-human animals and the natural world.

We then engage with Gabriela Steier's view of international food trade stakes in restoring the food system. Through an international and comparative law perspective, Chapter 10 explores the international legal framework that inhibits progressive reform of the food system. An outline of international treaties, including those administered by such bodies as the

World Trade Organization and the USA – Food and Drug Administration (FDA), are presented. Steier applies these international considerations of food regulation to food security, sustainability, and succulence contexts and reveals where current laws overlook opportunities for a restoration of food integrity.

A team of practitioners and researchers offers a dynamic chapter with perspectives on how plant-based food and farming are real solutions to climate chaos and healthy solutions for communities and local economies through integrity economics. In Chapter 11, Chaiti Seth, Sarah Pittoello, Roberto Gueli, and Av Singh discuss good local food itself as diverse, textured, and multi-flavoured. They offer poignant prose on how integrity and collaboration along with strong and caring relationships have become common threads in sustainable local and regional food production and consumption practices. They challenge the acceptance of industrialized agriculture, as it primarily feeds animals, cars, and the processed food industry. Through a neoliberal, free-market economy and radical capitalism gone wild, we have seen significant failures for the common good. In this chapter, a more nuanced and practical approach is taken to eating what is lighter for our bodies, minds, souls, and the planet. This chapter illuminates businesses, including community gardens, catering companies, small farms and cooperatives, locally owned grocery stores, and institutional food services that demonstrate how to build succulent, strong, sustainable food systems.

In Chapter 12, Sally Lipsky and Kathleen Kevany, in consultation with Nelson Campbell, examine the power of food movements for fuelling justice, health, and well-being. This chapter explores the psychological shifts and social change strategies that are contributing to a broader adoption of sustainable diets. This chapter shines light on the story behind thousands of Americans changing their food and health habits through the success of initiatives like PlantPure Nation and Healing America Together. The analysis includes discussions around the roles of various actors – health care, family, governments, and religious and social communities – in realizing the potential of succulent sustainability.

Succulent sustainability goes to school with Mary McKenna, Jessica Wall, and Suchita Roy. In Chapter 13 the authors trace the growing involvement of schools in plant-based initiatives connected to the food system, including growing and preparing food and composting food waste. Readers become informed about the skills and experience students gain that can be shared with their families. Inspiring examples from school-based learning show how engaging in food production and healthy eating habits by students can encourage positive social interactions and contribute to a vibrant school community. These educational programmes and policies are proving to enhance environmental responsibility, foster the enjoyment of plant-based eating, improve student learning and health, and strengthen school communities.

In the closing chapter, takeaway messages on succulent and sustainable lifestyles fuelled by plants are distilled. Kevany shares opportunities for integral analyses and collaborative strategies. Tools and techniques are provided to promote the adoption and enjoyment of plant-rich living. Readers are encouraged to engage in further learning and leading as *Vibrant Eaters & Leaders*.

Conclusion

With the cumulative damaging effects of unsustainable food production and consumption, turning a blind eye can no longer be tolerated. Our interconnected imbalances – aptly named wicked problems – will continue to evolve, yet such daunting issues pressure us to adapt quicker than earlier eras of human development. Now we must grapple with what is before us and strategize around actions that nurture life. Plant-based policies and lifestyles have become critical approaches to redress the vast detachment between agricultural policy, public health, and environmental sustainability. As this book demonstrates, substantive systems change and multi-faceted, cross-sectoral, and collaborative approaches are necessary to illuminate and update previously unquestioned assumptions. Together, we seek to guard against the malaise of specialism and reductionism, and bring to bear systems of systems thinking, a more integral view (Watkins & Wilber, 2015). We intend to expand beyond the reductionist approach towards a more holistic, integrated pattern of analyses and problem solving (Campbell & Jacobson, 2013). With trillions of dollars being required to reverse global warming and to care for largely lifestyle diseases, governments are seeking palatable strategies to reduce their political and economic burdens. What is needed now for governments to set a direction and take action on plant-based food systems? What could be more relevant than one of the greatest actions to reverse global warming while also helping to more effectively, efficiently, and ethically feed the world?

References

Alvaro, C., Jackson, L. A., Kirk, S., McHugh, T. L., Hughes, J., Chircop, A., . . . Lyons, R. F. (2010). Moving Canadian governmental policies beyond a focus on individual lifestyle: Some insights from complexity and critical theories. *Health Promotion International*, 26(1), 91–99.
Barnard, N. D., Scialli, A. R., Turner-McGrievy, G., Lanou, A. J., & Glass, J. (2005). The effects of a low-fat, plant-based dietary intervention on body weight, metabolism, and insulin sensitivity. *The American Journal of Medicine*, 118(9), 991–997.
Baur, G., & Stone, G. (2015). *Living the Farm Sanctuary life: The ultimate guide to eating mindfully, living longer, and feeling better every day*. New York, NY: Rodale Press.
Burlingame, B., & Dernini, S. (Eds.). (2012). *Sustainable diets and biodiversity: Directions and solutions for policy, research and action*. International Scientific Symposium, Biodiversity and Sustainable Diets United Against Hunger, Rome, Italy.

Campbell, N. (2015). *PlantPure nation* [Documentary film]. Mebane, NC: Plant-Pure, Inc.

Campbell, T. C., & Jacobson, H. (2013). *Whole: Rethinking the science of nutrition.* Dallas, TX: BenBella Books.

Cleveland, D. A. (2013). *Balancing on a planet: The future of food and agriculture* (Vol. 46). Berkeley, CA: University of California Press.

Collins English Dictionary (12th ed.). (2014). Glasgow, Scotland: HarperCollins.

Deckers, J. (2013). Obesity, public health, and the consumption of animal products. *Journal of Bioethical Inquiry, 10*(1), 29–38.

Djekic, I. (2015). Environmental impact of meat industry – Current status and future perspectives. *Procedia Food Science, 5*, 61–64.

Dodge, D., & Dion, R. (2011). *Chronic health care spending disease: A macro diagnosis and prognosis.* Ottawa, Canada: C.D. Howe Institute.

Gibbs, T., & Leech, G. M. (2009). *The failure of global capitalism: From Cape Breton to Colombia and beyond.* Halifax, Canada: Nimbus Publishing (CN).

Godfray, H. C. J., Beddington, J. R., Crute, I. R., Haddad, L., Lawrence, D., Muir, J. F., . . . Toulmin, C. (2010). Food security: The challenge of feeding 9 billion people. *Science, 327*(5967), 812–818. doi:10.1126/science.1185383

Gottlieb, R. (2001). *Environmentalism unbound: exploring new pathways for change.* Cambridge, MA: MIT Press.

Grant, J. D. (2012, September 2012). Food for thought . . . and health: Making a case for plant-based nutrition. *Canadian Family Physician, 58*(9), 917–919.

Hallström, E., Gee, Q., Scarborough, P., & Cleveland, D. A. (2017). A healthier US diet could reduce greenhouse gas emissions from both the food and health care systems. *Climatic Change, 142*(1–2), 199–212. doi:10.1007/s10584-017-1912-5

Hawken, P. (Ed.). (2017). *Drawdown: The most comprehensive plan ever proposed to reverse global warming.* New York, NY: Penguin Books. Retrieved from www.drawdown.org/solutions/food/plant-rich-diet

Horrigan, L., Lawrence, R. S., & Walker, P. (2002). How sustainable agriculture can address the environmental and human health harms of industrial agriculture. *Environmental Health Perspectives, 110*(5), 445–456.

Johnston, J. L., Fanzo, J. C., & Cogill, B. (2014). Understanding sustainable diets: A descriptive analysis of the determinants and processes that influence diets and their impact on health, food security, and environmental sustainability. *Advances in Nutrition, 5*(4), 418–429.

Joy, M. (2011). *Why we love dogs, eat pigs, and wear cows: An introduction to carnism.* San Francisco, CA: Conari Press.

Kevany, K. (2018, August 26). Eating as a political, spiritual, social act. *The Conversation.* Retrieved from https://theconversation.com/

Kevany, K. M., Baur, G., & Wang, G. C. (2018). Shifting food systems: Increasing well-being through plant-based approaches. *Explore: Journal of Science and Healing, 15*(2). Retrieved from www.explorejournal.com/article/S1550-8307(17)30397-X/fulltext

Lang, T. (2014). Sustainable diets: Hairshirts or a better food future? *Development, 57*(2), 240–256.

Levkoe, C. (2011). Towards a transformative food politics. *Local Environment, 16*(7), 687–705. doi:10.1080/13549839.2011.592182

Mason, P., & Lang, T. (2017). *Sustainable diets: How ecological nutrition can transform consumption and the food system.* Oxfordshire, UK: Taylor & Francis.

Meyer, J. H., & Land, R. (2005). Threshold concepts and troublesome knowledge (2): Epistemological considerations and a conceptual framework for teaching and learning. *Higher Education, 49*(3), 373–388.

Morland, K., Wing, S., Roux, A. D., & Poole, C. (2002). Neighborhood characteristics associated with the location of food stores and food service places. *American Journal of Preventive Medicine, 22*(1), 23–29.

Ornish, D., Magbanua, M. J. M., Weidner, G., Weinberg, V., Kemp, C., Green, C., . . . Haqq, C. M. (2008). Changes in prostate gene expression in men undergoing an intensive nutrition and lifestyle intervention. *Proceedings of the National Academy of Sciences, 105*(24), 8369–8374.

Poore, J., & Nemecek, T. (2018). Reducing food's environmental impacts through producers and consumers. *Science, 360*(6392), 987–992.

Riley, H., & Buttriss, J. L. (2011). A UK public health perspective: What is a healthy sustainable diet? *Nutrition Bulletin, 36*(4), 426–431.

Scrinis, G. (2007). From techno-corporate food to alternative agri-food movements. *Local-Global: Identity, Security, Community, 4,* 112–140.

Springmann, M., Godfray, H. C. J., Rayner, M., & Scarborough, P. (2016). Analysis and valuation of the health and climate change cobenefits of dietary change. *Proceedings of the National Academy of Sciences, 113*(15), 4146–4151.

Turner, C. (2011, October). The farms are not all right. *The Walrus*, pp. 34–44.

Tuttle, W. (2016). *World peace diet: Eating for spiritual health and social harmony.* New York, NY: Lantern Books.

Twells, L. K., Gregory, D. M., Reddigan, J., & Midodzi, W. K. (2014). Current and predicted prevalence of obesity in Canada: A trend analysis. *CMAJ Open, 2*(1), e18.

Walsh, B. (2009). The real cost of cheap food. *Time Magazine, 174*(8), 30–37.

Watkins, A., & Wilber, K. (2015). *Wicked & wise: How to solve the world's toughest problems.* Croydon, UK: Urbane Publications.

Weis, A. J. (2007). *The global food economy: The battle for the future of farming.* London, UK: Zed Books.

Weis, A. J. (2015). Meatification and the madness of the doubling narrative. *Canadian Food Studies/La Revue canadienne des études sur l'alimentation, 2*(2), 296–303.

World Health Organization (WHO). (2016). *Global report on diabetes.* Retrieved from http://apps.who.int/iris/bitstream/10665/204871/1/9789241565257_eng.pdf

Yasin, J., & Helms, M. M. (2010). A comparison of health-related expenditures: A multi-country comparison. *Academy of Health Care Management Journal, 6*(2), 1–19.

Part I

Stewarding our environment

2 Industrialized food systems

A look at food production, full-cost accounting, and consumer demand for protein in diets

Marcia M. English

Introduction

Food and agriculture are becoming forerunners in helping to shape global policies that impact on food security, human health, and climate change. In addition, a growing world population and increased urbanization have increased demand for more varied foods, which require additional supplies of natural resources. These changes have fostered the development of a modern food production system with output flows disconnected from input streams. Thus, in many instances, our modern food system is unsustainable and inefficient, with food waste accounting for one-third of all food produced. Increased awareness about the environmental, nutritional, and social impact of food has resulted in greater demands for transparency from the agri-food industry. A circular economy focused on efficiency and optimizing available resources is needed to feed the present and future generations in a sustainable manner. Illuminating hidden costs associated with commercial food production helps our understanding of the true costs of food, as often these are not readily reflected in price tags. In this chapter, we use a full-cost accounting model to provide a critical assessment of industrialized food production systems and estimate their impact on several agri-environmental indicators. In the examples provided, we place emphasis on the Canadian agri-food system. The challenges and opportunities of emerging prospects within the food system to reorient towards high-value foods and their hidden costs are also addressed.

The modern food system

The industrial model with perceived strengths and weaknesses

The transition from traditional agricultural practices to an industrialized global agri-food system has created a shift away from a food system which was defined by its emphasis on the responsible management of natural resources and diversity of ownership and cropping systems (Rosset, 2000). This system had few detrimental impacts on the environment (Sabaté,

Harwatt, & Soret, 2016). On the other hand, today's industrialized global agri-food system must confront challenges related to long-distance transportation of food, storage, and waste, as well as current agricultural practices that threaten biodiversity and increase resource degradation (Ingram & Porter, 2015).

Although some question the benefits of industrialized agriculture, its impact on the evolution of small farm agriculture cannot be ignored. Pre-industrialized agriculture consisted of simple farming based on animal-driven tools, circular exchanges of metabolic energy and labour-power, and self-supplied seeds and livestock progeny (Qualman, 2019). However, this system transitioned to high-powered machinery equipped for the large-scale production of food, with the use of synthetic and chemical fertilizers, and a linear seed-supply system characterized by intellectual property restrictions (Qualman, 2019; Sabaté, Sranacharoenpong, Harwatt, Wien, & Soret, 2015). This, in turn, led to several key changes in traditional agriculture, including less dependence on manual labour, greater variety and availability of food, and decreased time between harvesting and when the food was available for purchase (Harwatt & Soret, 2016). Improved production techniques increased yield and provided opportunities for food producers to explore innovative changes in food processing, preservation, and packaging in order to increase the shelf life and economic value of food. In addition, the use of chemical fertilizers, pesticides, and herbicides also changed the way in which production and pest control were carried out on farms (Goddard, Weersink, & Chen, 1993). Qualman (2019) describes these transitions in industrialized agriculture as outcomes of the "linearization" of agriculture, a process which disrupts circular flows between plants (or animals), humans, and the environment. Disrupted cycles of nutrients moving from soils to plants to humans or animals, and back to soils and plants again, and the labour-energy loops that connected people and animals to fields serve as key examples (Qualman, 2019).

Demographic shifts

In parallel with the rapid changes occurring on traditional farms, the agri-food system also had to adapt to meet several global changes, including, a growing world population, increasing urbanization (Hazell, 2018), and changing consumer demographics, taste profiles, and preferences (Goddard et al., 1993). Satterthwaite, Mcgranahan, and Tacoli (2010) defined urbanization as "the share of a nation's population living in urban areas" (p. 2819). Furthermore, these authors also purported that better economic opportunities are one of the key drivers of urbanization. A similar trend has been observed in Canada, where the number of Canadians living in rural areas has steadily declined since the 1940s (Figure 2.1). This migration trend has been linked to economic cycles and the activity in various economic sectors (Statistics Canada, 2018).

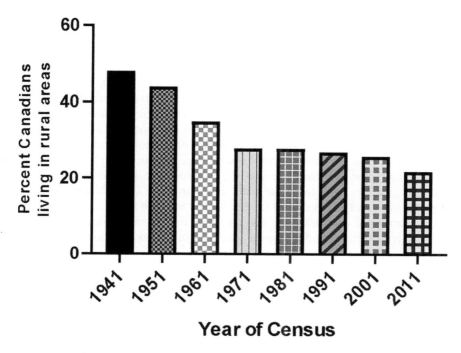

Figure 2.1 The overall decline in the proportion of Canadians living in rural areas of Canada

Source: Statistics Canada. (2015). *Proportion of Canadians living in rural areas.* Retrieved from https://www12.statcan.gc.ca/census-recensement/2011/as-sa/98-310-x/2011003/fig/fig3_2-1-eng.cfm

There can be little doubt that industrialization has not only affected the agri-food production system but also affected decision making at the farmer level. Hendrickson and James (2005) discussed three main changes in traditional agriculture: (1) standardization of crops and food products, (2) mass production, and (3) the concentration of commodity markets, and all three have direct bearing on farming behaviour and the structure of the agri-food system.

Standardization, as described by Wan, Zhang, Jiang, and Ji (2016), was implemented to increase the efficiency of the agri-food system by narrowing the range of tasks and roles involved in planting, processing, and managing crop production. However, what has happened is quite different from these expectations. For example, standardization with the use of electricity has facilitated the mass production of consumer food products in assembly lines and resulted in the production of large quantities of inexpensive foods with long shelf-lives which can be produced, stored, and transported with relative ease (Le, 2018). These foods are often rich in refined sugars and fats and low in fibre and micronutrients (Tilman & Clark, 2014).

On the other hand, concentration of commodity markets occurs when a small number of companies acquire a large market share of the industry (Wan, Zhang, Jiang, & Ji, 2016). The driving forces behind the concentration of commodity markets include (1) the growing dominance of large food retailers (such as the Canadian retailers Loblaws and Sobeys) in distribution channels, which impacts what happens in the agricultural marketplace, and by extension what happens to the diversity of the crops that make up those farms (Hendrickson & James, 2005), and (2) the liberalization of markets and the increasing stringent demands for food quality and safety (Gálvez-Nogales, 2010). Concentration in commodity markets and the formation of food chain clusters in the agri-food sector results in more economic power for a few companies that often are interconnected by activities involved in bringing agricultural products from the farm to the marketplace (Gálvez-Nogales, 2010). Hendrickson and James (2005) further argue that with fewer companies controlling more of the industry's market, including farmers' input (seeds and chemicals) and their products (crops and livestock), this situation leaves farmers with fewer options when faced with severe economic pressures, which, in turn, may lead to unethical decisions regarding land, seed, and labour use.

In addition to the farmers' ethical dilemma, there is also an associated risk of decreased net profit when surplus food supplies are available (Moschini, 2001). When analyzing the effects of globalization on the agri-food system, Anderson (2010) noted that fluctuations in crude oil prices can cause variation in food prices which threaten the success of small farms. This is because food crops are often bulky commodities, and given that global food supply chains have lengthened dramatically (as the physical distance from farm to plate has increased), this makes it costly to transport food across long distances, especially if it is perishable (Food and Agriculture Organization of the United Nations [FAO], 2017). Furthermore, this scenario can lead to an imbalance in the supply and demand of agricultural products, and lead to recurrent incapacity to provide sufficient remuneration for agri-food products (Brodeur & Clerson, 2015). In response to these market instabilities, many countries have implemented intervention measures, such as input subsides and agricultural insurance to provide a "safety net" for farmers (Brodeur & Clerson, 2015). This is also highlighted in Chapter 14. Over the past two decades, Canadian commodity price stabilization programmes have transitioned to programmes that stabilize the income of the farm unit as a whole (Skogstad, 2008). Two of the current assistance programmes for farmers in Canada include (1) the AgriStability programme, which offers support to farmers when they experience large margin decline, and (2) the AgriInsurance programme, which stabilizes a farmer's income by minimizing the financial impacts of production loss (Agriculture and Agri-Food Canada, 2018). Similar transitions have also occurred in the US and in the European Union, in which these countries decoupled assistance from current production decisions and moved away from market-price support and high-export subsidies, respectively (AAFC, 2017).

Importantly, these transitions have occurred as a result of serious unintended consequences of government support programs, leaving some stakeholders questioning the relevance of government intervention in agriculture (AAFC, 2017). Some of the unintended consequences include little desire to adopt new technologies on farms and a lack of innovation, which leads to uncompetitiveness in the marketplace. The generation of incentives for intensive production practices or expanding production on marginal lands have also been observed (AAFC, 2017). Together, these effects undermine efforts to build a stronger agricultural sector. In addition to these unintended consequences, increased urbanization, resulting in long workdays, provided more opportunities to consume "fast foods" – that is, foods that are energy-dense, nutrient-poor, and strongly associated with increased obesity (Burns & Inglis, 2007). In response to this consumer demand, energy-intensive food production has focused on generating more processed and prepared foods, the so-called cheaper foods (Satterthwaite et al., 2010; Tilman & Clark, 2014). But the production of "cheaper" foods have hidden costs that have impacted the environment, consumer health, and society as a whole (Lustig, 2017). Because these costs occur outside the marketplace, they are referred to as "externalities", and they are not included in the retail price of food products (Tegtmeier & Duffy, 2004). Externalities are subsidized and make the price of food appear "cheap" (Qualman, 2019; Walker, Rhubart-berg, Mckenzie, Kelling, & Lawrence, 2005).

Hidden costs of our current agri-food system

What information does true cost accounting in the present agri-food system capture?

The industrial approach to agriculture has resulted in the production of food that appears to cost less but comes at great cost to the health of the environment, the workers, and the public (Walker et al., 2005). Some of the negative environmental impacts of the current industrialized agri-food system include the use of chemical fertilizers that can leach into water sources and result in algal blooms, which are detrimental to some aquatic bottom dwellers (Horrigan, Lawrence, & Walker, 2002; Tilman & Clark, 2014). In addition, food systems have been reported to contribute between 19% and 29% of greenhouse gas (GHG) emissions (Vermeulen, Campbell, & Ingram, 2012). Industrialized agri-food systems are also detrimental to public health with excessive use of antibiotics in animal agriculture that is increasing bacterial resistance to antimicrobial agents (Horrigan et al., 2002). As is well argued in other chapters of this collection, diets rich in processed foods, refined sugars and fats, meat and dairy have contributed to the increased prevalence of chronic disease (Springmann, Godfray, Rayner, & Scarborough, 2016). Indeed, Popkin, Adair, and Ng (2013) describe a decrease in consumption of healthier diets and an increased consumption of more processed foods, a trend which started in the 1970s. In addition to the long-standing concerns about the environmental and public health sustainability of industrialized agriculture, the social costs are equally important, although they do not always obtain the same attention (Cullen et al., 2015). Important social costs may occur due to losses of family farms, or decline of rural communities, or loss of agricultural knowledge and skills (Hendrickson & James, 2005).

Growing public awareness of the negative effects of industrialized agriculture has prompted consumer demand for more sustainable food production. A recent FAO (2017) assessment of the true global costs of food estimates the annual total environmental cost at 2,100 billion US dollars (USD). The social costs were estimated to be even higher at 2,700 billion USD (TruCost, 2013), and these combined externalized costs amount to 4.8 trillion USD every year (FAO, 2015). These data help support the claim that there is no such thing as "cheap" food and suggests that a sustainable agri-food production system must include these costs when considering inputs and outputs (Walker et al., 2005). Steier (2011) suggests two ways to discourage large food corporations from excluding externalities in their food production costs. The first involves tort lawsuits against these corporations, whereas the second involves a shift in consumer demand for more sustainable food options instead of fast and "cheap" food options. Another approach to discourage companies from excluding the cost of externalities in their product prices is to use indicator-based tools or models that consider quality as well as social, economic, and public health aspects to monitor sustainability in agri-food systems (Peano, Migliorini, & Sottile, 2014). This approach would provide the evidence needed to help guide better decision making for policymakers and, ultimately, producer practices and consumer choices.

Indicator-based tools/models and their potential to monitor sustainability of agri-food systems

The current linearized agri-food system is not sustainable. Sustainable agri-food systems as described by Qualman (2019) are circular (i.e. utilizing cycles) and are built on recycling, and characterized by the use of current resources without compromising the ability of future generations to meet their own needs. Qualman (2019) further advocates that the pursuit of sustainability requires radical, transformative restructuring to the current linearize agri-food system (Qualman, 2019). The fact that the current agri-food system is unsustainable and that various stakeholders (FAO, 2017) have indicated a desire for change makes this an ideal time to transform contexts and operations of agri-food systems. Ensuring an adequate food supply for current and future generations while maintaining a healthy environment and successful, sustainable economies is a complex challenge (Daher & Mohtar, 2015). Although some progress has been made in understanding and quantifying the challenge that lies ahead, questions remain about how to obtain the true cost of food and how this knowledge can best be transferred to enable informed decisions by key stakeholders (policymakers, farmers, the food industry, and consumers). As a first step to address this issue, several indicator-based models have been applied to calculate the true cost of food production (Eosta, 2017). Some of the models that have been used include (1) true cost accounting (TCA) or full-cost accounting (FCA), (2) life-cycle analysis (LCA), (3) Sustainability Flower model, and (4) multi-indicator sustainability assessment. Each of these models will be briefly described next.

FCA is an economic tool focused on evaluating the environmental and social costs and benefits of activities associated with a product or process that is external to the market, with the aim of ensuring that the external costs associated with these activities are accounted for and reflected in the market price. In the case of the agri-food system, FCA can be very complex since many processes and outputs operate within many ecosystems, which necessitates a broad framework of analysis (Barg & Swanson, 2004). To add to the complexity, FCA does not only consider the negative impacts of the process but also includes benefits from activities that are not captured in the market. A second tool, LCA, was defined by Fava et al. (1991) as a process used to evaluate the environmental burden associated with a product, process, or activity. LCA is accomplished by identifying and quantifying energy and materials usage and environmental releases. The data are then used to access the impact of those energy and material releases on the environment over the entire life cycle of the product (Crosson et al., 2011). One key merit of the LCA tool is that it identifies upstream and downstream impacts arising from a process or activity which allows significant externalities to be identified (Bebbington, Gray, Hibbit, & Kirk, 2001). In this regard, LCA is similar to FCA.

On the other hand, the third tool, the Sustainability Flower, which was developed in 2009, is a management assessment tool that evaluates the impact of sustainable performance on six dimensions of the planet (soil, water, air, animals, plants, and energy), and three dimensions of people (cultural, social, and economic life) (Eosta, 2017). The Sustainability Flower model is different from the FCA and LCA tools in that it has a cultural component and focuses on soil (Soil & More, 2017). This framework has been used to monitor and manage the sustainability achievements of organic farmers in various countries, including South Africa, Argentina, and Costa Rica (Nature & More, 2019). The fourth tool, is a multi-indicator sustainability assessment tool based on the concept of "sustainable nutrition security" (SNS) and was proposed by (Gustafson et al., 2016). This tool uses a holistic approach to quantitatively characterize the performance of food systems through seven matrices of SNS (food nutrient adequacy, ecosystem stability, food affordability and availability, sociocultural well-being, food safety, resilience and waste, and loss reduction). Each of the seven matrices are based on a combination of multiple indicators that are combined to provide an overall score (0–100) (Chaudhary, Gustafson, & Mathys, 2018). The multi-indicator SNS tool is different from the previously mentioned tools in that it monitors the nutritional aspects of a food system, including the micronutrients, whose deficiency (the so-called hidden hunger) affects over two billion people in the world (Tulchinsky, 2010). Overall, each method has its merits, but one criticism of these indicator tools that has emerged is that different methodologies or approaches are applied for each method, which results in a lack of consistency in and comparability of the findings (Cullen et al., 2015). Nevertheless, some success has been achieved in quantifying the externalities in the agri-food sector, and a few examples on FCA will be highlighted in the next section.

Indicator-based tools to assess positive and negative externalities in the agri-food sector

Currently, studies that have evaluated agri-food systems using the FCA tool are rare. However, one of the first studies reported to use the FCA model to assess the environmental externalities for agriculture was a study done in the UK by Pretty (2008). Four features of externalities in agriculture were identified by Pretty (2008): (1) their costs are often neglected; (2) they often occur with a time lag; (3) they often damage groups whose interests are not well represented in political or decision-making processes; (4) the identity of the source of the externality is not always known. This work provided an aggregate cost of environmental externalities of 2.343 million pounds (£). This estimate amounted to £208 per hectare (ha) per year and was averaged across 11.2 million ha of arable land and permanent grassland. The externalities calculated were organized into seven categories, and the total cost for each category is shown in Table 2.1. Although a bit dated,

Table 2.1 Total external cost for UK agriculture in 1996

Cost Category for Externalities	Estimated Costs, UK (£ Million)
1 Damage to natural capital, water	231
2 Damage to natural capital, air	1,113
3 Damage to natural capital, soil	96
4 Damage to natural capital, biodiversity, and landscapes	27 1
5 Damage to human health, pesticides	Not able to calculate costs
6 Damage to human health, nitrates	776
7 Damage to human health, micro-organisms, and other diseases.	

Source: Pretty, J. (2008). Agricultural sustainability: concepts, principles and evidence. *Philosophical Transactions: Biological Sciences, 363*(1491), 447–465. http://doi.org/10.1098/rstb.2007.2163; Barg, S., & Swanson, D. (2004). *Full-cost accounting for agriculture.* International Institute for Sustainability. Retrieved from www.iisd.org/sites/default/files/publications/natres_full_cost_agri.pdf. Used with permission.

the information shows that the areas with the greatest impact were damage to natural capital of air and water, and damage to human health from micro-organisms and other diseases. Similar trends have also been observed recently (Jongeneel, Polman, & van Kooten, 2016).

FCA analysis undertaken by Barg and Swanson (2004) with the International Institute for Sustainable Development (IISD) and the follow-up report in 2005 (Barg, Swanson, & Venema, 2005) used the impact pathway approach to evaluate the externalities in agriculture in Canada. The impact pathway approach is applicable in many FCA exercises and is an analysis method that takes into account the route by which the actual damage or benefit takes place (Barg et al., 2005). This approach consists of four main stages: (1) identifying pathway constituents associated with an agri-environment indicator, (2) determining how pathway constituents are dispersed or transported to the location of impact in an ecosystem, (3) relating the concentration of the pathway constituent at the location of impact to specific environmental or human well-being impacts, and (4) determining the costs associated with the specific environmental or human well-being impacts (Barg et al., 2005). The 2004 and 2005 IISD reports were designed to explore the conceptual methods and data needs and gaps associated with the valuation of indicator change.

In their report, Barg et al. (2005) applied the impact pathway approach to explore changes in five different agri-environmental indicators, including (1) risk of water erosion – soil quality category, (2) risk of water contamination by phosphorous – water quality category, (3) greenhouse gas (GHG) emissions – ecosystems atmosphere emissions category, (4) energy use efficiency – eco-efficiency category, and (5) wildlife habitat – agriculture biodiversity category. However, these authors developed the methods for the soil quality category with the intent that the developed methods could then be applied to the remaining agri-environment indicators (Brag et al., 2005). A summary of the soil quality externalities is presented here. Risks of water erosion (ranging from tolerable, low, moderate, high, to severe) for the provinces with the largest amount of cropland area in Canada were determined. The highest ratings for risk of water erosions were observed at the tolerable level (<6 tonnes per ha per year), and the data are as follows: 90%, 83%, and 89% for Saskatchewan, Alberta, and Manitoba, respectively. Total off-site damage from soil particles (i.e. increased sediment concentration in a waterway, including ditch cleaning and road services) were estimated at CAD $14.11 per tonne of erosion per year (Barg et al., 2005). Water erosion also results in the transport of nutrients and other contaminants, such as pesticides, to off-farm waterways which can also impact certain aspects of human well-being (including reduced value of water bodies for recreational activities), and some ecosystems, such as changes in species composition (Barg et al., 2005).

Reorienting agri-foods towards high-value foods that address hidden costs

The industrialized agri-food system has four main activities: (1) production, (2) processing and packaging, (3) retailing and distributing, and (4) consuming (Ingram, 2011). Sustainable agriculture would involve carrying out the four main activities of agri-food systems in ways that meet the need of producers and consumers without compromising the ability of future generations to meet their own needs. In principle, these activities would be designed to promote environmental and public health, as well as social equity, along with being resource conserving and commercially competitive. Renewed interests in alternative systems of agricultural production, and particularly alternatives that lower GHG emissions, are encouraging. They promote biodiversity amongst plants and animals, and do not undermine natural resources, including land, water, and soil (Chaudhary et al., 2018). Although there is growing agreement about how to fully achieve a sustainable agri-food system, organic farming and adopting a plant-based diet have received increased attention as strategies for stewarding the planet's resources.

Organic farming

The practice of organic farming is not new and predates other approaches to "environmentally friendly" farming. It may be defined as a holistic approach to agriculture which aims to progress towards an entire production, processing, and food distribution chain which is both socially just and ecologically responsible (Rigby & Ca, 2001). A growing number of studies have compared the environmental impacts of the same products produced in organic versus conventional agriculture (Meier et al., 2015). Overall, organically grown foods demonstrate a lower environmental impact on a per area and per year basis. However, lower yields of organic farming can lead to a higher environmental impact on a per product basis (Tuomisto, Hodge, Riordan, & Macdonald, 2012). As interest in organic farming is renewed, Canadian farmers are adapting their production methods to meet the demand for more sustainably produced food (Statistics Canada, 2017). Between 2011 and 2016, there was a 4.6% increase in organic farms in Canada, which represented 2.2% and 2.0% of all farms in Canada in 2016 and 2011, respectively (Statistics Canada, 2017). Consumers can be willing to pay more for organic foods when these products are viewed as more nutritious, better for the environment, or healthier than traditionally raised foods (Aranson, 2015). In 2016, Quebec had the highest number of organic farms in Canada, and family-owned farms such as Canadian Organic Maple (in New Brunswick, Canada) are leading the way by being the single-largest organic maple producers in the world (Statistics Canada, 2017). In 2012, Canada's organic market was worth an estimated $5.4 billion Canadian dollars (CAD) (the Canadian Organic Trade Association [COTA], 2017).

Consumer demand for plant proteins in their diets

Consumers more frequently connect diet and health (Chaudhary et al., 2018). In addition, increased interests to generate fewer environmental impacts have left key stakeholders in pursuit of new ways to shift to more sustainable agriculture and food production systems (Henchion, Hayes, Mullen, Fenelon, & Tiwari, 2017). To date, several life-cycle assessment studies have examined the environmental impact of a variety of fruits (Warner et al., 2010) and vegetables (Zafiriou et al., 2012). Amongst the main food groups, food proteins from plant sources are of interest because of their nutritional value and their eco-friendly carbon footprint (Henchion et al., 2017), and more countries, including Canada, are emphasizing greater consumption of plant food in their national food guidelines, as noted in Chapter 10. Some plants, including pulses (the dried seeds of leguminous plants such as peas, chickpeas, and lentils), have the unique ability to fix nitrogen – i.e., they absorb nitrogen from the atmosphere into their roots, and bacteria present in their roots converts the atmospheric nitrogen to ammonia. The ammonia is then converted into organic compounds that are used by the plant for growth, which in turn reduces their requirement for fertilizers. This natural ability decreases the requirement for fertilizers, which in turn contributes to the low carbon footprint of these plant-protein sources (Pulse Canada, 2019). Marine plants such as seaweed and algae also represent promising future protein sources.

A long-standing concern of industrialized agriculture has been to mitigate the carbon footprint of livestock farming because relative to animal-based foods, plant-based foods have lower GHG emissions and require less inputs of land and water (Tilman & Clark, 2014). Both the United Nations and the Food and Agriculture Organization are advocating for more sustainable diets, which include plant sources of protein to mitigate greenhouse gas emissions (FAO, 2018). Moving to a plant-based diet has been suggested as a course of action to reduce the environmental impact of food production and consumption by as much as 46% to 74% (Harwatt, Sabaté, Eshel, Soret, & Ripple, 2017). The narrative in Canada as evidenced by the newly revised Food Guide, encourages people to increase consumption of plant-based foods, which aligns with these global agenda themes. However, to achieve this goal in a sustainable manner poses an immediate challenge. Pulses, such as dried beans and chickpeas, are especially good candidates because they are rich in nutrients, low in fertilizer requirements, and readily produced in Canada (Hossain et al., 2017).

Reliance on meat protein sources to cater to the growing demand is unsustainable and, based on the earlier analyses, does not show itself to be an attractive solution. Several innovative approaches to incorporate plant-based products in the Canadian marketplace already have been initiated (see Chapter 4). For example, Lightlife, a subsidiary of Maple Leaf Foods Inc., has recently launched a plant-based burger (Kevany, 2018). In addition, in 2018, the Plant-Based Foods of Canada industry organization was formed to help support the regulatory and market interests of plant food companies in Canada, including Daiya Foods, Danone, Earth's Own Food, Ripple Foods, and Lightlife Foods (Plant-Based Foods of Canada).

The environmental cost of protein food choices

Legislation across the globe is creating awareness of the socio-economic impact of food and food systems, and determining *the true cost* of agriculture and food processing using economic models. A recent study by Sabaté et al. (2015) evaluated the resource efficiency and environmental impact of producing 1 kg of edible protein from two plant-protein sources (kidney beans and almonds) and three animal-protein sources (eggs, chicken, and beef). These authors found a significantly lower impact on the agricultural inputs (water, energy, fertilizers, and pesticides) to produce 1 kg of protein from this plant source compared to that of beef. It was also observed that producing 1 kg of protein from beef also produced more waste compared to the other animal-protein sources (eggs and chicken) studied. The authors concluded that more environmentally friendly plant-based proteins could potentially reduce the environmental footprint associated with animal-protein foods.

Recommendations and conclusion

Anticipated population growth and the impacts of climate change require more details on measuring what matters in the various food supply chains, which would help in making decisions and informing shifts that are needed. Increased consumer awareness about the link between diet and health has resulted in a greater demand for healthy, nutrient-dense foods. Reliance on meat protein sources to cater to the growing demand is unsustainable, with negative environmental and climatic impacts. Several alternative protein sources have been identified with a keen focus on plant proteins. What is lacking in one plant-protein source can be mitigated by cereal-pulse combinations and supplementation. The substitution of beef with pulses may help reduce the environmental footprint. In addition, public policies that encourage a shift towards more plant-based diets will help to support individual action in this area. We pay for food well beyond the grocery store checkout; we pay for food in our utility bills and taxes, and in our declining environmental and personal health. Thus, the need for better information for decision making is a key reason to determine the true costs of the current industrialized agri-food system. Farmers, consumers, and policymakers would benefit from having this information.

References

Agriculture and Agri-Food Canada. (2017). *Challenges facing Canadian agriculture*. Retrieved from www5.agr.gc.ca/resources/prod/doc/cb/apf/pdf/bg_con_comp_e.pdf

Agriculture and Agri-Food Canada. (2018). *Youth in agriculture.* Retrieved April 12, 2019, from www.agr.gc.ca/eng/programs-and-services/youth-in-agriculture/?id=1391690826829

Anderson, K. (2010). Globalization's effects on world agricultural trade, 1960–2050. *Philosophical Transactions of the Royal Society B, 365,* 3007–3021. http://doi.org/10.1098/rstb.2010.0131

Aranson, R. (2015). *Consumers want organic, so why are farmers wary?* Retrieved April 2, 2019 from http://www.producer.com/2015/01/consumers-want-organic-so-why-are-farmers-wary/

Barg, S., & Swanson, D. (2004). *Full cost accounting for agriculture.* International Institute for Sustainability. Retrieved from www.iisd.org/sites/default/files/publications/natres_full_cost_agri.pdf

Barg, S., Swanson, D., & Venema, H. D. (2005). Full cost accounting for agriculture – Year 2 report. *Changes,* pp. 1–130.

Bebbington, J., Gray, R., Hibbit, C., & Kirk, E. (2001). *Full cost accounting: an agenda for action (Report).* Retrieved from https://www.icmap.com.pk/downloads/research-studies/a1_fca.pdf

Brodeur, C., & Clerson, F. (2015). *Is government intervention in agriculture still relevant in the 21st century?* (Final Report). Québec, Canada.

Burns, C. M. Ã., & Inglis, A. D. (2007). Measuring food access in Melbourne: Access to healthy and fast foods by car, bus and foot in an urban municipality in Melbourne. *Health & Place, 13,* 877–885. http://doi.org/10.1016/j.healthplace.2007.02.005

Chaudhary, A., Gustafson, D., & Mathys, A. (2018). Multi-indicator sustainability assessment of global food systems. *Nature Communications, 9,* 1–13. http://doi.org/10.1038/s41467-018-03308-7

Canada Organic Trade Association (COTA). (2017). *Highlights from COTA's 2017 consumer report.* Retrieved April 3 from https://www.cog.ca/home/about-organics/organic-statistics/

Crosson, P., Shalloo, L., Brien, D. O., Lanigan, G. J., Foley, P. A., Boland, T. M., . . . Kenny, D. A. (2011). A review of whole farm systems models of greenhouse gas emissions from beef and dairy cattle production systems. *Animal Feed Science and Technology, 166,* 29–45. http://doi.org/10.1016/j.anifeedsci.2011.04.001

Cullen, S., Holden, P., Kazi, N., Martin, R., Perry, M., Richardson, R., . . . Young, R. (2015). *Examining the social, environmental, and health impacts of production food: True cost accounting report,* November 2015. Retrieved from https://futureoffood.org/wp. . ./The-Real-Cost-of-Food-Food-Tank-pdf.

Daher, B. T., & Mohtar, R. H. (2015). Water – energy – food (WEF) Nexus tool 2.0: Guiding integrative resource planning and decision-making. *Water International, 40,* 748–771. http://doi.org/10.1080/02508060.2015.1074148

Eosta. (2017). *True cost accounting for food, farming and finance.* Retrieved from www.natureandmore.com/files/documenten/tca-fff-report.pdf

FAO. (2015). *Natural capital impacts in agriculture.* Rome, Italy: FAO. Retrieved from www.fao.org

FAO. (2017). *The future of food and agriculture – Trends and challenges.* Rome, Italy: FAO. Retrieved from www.fao.org/3/a-i6583e.pdf

FAO. (2018). *The future of food and agriculture – Alternative pathways to 2050* [Summary version]. Rome, Italy: FAO, p. 60. Retrieved from www.fao.org/publications/fofa/en/

28 *Marcia M. English*

Fava, J, Consoli F., Denison, R., Dickson, K., Mohin, T., & Vigon, B. (1991). *A conceptual framework for life-cycle assessment. Workshop Report. Society of Environmental Toxicology and Chemistry (SETAC)*. Pensacola Florida, United States of America. February 1–7. Retrieved from https://pdfs.semanticscholar.org/8ca0/ac01b77b5f68a96df0de7b4d59cfc827b125.pdf

Gálvez-Nogales, E. (2010). *Agro-based clusters in developing countries: Staying competitive in a globalized economy*. Retrieved from www.fao.org/docrep/012/i1560e/i1560e.pdf

Goddard, E., Weersink, A., & Chen, K. (1993). Economics of structural change in agriculture. *Canadian Journal of Agricultural Economics, 41*, 475–489.

Gustafson, D., Gutman, A., Leet, W., Drewnowski, A., Fanzo, J., & Ingram, J. (2016). Seven food system metrics of sustainable nutrition security. *Sustainability, 8*, 1–17. http://doi.org/10.3390/su8030196

Harwatt, H., & Soret, S. (2016). Environmental nutrition: A new frontier for public health. *American Journal of Public Health, 106*(5), 815–821. http://doi.org/10.2105/AJPH.2016.303046

Harwatt, H., Sabaté, J., Eshel, G., Soret, S., & Ripple, W. (2017). Substituting beans for beef as a contribution toward US climate change targets. *Climate Change, 143*, 261–270. http://doi.org/10.1007/s10584-017-1969-1

Hazell, P. B. R. (2018). Urbanization, agriculture, and smallholder farming. In R. Sessaj & P. Pingali (Eds.), *Agriculture & food systems to 2050: Global trends, challenges and opportunities*. World Scientific Series in Grand Public Policy Challenges of the 21st Century (2nd ed., pp. 137–160). Singapore: World Scientific.

Henchion, M., Hayes, M., Mullen, A., Fenelon, M., & Tiwari, B. (2017). Future protein supply and demand: Strategies and factors influencing a sustainable equilibrium. *Foods, 6*(7), 53. http://doi.org/10.3390/foods6070053

Hendrickson, M. K., & James, H. S. (2005). The ethics of constrained choice: How the industrialization of agriculture impacts farming and farmer behavior. *Agricultural and Environmental Ethics, 18*(3), 269–291. http://doi.org/10.1007/s10806-005-0631-5

Horrigan, L., Lawrence, R. S., & Walker, P. (2002). How sustainable agriculture can address the environmental and human health harms of industrial agriculture. *Environmental Health Perspectives, 110*(5), 445–456.

Hossain, Z., Wang, X., Hamel, C., Knight, J. D., Morrison, M. J., & Gan, Y. (2017). Biological nitrogen fixation by pulse crops on semiarid Canadian prairies. *Canadian Journal of Plant Science, 131*, 119–131.

Ingram, J. (2011). A food systems approach to researching food security and its interactions with global environmental change. *Food Security, 3*, 417–431. http://doi.org/10.1007/s12571-011-0149-9

Ingram, J. S. I., & Porter, J. R. (2015). Plant science and the food security agenda. *Nature Plants, 1*, Article No. 15173. https://doi.org/10.1038/nplants.2015.173

Jongeneel, R., Polman, N., & van Kooten, C. (2016). *How important are agricultural externalities? A framework for analysis and application to Dutch agriculture* (Working Paper 2016-04). Retrieved from http://web.uvic.ca/~repa/publications/REPA working papers/WorkingPaper2016-04.pdf

Kevany, K. M. (2018, April 12). How to make global food systems more sustainable. *The Conversation*. Retrieved from https://theconversation.com/

Le, B. (2018). *Science meets food "Human Rights and Food: The Impact of Food Technology on Global Health"*. Retrieved April 1, 2019 from http://sciencemeetsfood.org/human-rights-food-impact-food-technology-global-health/

Lustig, R. (2017). Processed food – An experiment that failed. *Journal of American Medical Association*, *171*(3), 212–213. http://doi.org/10.1001/jamapediatrics.2016.3868

Meier, M. S., Stoessel, F., Jungbluth, N., Juraske, R., Schader, C., & Stolze, M. (2015). Environmental impacts of organic and conventional agricultural products – Are the differences captured by life cycle assessment? *Journal of Environmental Management*, *149*, 193–208. http://doi.org/10.1016/j.jenvman.2014.10.006

Moschini, G. C. (2001). Biotech – Who wins? Economic benefits and costs of biotechnology innovations in agriculture. *Estey Centre Journal of International Law and Trade Policy*, *2*(1), 93–117.

Nature & More (2019). *The true cost of food*. Retrieved from https://www.natureandmore.com/en/growers

Peano, C., Migliorini, P., & Sottile, F. (2014). A methodology for the sustainability assessment of agri-food systems: An application to the Slow Food Presidia project. *Ecology and Society*, *19*(4), 1–11. http://doi.org/10.5751/ES-06972-190424

Popkin, B. M., Adair, L. S., & Ng, S. W. (2013). Now and then: The global nutrition transition: The pandemic of obesity in developing countries. *Nutrition Reviews*, *70*(1), 3–21. http://doi.org/10.1111/j.1753-4887.2011.00456.x.NOW

Pretty, J. (2008). Agricultural sustainability: Concepts, principles and evidence. *Philosophical Transactions: Biological Sciences*, *363*(1491), 447–465. http://doi.org/10.1098/rstb.2007.2163

Pulse Canada (2019). *Environmental sustainability*. Retrieved from http://www.pulsecanada.com/food-industry/pulse-benefits/sustainability/

Qualman, D. (2019). *Civilization critical: Energy, food, nature and the future*. Halifax, Canada: Fernwood Publishing.

Rigby, D., & Ca, D. (2001). Organic farming and the sustainability of agricultural systems. *Agricultural Systems*, *68*, 21–40.

Rosset, P. (2000). The multiple functions and benefits of small farm agriculture in the context of global trade negotiations. *Development*, *43*, 77–82.

Sabaté, J., Sranacharoenpong, K., Harwatt, H., Wien, M., & Soret, S. (2015). The environmental cost of protein food choices. *Public Health Nutrition*, *18*(11), 2067–2073. http://doi.org/10.1017/S1368980014002377

Sabaté, J., Harwatt, H., & Soret, S. (2016). Environmental nutrition: A new frontier for public health. *American Journal of Public Health*, *106*(5), 815–821. doi: 10.2105/AJPH.2016.303046

Satterthwaite, D., Mcgranahan, G., & Tacoli, C. (2010). Urbanization and its implications for food and farming. *Philosophical Transactions of the Royal Society B*, *365*, 2809–2820. http://doi.org/10.1098/rstb.2010.0136

Skogstad, G. (2008). Canadian agricultural programs and paradigms: The influence of international trade agreements and domestic factors. *Canadian Journal of Agricultural Economics*, *56*, 493–507.

Soil & More (2017). *Sustainability flower*. Retrieved from https://www.soilandmore.com/about-us/sustainability-flower

Springmann, M., Godfray, H. C. J., Rayner, M., & Scarborough, P. (2016). Analysis and valuation of the health and climate change cobenefits of dietary change. *Proceedings of the National Academy of Sciences*, *113*(15), 4146–4151. http://doi.org/10.1073/pnas.1523119113

Statistics Canada. (2015). *Proportion of Canadians living in rural areas*. Retrieved April 1, 2019 from https://www12.statcan.gc.ca/census-recensement/2011/as-sa/98-310-x/2011003/fig/fig3_2-1-eng.cfm

Statistics Canada. (2017). *Growing opportunity through innovation in agriculture.* Retrieved April 2, 2019 from https://www150.statcan.gc.ca/n1/pub/95-640-x/2016001/article/14816-eng.htm

Statistics Canada. (2018). *Canada's rural population since 1851.* Retrieved April 1, 2019 from https://www12.statcan.gc.ca/census-recensement/2011/as-sa/98-310-x/98-310-x2011003_2-eng.cfm

Steier, G. (2011). Externalities of industrial food production: The costs of profit. *The Dartmouth Law Journal, 9,* 163–197. Retrieved from http://ssrn.com/abstract=2115533

Tegtmeier, E. M., & Duffy, M. D. (2004). External costs of agricultural production in the United States. *International Journal of Agricultural Sustainability, 2*(1), 1–20.

Tilman, D., & Clark, M. (2014). Global diets link environmental sustainability and human health. *Nature, 515*(7528), 518–522. http://doi.org/10.1038/nature13959

TruCost. (2013). *TEEB for Business coalition study, "natural capital at risk – the top 100 externalities of business".* Retrieved April 1, 2019, from https://www.trucost.com/trucost-news/teeb-business-coalition-study-shows-multi-trillion-dollar-natural-capital-risk-underlying-urgency-green-economy-transition-2/

Tulchinsky, T. H. (2010). Micronutrient deficiency conditions: Global health issues. *Public Health Reviews, 32*(1), 243–255.

Tuomisto, H. L., Hodge, I. D., Riordan, P., & Macdonald, D. W. (2012). Does organic farming reduce environmental impacts? A meta-analysis of European research. *Journal of Environmental Management, 112*(834), 309–320. http://doi.org/10.1016/j.jenvman.2012.08.018

Vermeulen, S. J., Campbell, B. M., & Ingram, J. S. I. (2012). Climate change and food systems. *Annual Review of Environment and Resources, 37,* 195–222. http://doi.org/10.1146/annurev-environ-020411-130608

Walker, P., Rhubart-berg, P., Mckenzie, S., Kelling, K., & Lawrence, R. S. (2005). Public health implications of meat production and consumption [Invited paper]. *Public Health Nutrition, 8*(4), 348–356. http://doi.org/10.1079/PHN2005727

Wan, N., Zhang, M., Jiang, J., & Ji, X. (2016, October). An ecological method to understand agricultural standardization in peach orchard ecosystems. *Nature Scientific Reports, 6,* 1–9. http://doi.org/10.1038/srep21675

Warner, D., Davies, D., Hipps, N., Osborne, N., Tzilivakis, J., & Lewis, K. (2010). Greenhouse gas emissions and energy use in UK-grown short-day strawberry (*Fragaria xananassa* Duch) crops. *The Journal of Agricultural Science, 148*(6), 667–681. doi:10.1017/S0021859610000493

Zafiriou, P., Mamolos, A., Menexes, G., Siomos, A., Tsatsarelis, C., & Kalburtji, K. (2012). Analysis of energy flow and greenhouse gas emissions in organic, integrated and conventional cultivation of white asparagus by PCA and HCA: Cases in Greece. *Journal of Cleaner Production, 29–30,* 20–27. doi:10.1016/j.jclepro.2012.01.040

3 The solution on our plates

Why sustainable plant-based diets are needed to reverse the food-climate-health-equity crisis

David A. Cleveland

Introduction

What do we want from our food system? I assume that most of us want food that is delicious and nutritious, environment and climate friendly, and in ethical and just ways supports our human and non-human communities. The food system that both drives our diets and is driven by them jeopardizes all of these goals by creating a food-climate-health-equity crisis (Figure 3.1). That means that what we choose to eat is not just a personal decision – it's an existential choice for our species and the earth.

In 2019, the world's food system strives to feed 7.7 billion people daily, but has large and unsustainable negative effects, including deteriorating human health, soaring health-care costs, increasing inequity, animal suffering, ecological destruction, and anthropogenic climate change (ACC). Yet the broad impacts of the food system remain noticeably absent from the policies of most governments or the mind-sets of non-governmental organizations (NGOs) and corporations, and from the daily food choices of most people. Is diet change needed to avert catastrophe?

In this chapter, I answer questions about the relationship of our diets, especially in the global North, to the food-climate-health-equity crisis and evaluate the potential of sustainable – in terms of environmental (focusing on climate, health, and social indicators) – plant-based diets (SPBDs) as a necessary part of the solution to the crisis. I also give examples in the third section of potential and existing efforts to move towards SPBDs.

Are more plant-based diets needed to solve the food-climate-health-equity crisis?

Since the Neolithic revolution that marked the transition from foraging to agriculture beginning about 12,000 years ago, the human response to increasing demand for food and other resources from a growing population with increasing consumption rates has been to increase production – a *supply-side solution* which has had increasing negative environmental and social impacts, including ACC, human sickness and death, and inequity (Cleveland, 2014).

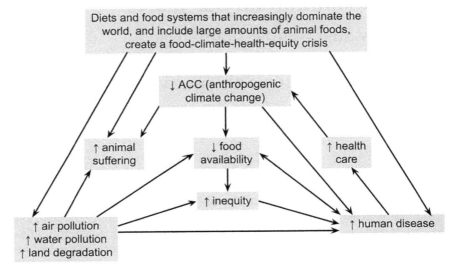

Figure 3.1 Our diets are driving the food-climate-health-equity crisis

Source: © 2019 David A. Cleveland, used with permission.

This Neolithic supply-side strategy has led to prioritizing production over human and environmental health, with impacts close to or already exceeding the limits of sustainable social systems and the planetary boundaries for many biophysical systems, including the climate (Steffen et al., 2018). The human impacts on the planet are so large that a new epoch, the Anthropocene, has been suggested, and the term is now in wide use (Ruddiman, Ellis, Kaplan, & Fuller, 2015). Our food system is the largest contributor (Willett et al., 2019).

The Neolithic supply-side strategy is no longer viable in the Anthropocene. Therefore, we need *demand-side solutions* that reduce demand on social and biophysical systems; don't require extensive research, technology development, or resources; and can make a major difference over the short term. It is important to understand whether changing to SPBDs is one of many mitigation strategies to choose from, or whether it is *required* to successfully reverse the food-climate-health-equity crisis.

SPBDs are needed to avert climate catastrophe

One of the largest and most threatening impacts on the earth is the human impact on the climate, mostly via greenhouse gas emissions (GHGE). There is virtually complete consensus amongst scientists that humans have caused an increase in GHGE, leading to an accumulation of greenhouse gases in the atmosphere, the main cause of increasing average global temperatures and increasing weather extremes. The 2015 Paris Agreement was created to keep "the increase in the global average temperature to well below 2°C above pre-industrial levels and to pursue efforts to limit the temperature increase to 1.5°C above pre-industrial levels" (UNFCCC, 2015) in order to avoid catastrophic effects on the earth's ecosystems and human society. The current average global temperature is 1.0°C over pre-industrial levels. To limit warming to 1.5°C will require a reduction in GHGE far beyond the national commitments in the Paris Agreement and system changes at a scale that have no "documented historic precedent" and will still bring large negative impacts, although less than with 2°C (IPCC, 2018, p. 17). If we don't stabilize and reduce GHGE to slow and reverse these trends, they will lead to environmental and social catastrophe. While I focus on the effect of the food system on the climate, climate change is also making it more difficult to produce food (FAO, 2016).

Food system GHGE probably began ~7,000 years ago as a result of land clearing and animal domestication (Ruddiman et al., 2015). Our global food system contributes a large share of current GHGE. While estimates vary due to the use of different system boundaries, as well as other assumptions, it likely accounts for at least 25%–30% of total anthropogenic emissions. Vermeulen, Campbell, and Ingram's (2012) commonly cited estimate is that global food systems contribute 19%–29% of total GHGE (p. 198).

Animal foods currently account for most food system GHGE, with livestock alone comprising 14.5% of all anthropogenic emissions (Gerber et al., 2013). An analysis of 120 life-cycle assessment publications found that plant foods (e.g. grains, soy and other legumes, refined sugars, oils, and fruits and vegetables) had relatively low to very low GHGE per kcal, per gram of protein, and per serving, compared with animal foods (meat, fish, and dairy), especially ruminant meat, which, for example, has emissions per gram of protein about 250 times those of legumes (Tilman & Clark, 2014). As a consequence, animal foods have a disproportionately large effect on food waste emissions: for example, in the USA, animal foods account for 33% of food wasted at the retail and consumer levels, yet this waste produces 74% of the GHGE of all food wasted at these levels (Heller & Keoleian, 2015).

Animal food production emits a large proportion of anthropogenic methane and nitrous oxide, greenhouse gases that have a 100-year global warming potential, respectively, of 34 and 298 times that of CO_2 (Myhre et al., 2013, p. 714). In the USA in 2016, agriculture accounted for 80% of nitrous oxide emissions, mostly from soil, and 30% of methane emissions, 94% of which is from enteric fermentation of ruminants and manure management (calculated using data in EPA, 2018). Because methane has a short life span in the atmosphere, with a 20-year global warming potential of 86, which is considered high by analysts estimating different gases, reducing the rate of methane emissions is especially important for achieving climate change mitigation over the shorter term (Balcombe, Speirs, Brandon, & Hawkes, 2018; Godfray et al., 2018).

Our food system also emits CO_2 from the use of fossil fuels to produce and transport inputs, such as fertilizer and irrigation water, to power farm machinery and to produce, transport, process, store, and prepare food. In 2007, the food system accounted for 13.6% of all fossil fuel CO_2 emissions in the USA economy (Canning, Rehkamp, Waters, & Etemadnia, 2017).

Because animal foods have higher GHGE than plant foods, diets containing them are also higher in GHGE. In the UK, for example, the self-reported diets of 65,000 people showed that a high meat eater had 1.9 times and a medium meat eater 1.5 times the GHGE of a lacto-ovo-vegetarian, and that an average meat eater had about 2 times and a high meat eater 2.5 times the GHGE of a vegan eater (Scarborough et al., 2014).

While changing the food system is absent from many climate change mitigation strategies, a growing body of research supports food system change, including diet change, as an effective strategy. Diet change, emphasizing reducing animal product consumption, is also beginning to be promoted as a policy, mostly by NGOs such as Friends of the Earth, Center for Biological Diversity, and the Natural Resources Defense Council.

Increasingly the scientific community supports the evidence that more SPBDs are needed to avert a climate crisis and that there is a positive correlation between health benefits and lower GHGE for many foods and diets (Cleveland & Gee, 2017; Hallström, Carlsson-Kanyama, & Börjesson, 2015; Swinburn et al., 2019; Willett et al., 2019). One of the earliest analyses of the role of healthier diets in meeting climate mitigation targets found that for the UK, agricultural technology improvements and a 30% reduction in livestock production would be needed to meet the 2050 target of 80% reduction in the level of 1990 emission (Friel et al., 2009). Less meat consumption would lower dietary saturated fat and cholesterol, resulting in a 15% reduction in the burden of coronary artery disease (Friel et al., 2009). A global plant-based diet could, by 2050, prevent about 11,600,000 deaths per year, 23.6% of total deaths amongst adults, and reduce GHGE by 80% (Willett et al., 2019, pp. 15, 26).

Bajželj et al. (2014) found similar results using different methods, a model relating global land use and agricultural biomass flow. They compared the annual GHGE of different scenarios in relation to the estimated GHGE threshold for 2050 required to stay under a 2°C increase in average global temperature (Bajželj et al., 2014). They found that if no changes are made in the food system, its GHGE alone would almost reach this threshold, meaning that all sources of GHGE other than food would have to reduce emissions to almost zero to stay under 2°C (Figure 3.2, A). Even the scenario that improved yield by increasing irrigation and fertilizer application efficiency, plus a 50% reduction in food waste, reached half of the GHGE threshold by 2050 (Figure 3.2, B). Only by adding diets with reduced meat and dairy was food system GHGE lowered to one-quarter of the threshold – the level

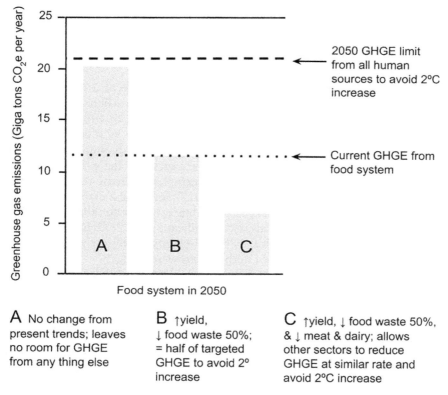

Figure 3.2 Moving to more sustainable plant-based diets is needed to avert climate catastrophe. Based on (Bajželj et al., 2014)

Source: © 2019 David A. Cleveland, used with permission.

required for a pro rata reduction in GHGE to stay below a 2°C increase over pre-industrial temperature (Figure 3.2, C).

SPBDs are needed to reverse the pandemic of deadly non-communicable diseases

Our diets have become increasingly unhealthy due to rising consumption of meat and dairy, saturated fats, sugar-sweetened beverages, refined grains, and processed and prepared foods, as well as decreasing consumption of healthier foods, such as fruits, vegetables, whole grains, and legumes (Willett et al., 2019).

The spread of unhealthy diets in the industrial countries of the global North, and then to the global South, is part of a major human nutrition transition (Popkin, 2006). Along with other factors, such as lack of physical activity, these diets are an important driver of a pandemic of non-communicable diseases (NCDs) – including cancers, type 2 diabetes, and cardiovascular disease (Popkin, 2006). Even though life expectancies are increasing in industrialized societies as age-specific mortality for NCDs declines, the years lived with debilitating disease are increasing, such as in Denmark (Andersson & Vasan, 2017).

Many animal foods increase the risk of NCDs like type 2 diabetes, cancer, and cardiovascular disease (Bouvard et al., 2015; Micha et al., 2017; Schwingshackl et al., 2017; Talaei, Wang, Yuan, Pan, & Koh, 2017), and almost all the nutrients provided by animal foods can be found in healthy plant foods (USDA & HHS, 2015a). While consumption of unhealthy plant foods like refined grains and added sugars increase the risk for NCDs, healthy plant foods, such as fruits and vegetables, decrease the risk of cardiovascular disease, cancer (Aune et al., 2017), and type 2 diabetes (Toumpanakis, Turnbull, & Alba-Barba, 2018). Many, though not all, components of unhealthy diets are also foods with significantly larger GHGE relative to healthier foods. Because of this, SPBD offer opportunities for health and climate co-benefits, as discussed in the previous section.

However, more plant-based diets don't always optimize climate and health co-benefits. For example, one study of 100 dietary patterns found that reduced GHGE from diets were associated with poorer health indicators, because some low GHGE diets, which are low in animal foods, saturated fat, and salt, are often also low in essential micronutrients and high in sugar, which has large negative health effects but relatively small GHGE (Payne, Scarborough, & Cobiac, 2016).

In addition to food system GHGE from unhealthy animal foods, there are GHGE from the health-care costs for diet-related NCDs. It has been estimated that the global health-care costs for NCDs could reach $47 trillion by 2030 (Bloom et al., 2011), and that in the USA, all NCDs will cost $265,000 per person from 2015–2050, a total of $95 trillion (Chen, Kuhn, Prettner, & Bloom, 2018). For example, type 2 diabetes is a major cause of renal failure, leading to the need for dialysis according to the US National Institutes of Health, making diabetes a very greenhouse gas intensive disease – in the USA about 9.7% of adults had diabetes in 2017, with annual per capita health-care expenditures 2.3 times higher than people without diabetes, costing an estimated $327 billion that year (ADA, 2018).

To estimate the climate and health co-benefits of more SPBDs, Hallström and colleagues created counterfactual healthy alternative diets (HADs) based on dietary recommendations and the foods with very strong evidence of their effect on NCDs (Hallström, Gee, Scarborough, & Cleveland, 2017) (Figure 3.3). We found that for the healthiest diet (HAD-3) which eliminated all red and processed meat, the relative risk of coronary heart disease, type 2 diabetes, and colorectal cancer decreased 29%–45%, and health-care costs reduced by $93 billion out of a total cost of $230 billion for those three diseases, which in turn reduced GHGE by 84 kg per person

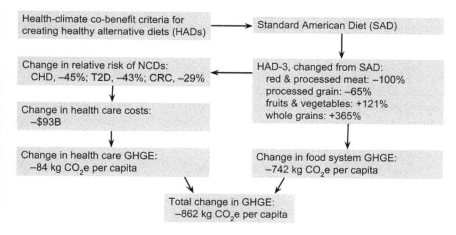

Figure 3.3 Healthier, more plant-based diets can reduce health-care costs and their greenhouse gas emissions. Based on (Hallström et al., 2017)

Source: © 2019 David A. Cleveland, used with permission.

per year. The decreases in GHGE from both food and health-care systems with HAD-3 were equal to 23% of the USA Climate Action Plan (Executive Office of the President, 2013) goal of a 17% reduction below USA 2005 net emission levels by 2020.

While reduction in health-care GHGE was only 10% of the total reduction in GHGE due to dietary change (the other 90% was from the food system), it underestimates the potential for healthy diets to reduce GHGE from the health-care system. This is because we didn't include many diseases (e.g. hypertension, stroke, and forms of cancer other than colorectal cancer) associated with the foods changed in the diets and many potential diet-disease links for foods not changed in the HADs (e.g. added sugar and dairy) that are associated with NCDs due to a lack of quality data. As these data become available, estimates of GHGE from the care of food-related NCDs will increase.

SPBDs are needed to reduce inequality and suffering

The recent *Lancet* report on the global syndemic of obesity, undernutrition, and ACC states the need to recognize that the world system currently incentivizes business to drive this syndemic and prevents policies to counter business as usual – a classic case of market failure where profits are privatized and costs externalized onto society, with the poorest suffering the most (Swinburn et al., 2019, p. 32). Food companies are often aided by governments: for example, in the USA, low-income and minority groups eat the most government-subsidized, obesogenic commodities and have the highest risk for associated NCDs (Siegel et al., 2016) (Figure 3.4).

Vulnerable minority and low-income communities are targeted with advertising for junk food by corporations. For example, in the USA, advertising nutritionally poor products (e.g. fast food, candy, sugary drinks, and snacks) is almost exclusively targeted to black and Hispanic youth (Harris, Frazier, Kumanyika, & Ramirez, 2019), a contributing cause of significantly higher rates of obesity – black (22%), Hispanic (26%) – compared with whites (14%) (Hales, Carroll, Fryar, & Ogden, 2017). In the USA, lower food security is strongly related to the risk of diet-related and other NCDs (Gregory & Coleman-Jensen, 2017).

Because resources are increasingly limited in the Anthropocene, reduced consumption by over-consumers is needed to make food resources available to under-consumers. If food over-consuming and GHGE over-producing populations like those of the USA reduced their food consumption, it could free up resources for under-consuming populations with very low GHGE, like that of Haiti, whose overall well-being would also increase (Figure 3.5). Because animal foods produce the majority of food GHGE and much of the food-related NCDs, this shift would mean a global move towards more SPBDs (e.g. Willett et al., 2019). Importantly, the well-being of over-consuming populations would not have to decrease, as shown by the example of Costa Rica, which, compared with the USA, has almost eight times lower GHGE per capita, over five times lower GDP per capita, 23% less food energy, and 42% less ruminant meat available per capita, yet slightly

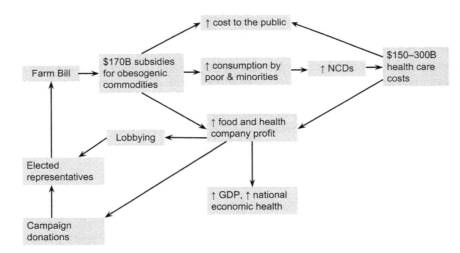

Figure 3.4 The links amongst USA government agricultural subsidies, private profits, disease, and inequality. Based in part on (Siegel et al., 2016)

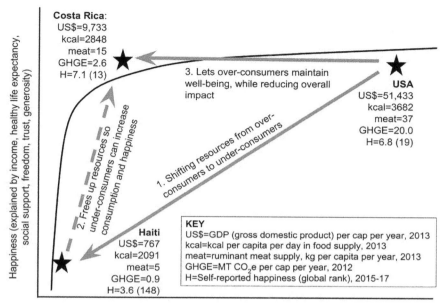

Figure 3.5 More plant-based diets can increase global equity

Sources: GDP: (World Bank, 2019); kcal and meat: (FAOSTAT, 2018); GHGE: (EDGAR, 2016); HI: (Helliwell, Layard, & Sachs, 2018: Statistical Appendix 1 for Chapter 2, pp. 28–30). © 2019 David A. Cleveland, used with permission.

higher self-reported happiness (explained by income, healthy life expectancy, social support, freedom, trust, and generosity). This pattern follows the well-known economic principle that each equal increase in consumption provides less value to consumers whose consumption is already relatively high than to ones that are relatively low.

How could diet change actually happen?

At the macro-level, the food system determines the biophysical, economic, and sociocultural parameters within which people make food and diet choices, and at the individual level, these choices are also influenced by people's unique environments and personal characteristics (cf. Garnett, Mathewson, Angelides, & Borthwick, 2015, pp. 18–19) (Figure 3.6).

The major obstacle to increasing SPBDs at the macro-level is the economic and political power of the food industry, which controls so much of our food and diet choice contexts in part through its corrupting influence on governments, civil organizations, and university researchers (Nestle, 2018;

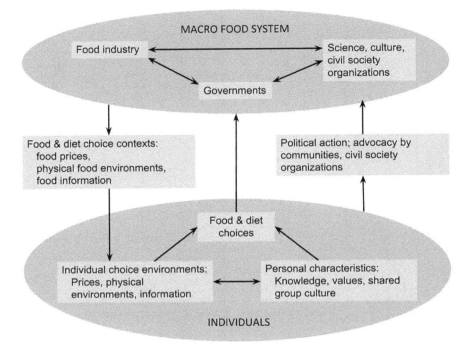

Figure 3.6 Some important variables and processes determining food and diet choice

Swinburn et al., 2019, p. 32). Many government bodies and NGOs believe they need to rely on public-private partnerships to implement nutrition programmes, with for-profit businesses even seen as leaders (Koh, Singer, & Edmondson, 2019), which can lead to subversion of the public-serving mission of the public-sector bodies (Marks, 2017; Nestle, 2018).

At the individual level, a major challenge is people's reluctance to change their diets, which is compounded by the food industry's creation of physical food environments dominated by inexpensive, unhealthy, addictive foods, and its aggressive advertising that dominates food information.

In the following sections, I give some examples of how changes in individual choice environments and personal characteristics, influenced by changes in the macro food system, could move us towards SPBDs.

Prices

Internalizing negative externalities to the food industry (for example, by taxing animal foods and junk foods based on their GHGE or negative health effects) and subsidizing low GHGE, healthy plant foods are ways to move towards SPBDs, since as we have seen, animal foods have negative health effects and the highest GHGE.

Taxes on soda and other sugar-sweetened beverages (SSBs) based on their negative health effects show the potential for taxing animal foods. SSB taxes have been instituted in a number of sites globally and approved by voters in several USA cities, despite strong opposition from the SSB industry, and they have had generally promising results (Redondo, Hernández-Aguado, & Lumbreras, 2018). The first USA SSB tax, implemented in 2015 in Berkeley, California, was followed by an average 52% decrease in SSB consumption and a 29% increase in water consumption in 2015–2017 (Lee et al., 2019). While most life-cycle assessments show sugar having low GHGE, added sugar in the diet is a major cause of obesity, diabetes, and associated health care, as described earlier, which means that sugar makes contributions to GHGE through the health-care system.

A model of the effects in 2020 of taxes on all unhealthy food commodities globally, including using tax revenues to increase the availability of fruits and vegetables, reduced GHGE by 8.6% – two-thirds due to reduced beef consumption and one-quarter due to reduced milk consumption (Springmann et al., 2017). A tax on saturated fat from October 2011 to January 2013 in Denmark resulted in a 4.0% reduction in saturated fat intake, as well as a decrease in salt and increase in vegetable consumption for most people (Smed, Scarborough, Rayner, & Jensen, 2016). Since most saturated fat in the diet is in animal foods, this tax would also decrease GHGE.

Physical environments

Food environments are often dominated by unhealthy animal and other foods but can be managed to increase the availability of plant-based food and decrease the availability of animal foods. Many K–12 schools are implementing policies for healthier, more plant-based, less GHGE intensive meals. For example, the Oakland Unified School District reduced total meat in its school food by almost 30%, resulting in a 14% reduction in GHGE, in spite of a slight increase in beef (Hamerschlag & Kraus-Polk, 2017). In 2019, the California Climate-Friendly Food Program bill was introduced in the state legislation to encourage public schools to provide plant-based food and milk options to pupils to "support California's climate change mitigation goals, and to promote the consumption of healthy food" (California Government, 2019).

Changed food environments resulting in rapid changes in health are also not rare. The North Karelia Project in Finland is a well-known example of a shift towards a more plant-based food environment with dramatic health results (Puska & Stahl, 2010). In response to a very high incidence of cardiovascular mortality in a dairy farm region, the Finish government instituted a campaign to change diets in 1972, including reducing or eliminating subsidies for dairy foods, encouraging dairy farmers to switch to cultivating wild berries, and developing alternative sources of oil from plants. Despite strong opposition from the national dairy industry, dramatic changes in diet resulted and were associated with equally dramatic improvements in health, including an 85% reduction in heart disease mortality by 2005.

Information and knowledge

Research has shown that providing missing information is often not sufficient to change behaviour but can do so if it resonates with or changes values. An experiment with US consumers demonstrated their lack of knowledge of the GHGE of foods, which they most underestimated for animal foods (Camilleri, Larrick, Hossain, & Patino-Echeverri, 2019). When they were provided labels with information on the GHGE of canned vegetable and beef soup, they chose the vegetable soup that had lower emissions more often. An experiment comparing the effects of two, two-quarter freshman year courses on university student food choice found that information about the climate effects of animal foods led to decreased consumption (Jay et al., 2019). Students in a course on the environmental impact of the food system had similar diets as students in a course on cosmology and evolution at the beginning of the courses, but at the end, food systems students reported diets 309 kg CO_2e per person per year lower (a 17% reduction), mostly due to lower beef consumption, which declined from 3.5 to 2.5 servings per week).

Dietary guidelines issued by governments are an important source of information for consumers and in guiding policy, and there is increasing movement towards including climate and other environmental impacts of the food system as criteria in creating dietary guidelines, although there is pushback from the food industry (Gonzalez Fischer & Garnett, 2016). In the USA, the Dietary Guidelines Advisory Committee recommended basing dietary recommendations on environmental impact as well as health (USDA & HHS, 2015b) in the new edition of the Dietary Guidelines for Americans (USDA & HHS, 2015a), but this was rejected by the government, most likely because of pressure from the food industry, especially the meat industry (Gonzalez Fischer & Garnett, 2016, pp. 37–38).

Values

Psychological experiments support the hypothesis that tapping into peoples' sense of fairness and worth can motivate diet change. Experiments with adolescents used an exposé treatment for one group that presented data on food company manipulation of their food choices, while a comparison group received only information on the negative health effects of their food choices. The exposé group saw healthy eating as aligned with the values of autonomy and social justice, and significantly increased their healthy food choices, compared with the control group members, who did not change their food choices (Bryan et al., 2016).

Documentary filmmaker Richard Ray Perez tells a story from his childhood in 1960s California. Young Perez asked his head start teacher why the teacher was not eating the grapes in his lunch (Aguilar, 2014). The teacher told Perez it was because of the United Farm Worker boycott to demand improvement in the unjust working conditions of farm workers. All of a sudden, the grapes, which had only been a source of personal pleasure, activated Perez's value of social justice – he stopped eating his grapes.

Conclusion

There is a food-climate-health-equity crisis that threatens the future of humanity and many other organisms that live on Earth. Our diets, and the food systems they are both driven by and support, are key causes of this crisis. Fortunately, many foods have both positive health and climate environment impacts, and can promote social equity by reducing the overall demand for food and resources. These foods are mostly plant based, and by replacing animal foods, they can reduce the suffering of domestic animals (through reduced demand) as well as wild animals (due to lower demands for land). *The information in this chapter supports the conclusion that change to more SPBDs is a key demand-side solution and is required as part of any strategy to reverse the food-climate-health-equity crisis* (Figure 3.7).

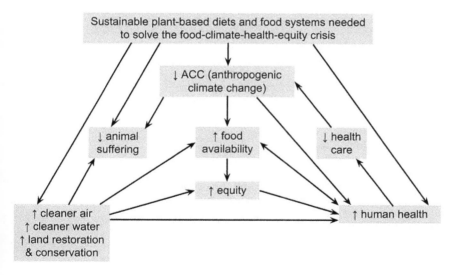

Figure 3.7 Sustainable plant-based diets are needed to avert the food-climate-health-equity crisis

Source: © 2019 David A. Cleveland, used with permission.

We can all choose more SPBDs and advocate for policies to move to more SPBDs, including countering the negative influence of the mainstream food industry.

One key is changing values. Will the new empirical realities of the food-climate-health-equity crisis in the Anthropocene activate values that can drive diet change, for example, by expanding the ways in which food can give us pleasure? Like Perez's epiphany about the grapes in his lunch, we need to empathize with all of the processes that bring food to our plates and make our personal choices and social advocacy responsive to our goals for food that promotes a habitable climate and environment, healthy people, social justice, and animal welfare, as well as being delicious.

Acknowledgements

I thank Daniela Soleri, Kathleen Kevany, and one anonymous reviewer for valuable comments on drafts, as well as the students and Teaching Assistants in my Diet and Global Climate Change course at UCSB for many enlightening discussions, including challenging my assumptions.

Competing interests

I have no competing interests.

References

ADA. (2018). Economic costs of diabetes in the U.S. in 2017. *Diabetes Care, 41*, 917–928. doi:10.2337/dci18-0007

Aguilar, C. (2014, April 24). *Dir. Richard Ray Perez on "Cesar's Last Fast" Part 2: An imperfect man capable of great things*. Retrieved from www.indiewire.com/2014/04/dir-richard-ray-perez-on-cesars-last-fast-part-2-an-imperfect-man-capable-of-great-things-168721/

Andersson, C., & Vasan, R. S. (2017). Epidemiology of cardiovascular disease in young individuals. *Nature Reviews Cardiology* [Advance online publication]. doi:10.1038/nrcardio.2017.154

Aune, D., Giovannucci, E., Boffetta, P., Fadnes, L. T., Keum, N., Norat, T., . . . Tonstad, S. (2017). Fruit and vegetable intake and the risk of cardiovascular disease, total cancer and all-cause mortality – A systematic review and dose-response meta-analysis of prospective studies. *International Journal of Epidemiology, 46*(3), 1029–1056. doi:10.1093/ije/dyw319

Bajželj, B., Richards, K. S., Allwood, J. M., Smith, P., Dennis, J. S., Curmi, E., . . . Gilligan, C. A. (2014). Importance of food-demand management for climate mitigation. *Nature Climate Change, 4*, 924–929. doi:10.1038/nclimate2353

Balcombe, P., Speirs, J. F., Brandon, N. P., & Hawkes, A. D. (2018). Methane emissions: Choosing the right climate metric and time horizon. *Environmental Science: Processes & Impacts, 20*(10), 1323–1339. doi:10.1039/C8EM00414E

Bloom, D. E., Cafiero, E. T., Jané-Llopis, E., Abrahams-Gessel, S., Bloom, L. R., Fathima, S., . . . Weinstein, C. (2011). *The global economic burden of non-communicable diseases.* Retrieved from http://apps.who.int/medicinedocs/en/m/abstract/Js18806en/

Bouvard, V., Loomis, D., Guyton, K. Z., Grosse, Y., Ghissassi, F. E., Benbrahim-Tallaa, L., . . . Straif, K. (2015). Carcinogenicity of consumption of red and processed meat. *The Lancet Oncology, 16*(16), 1599–1600. http://dx.doi.org/10.1016/S1470-2045(15)00444-1

Bryan, C. J., Yeager, D. S., Hinojosa, C. P., Chabot, A., Bergen, H., Kawamura, M., . . . Steubing, F. (2016). Harnessing adolescent values to motivate healthier eating. *Proceedings of the National Academy of Sciences, 113*(39), 10830–10835. doi:10.1073/pnas.1604586113

California Government. (2019, February 12). *AB-479. School meals: Plant-based food and milk options: California climate-friendly food program.* Retrieved from www.leginfo.legislature.ca.gov/faces/billNavClient.xhtml?bill_id=201920200AB479

Camilleri, A. R., Larrick, R. P., Hossain, S., & Patino-Echeverri, D. (2019). Consumers underestimate the emissions associated with food but are aided by labels. *Nature Climate Change, 9*(1), 53–58. doi:10.1038/s41558-018-0354-z

Canning, P., Rehkamp, S., Waters, A., & Etemadnia, H. (2017). *The role of fossil fuels in the U.S. food system and the American diet, ERR-224.* Retrieved from www.ers.usda.gov/publications/pub-details/?pubid=82193

Chen, S., Kuhn, M., Prettner, K., & Bloom, D. E. (2018). The macroeconomic burden of noncommunicable diseases in the United States: Estimates and projections. *PLoS One, 13*(11), e0206702. doi:10.1371/journal.pone.0206702

Cleveland, D. A. (2014). *Balancing on a planet: The future of food and agriculture.* Berkeley, CA: University of California Press.

Cleveland, D. A., & Gee, Q. (2017). Plant based diets for mitigating climate change. In F. Mariotti (Ed.), *Vegetarian and plant-based diets in health and disease prevention* (pp. 135–156). Waltham, MA: Academic Press/Elsevier.

EDGAR. (2016). *GHG time series 1990–2012 per capita emissions for world countries.* Retrieved from http://edgar.jrc.ec.europa.eu/overview.php?v=GHGts_pc1990-2012

EPA. (2018). *Inventory of U.S. greenhouse gas emissions and sinks: 1990–2016.* Retrieved from www.epa.gov/ghgemissions/inventory-us-greenhouse-gas-emissions-and-sinks-1990-2016

Executive Office of the President. (2013). *The President's climate action plan.* Washington, DC: The White House.

FAO. (2016). *The state of food and agriculture 2016 (SOFA): Climate change, agriculture and food security.* Rome, Italy: FAO. Retrieved from www.fao.org/publications/card/en/c/18679629-67bd-4030-818c-35b206d03f34/

FAOSTAT. (2018). *Food and agriculture data.* Retrieved from http://www.fao.org/faostat/en/#home

Friel, S., Dangour, A. D., Garnett, T., Lock, K., Chalabi, Z., Roberts, I., . . . Haines, A. (2009). Public health benefits of strategies to reduce greenhouse-gas emissions: Food and agriculture. *The Lancet, 374*(9706), 2016–2025. Retrieved from http://linkinghub.elsevier.com/retrieve/pii/S0140673609617530

Garnett, T., Mathewson, S., Angelides, P., & Borthwick, F. (2015). *Policies and actions to shift eating patterns: What works?* Food Climate Research

Network. Retrieved from www.fcrn.org.uk/fcrn-publications/reports/policies-and-actions-shift-eating-patterns-what-works

Gerber, P. J., Steinfeld, H., Henderson, B., Mottet, A., Opio, C., Dijkman, J., . . . Tempio, G. (2013). *Tackling climate change through livestock – A global assessment of emissions and mitigation opportunities.* Retrieved from www.fao.org/ag/againfo/resources/en/publications/tackling_climate_change/index.htm

Godfray, H. C. J., Aveyard, P., Garnett, T., Hall, J. W., Key, T. J., Lorimer, J., . . . Jebb, S. A. (2018). Meat consumption, health, and the environment. *Science*, *361*(6399), eaam5324. doi:10.1126/science.aam5324

Gonzalez Fischer, C., & Garnett, T. (2016). *Plates, pyramids and planet – Developments in national healthy and sustainable dietary guidelines: A state of play assessment.* Retrieved from www.fcrn.org.uk/fcrn-publications/reports/plates-pyramids-and-planet-%E2%80%93-developments-national-healthy-and-sustainable

Gregory, C., & Coleman-Jensen, A. (2017). *Food insecurity, chronic disease, and health among working-age adults* (Economic Research Report No. ERR-235). Retrieved from https://www.ers.usda.gov/webdocs/publications/84467/err-235.pdf?v=0

Hales, C., Carroll, M., Fryar, C., & Ogden, C. (2017). *Prevalence of obesity among adults and youth: United States, 2015–2016* (NCHS Data Brief, No. 288). Hyattsville, MD: National Center for Health Statistics. Retrieved from www.cdc.gov/nchs/data/databriefs/db288.pdf

Hallström, E., Carlsson-Kanyama, A., & Börjesson, P. (2015). Environmental impact of dietary change: A systematic review. *Journal of Cleaner Production*, *91*, 1–11.

Hallström, E., Gee, Q., Scarborough, P., & Cleveland, D. A. (2017). A healthier US diet could reduce greenhouse gas emissions from both the food and health care systems. *Climatic Change*, *142*(1–2), 199–212. doi:10.1007/s10584-017-1912-5

Hamerschlag, K., & Kraus-Polk, J. (2017). *Shrinking the carbon and water footprint of school food: A recipe for combating climate change. A pilot analysis of Oakland unified school district's food programs.* Retrieved from www.foe.org/projects/food-and-technology/good-food-healthy-planet/school-food-footprint

Harris, J. L., Frazier, W., Kumanyika, S., & Ramirez, A. G. (2019). *Increasing disparities in unhealthy food advertising targeted to Hispanic and Black youth.* Retrieved from http://uconnruddcenter.org/files/Pdfs/TargetedMarketingReport2019.pdf

Heller, M. C., & Keoleian, G. A. (2015). Greenhouse gas emission estimates of U.S. dietary choices and food loss. *Journal of Industrial Ecology*, *19*(3), 391–401. doi:10.1111/jiec.12174

Helliwell, J. F., Layard, R., & Sachs, J. D. (2018). *World happiness report 2018.* New York: Sustainable Development Solutions Network (SDSN).

IPCC. (2018). Summary for policymakers. In V. Masson-Delmotte, P. Zhai, H.-O. Pörtner, D. Roberts, J. Skea, P. R. Shukla . . . T. Waterfield (Eds.), *Global warming of 1.5°C: An IPCC special report on the impacts of global warming of 1.5°C above pre-industrial levels and related global greenhouse gas emission pathways, in the context of strengthening the global response to the threat of climate change, sustainable development, and efforts to eradicate poverty* (Glossary). Geneva, Switzerland: World Meteorological Organization.

Jay, J. A., D'Auria, R., Nordby, C., Rice, D. A., Cleveland, D. A., Friscia, A., . . . Wesel, E. (2019). Reduction of the carbon footprint of college freshman diets after a food-based environmental science course. *Climatic Change*. doi:10.1007/s10584-019-02407-8

Koh, H. K., Singer, S. J., & Edmondson, A. C. (2019). Health as a way of doing business. *JAMA, 321*(1), 33–34. doi:10.1001/jama.2018.18935

Lee, M. M., Falbe, J., Schillinger, D., Basu, S., McCulloch, C. E., & Madsen, K. A. (2019). Sugar-sweetened beverage consumption 3 years after the Berkeley, California, sugar-sweetened beverage tax. *American Journal of Public Health, 109*(4), 637–639. doi:10.2105/ajph.2019.304971

Marks, J. H. (2017). Caveat partner: Sharing responsibility for health with the food industry. *American Journal of Public Health, 107*, 360–361. doi:10.2105/AJPH.2016.303645

Micha, R., Shulkin, M. L., Peñalvo, J. L., Khatibzadeh, S., Singh, G. M., Rao, M., . . . Mozaffarian, D. (2017). Etiologic effects and optimal intakes of foods and nutrients for risk of cardiovascular diseases and diabetes: Systematic reviews and meta-analyses from the nutrition and chronic diseases expert group (NutriCoDE). *PLoS One, 12*(4), e0175149. doi:10.1371/journal.pone.0175149

Myhre, G., Shindell, D., Bréon, F.-M., Collins, W., Fuglestvedt, J., Huang, J., . . . Zhang, H. (2013). Anthropogenic and natural radiative forcing. In T. F. Stocker, D. Qin, G.-K. Plattner, M. Tignor, S. K. Allen, J. Boschung . . . A. Nauels (Eds.), *Climate change 2013: The physical science basis. Contribution of Working Group I to the Fifth Assessment Report of the Intergovernmental Panel on Climate Change* (pp. 659–740). Cambridge, UK: Cambridge University Press.

Nestle, M. (2018). *Unsavory truth: How food companies skew the science of what we eat.* New York, NY: Basic Books.

Payne, C. L. R., Scarborough, P., & Cobiac, L. (2016). Do low-carbon-emission diets lead to higher nutritional quality and positive health outcomes? A systematic review of the literature. *Public Health Nutrition, 19*(14), 2654–2661. doi:10.1017/S1368980016000495

Popkin, B. M. (2006). Global nutrition dynamics: The world is shifting rapidly toward a diet linked with noncommunicable diseases. *The American Journal of Clinical Nutrition, 84*(2), 289–298. Retrieved from <Go to ISI>://000239674300004

Puska, P., & Stahl, T. (2010). Health in all policies – The Finnish initiative: Background, principles, and current issues. *Annual Review of Public Health, 31*, 315–328. Palo Alto, CA: Annual Reviews.

Redondo, M., Hernández-Aguado, I., & Lumbreras, B. (2018). The impact of the tax on sweetened beverages: A systematic review. *The American Journal of Clinical Nutrition, 108*(3), 548–563. doi:10.1093/ajcn/nqy135

Ruddiman, W. F., Ellis, E. C., Kaplan, J. O., & Fuller, D. Q. (2015). Defining the epoch we live in. *Science, 348*(6230), 38–39. doi:10.1126/science.aaa7297

Scarborough, P., Appleby, P., Mizdrak, A., Briggs, A. M., Travis, R., Bradbury, K., . . . Key, T. (2014). Dietary greenhouse gas emissions of meat-eaters, fish-eaters, vegetarians and vegans in the UK. *Climatic Change, 125*(2), 179–192. doi:10.1007/s10584-014-1169-1

Schwingshackl, L., Hoffmann, G., Lampousi, A.-M., Knüppel, S., Iqbal, K., Schwedhelm, C., . . . Boeing, H. (2017). Food groups and risk of type 2 diabetes mellitus: A systematic review and meta-analysis of prospective studies. *European Journal of Epidemiology, 32*(5), 363–375. doi:10.1007/s10654-017-0246-y

Siegel, K. R., McKeever Bullard, K., Imperatore, G., Kahn, H. S., Stein, A. D., Ali, M. K., . . . Narayan, K. M. (2016). Association of higher consumption of foods derived from subsidized commodities with adverse cardiometabolic risk among us adults. *JAMA Internal Medicine*, *176*(8), 1124–1132. doi:10.1001/jamainternmed.2016.2410

Smed, S., Scarborough, P., Rayner, M., & Jensen, J. D. (2016). The effects of the Danish saturated fat tax on food and nutrient intake and modelled health outcomes: An econometric and comparative risk assessment evaluation. *European Journal of Clinical Nutrition*, *70*(6), 681–686. doi:10.1038/ejcn.2016.6

Springmann, M., Mason-D'Croz, D., Robinson, S., Wiebe, K., Godfray, H. C. J., Rayner, M., . . . Scarborough, P. (2017). Mitigation potential and global health impacts from emissions pricing of food commodities. *Nature Climate Change*, *7*, 69–74.

Steffen, W., Rockström, J., Richardson, K., Lenton, T. M., Folke, C., Liverman, D., . . . Schellnhuber, H. J. (2018). Trajectories of the Earth system in the Anthropocene. *Proceedings of the National Academy of Sciences*, *115*(33), 8252–8259. doi:10.1073/pnas.1810141115

Swinburn, B. A., Kraak, V. I., Allender, S., Atkins, V. J., Baker, P. I., Bogard, J. R., . . . Dietz, W. H. (2019). The global syndemic of obesity, undernutrition, and climate change: The Lancet Commission report. *The Lancet*, *393*(10173), 791–846. doi:10.1016/S0140-6736(18)32822-8

Talaei, M., Wang, Y.-L., Yuan, J.-M., Pan, A., & Koh, W.-P. (2017). Meat, dietary heme iron, and risk of type 2 diabetes mellitus: The Singapore Chinese health study. *American Journal of Epidemiology*, *186*(7), 824–833. doi:10.1093/aje/kwx156

Tilman, D., & Clark, M. (2014). Global diets link environmental sustainability and human health. *Nature*, *515*(7528), 518–522. doi:10.1038/nature13959

Toumpanakis, A., Turnbull, T., & Alba-Barba, I. (2018). Effectiveness of plant-based diets in promoting well-being in the management of type 2 diabetes: A systematic review. *BMJ Open Diabetes Research & Care*, *6*(1), e000534. doi:10.1136/bmjdrc-2018-000534

UNFCCC. (2015). *Adoption of the Paris agreement* (Report No. FCCC/CP/2015/L.9/Rev.1). Retrieved from http://unfccc.int/resource/docs/2015/cop21/eng/l09r01.pdf

USDA, & HHS. (2015a). *2015–2020 Dietary guidelines for Americans* (8th ed.). Retrieved from http://health.gov/dietaryguidelines/2015/guidelines/

USDA, & HHS. (2015b). *Scientific report of the 2015 dietary guidelines advisory committee*. Retrieved from www.health.gov/dietaryguidelines/2015-scientific-report/

Vermeulen, S. J., Campbell, B. M., & Ingram, J. S. I. (2012). Climate change and food systems. In A. Gadgil & D. M. Liverman (Eds.), *Annual review of environment and resources* (Vol. 37, pp. 195–222). Palo Alto, CA: Annual Reviews.

Willett, W., Rockström, J., Loken, B., Springmann, M., Lang, T., Vermeulen, S., . . . Murray, C. J. L. (2019). Food in the Anthropocene: The EAT – Lancet Commission on healthy diets from sustainable food systems. *The Lancet*, *393*(10170), 447–492. https://doi.org/10.1016/S0140-6736(18)31788-4

World Bank. (2019). *Data bank: World Development Indicators*. Retrieved from https://databank.worldbank.org/data/reports.aspx?source=2&series=NY.GDP.PCAP.CD&country

4 Beyond halos and technofixes

Considering meat alternatives and their potential for meaningful food systems change

Haley Swartz and Linnea Laestadius

Introduction

In August 2018, the North American Meat Institute (NAMI), a trade association for livestock producers, and Memphis Meats, a biotechnology company specializing in cultured meat production, jointly sent a letter to the Trump administration requesting clarity on the regulation of cultured meat products (Valeti & Carpenter, 2018). Cultured meats pose a distinct and novel regulation conundrum because they are created by culturing animal cells in a sterile environment *outside* of an animal. This collaboration of two unlikely partners – disparate in ideology but unified in their search of economic gain – was an anomaly. Valeti and Carpenter (2018) wrote,

> As an industry, we are uncompromising on product safety and we recognize the importance of consumer transparency. We support a fair and competitive marketplace that lets consumers decide what food products make sense for them and their families, and the existing regulatory framework can achieve these goals.
>
> (p. 1)

The two federal agencies responsible for regulation of the US food supply – the Food and Drug Administration (FDA) and US Department for Agriculture (USDA) – jointly held a public meeting in October 2018 for all stakeholders to discuss the path ahead for US, and potentially global, regulation of the cultured meats market. In November 2018, the two agencies issued a joint press release stating that they will share regulatory authority over these products, with oversight moving from the FDA to the USDA at the cell harvest stage. The administration also felt that additional legislation specific to cultured meat was unnecessary (USDA, 2018).

The evolving discussion over the regulation of animal meat alternatives reflects the nuances of their production, as well as the seeming inevitability of their expansion in the US. Despite its pre-market status, several state lawmakers have now introduced legislation that prohibits cell-cultured meat products from using the term "meat" on its label (Bloch, 2019). Plant-based meat alternatives already have a common presence in modern Western diets. Nielsen data indicates that sales of plant-based alternatives grew 17% in just one year, with a revenue totalling $3.7 billion in 2017 (Good Food Institute, 2018). These trends indicate a need to explore the role of meat alternatives in creating sustainable and healthful diets.

As outlined in the other chapters of this collection, traditional animal meat production poses many concerns, including natural resource protection (Chapter 3), health-promoting approaches (Chapters 5–7), fair and living wages (Chapter 11), and animal welfare (Chapters 8–9), for consumers and producers alike. In the 1980s, producers responded to the demand for new types of protein by introducing meat alternatives (Prichep, 2017). However, the market fundamentally shifted in the 2010s with two technological developments: (1) improvements to the taste and texture of *plant-based meat alternatives* to become more "meat-like", expanding product appeal to a broader segment of consumers, and (2) the use of cellular biotechnology to create *cultured meats* (Aiking, 2011; L. M. Keefe, 2018), described in Table 4.1.

Multiple producers of novel plant-based meat alternatives, often touting their resemblance to animal meat, have now entered the market and have seen rapid growth. For example, in November 2018, the meat alternative company Beyond Meat announced a $100 million initial public offering

Table 4.1 Meat alternative terminology by method of production

Term	Similar Terms	Definition	Example
Plant-based meat alternative	Imitation meat, fake meat, meat substitute, alternative protein, artificial meat, novel protein food, novel vegetal protein, meat replacement	Alternative to animal products that use primarily plant-based ingredients (e.g. soy or pea proteins), which are processed to resemble meat	Beyond Meat, Impossible Foods
Cultured meat	Cell-cultured meat, lab-grown meat, *in vitro* meat, synthetic meat, clean meat, cellular agriculture	Alternative to animal products using biotechnology methods to harvest animal cells, which are then cultured and later processed into a meat product	Memphis Meats, Finless Foods

Source: Authors own work, created for this volume

(Rowland, 2018). Though cultured meat products are not yet widely available, they may enter the market as early as 2022 (L. M. Keefe, 2018).

Proponents argue that these products can answer growing consumer demand for foods that are just as tasty as animal meats but less damaging to both human and environmental health. This message can be distilled into two intersecting psychological effects, illustrated in Figure 4.1. First, the *health halo effect* may lead consumers to fail to fully explore the implications of their food choices or rest on their laurels after a small dietary change. News coverage of the developing industry has largely perpetuated the assumptions that support health halos. One recent review found that media coverage of cultured meat presented it as the *best* solution for the future (Hocquette, 2016). This statement is indicative of a *technofix* mentality, which reinforces the halo effect. While many of these types of claims appear to be valid, and in a growing number of instances verifiable, this chapter illuminates that technologically advanced meat alternatives are not a panacea for the range of production issues in the modern food system. Further, environmental impact assessments and clinical nutrition studies are neither required by the FDA nor are they always made publicly available: companies largely consider this information confidential. Accordingly, these novel foods must be critically and fairly examined across a range of measures to ensure that producers are engaging in ethical practices and accurate marketing. To contextualize the limitations of novel meat alternatives, this chapter explores the evidence underlying these two product categories in the

Technofix	The process by which consumers perceive a food to be healthier than it may be due to the presence of health-promoting labels or branding, which then deters them from seeking further information to support or reject their view (Williams, 2008; Leathwood, Richardson, Sträter, Todd, & van Trijp, 2007).
Health Halo	The philosophy that long-standing food systems problems can be easily solved through advancements in science and engineering, often overlooking potential trade-offs or unintended consequences (Husemann & Husemann, 2011; Scott, 2011). The emerging "halo effect" is depicted in Figure 4.1.

Figure 4.1 Definitions of halo effect and technofix.

Source: Created by author, adapted from Williams, 2005 and Husemann and Husemann, 2011.

following dimensions: nutrition and health, environmental sustainability, food safety, farmed animals, and business practices. These five dimensions are highlighted not to favour one product category over another, but to promote close and transparent examinations of technological interventions that seek to improve the food system.

Current state of the evidence

Nutrition and health

The meat alternative market has been cited as the *next protein transition*, representing the most recent in a series of fundamental dietary shifts in Western countries towards protein-rich foods (Aiking & de Boer, 2018). However, emerging research is unclear about the nutritional profiles of meat alternatives in comparison to traditional meats or unprocessed plant-based proteins. For example, while protein-equivalent, plant-based alternatives to beef may offer an equivalent or improved nutritional impact (including full lipid profiles, key vitamins, minerals, and micronutrients), many of the ingredients used to create meat alternatives are new to human diets and research has not established their long-term nutritional or health impact (e.g. soy protein concentrate, pea protein isolate) (Eshel, Shepon, Noor, & Milo, 2016; Friends of the Earth, 2018). Novel meat alternatives may also be at odds with the clean label movement, which emphasizes eating "real food" made only with ingredients that are easily pronounced and with no artificial ingredients or synthetic chemicals (Go Clean Label, 2019). Whereas consumers can choose grass-fed animal meat or a two-ingredient bowl of organic rice and beans, novel meat alternatives may have a dozen or more ingredients ranging from additives (e.g. caramel colour, maltodextrin) to processing aids that are not required to be listed on food package ingredient labels (e.g. antibiotics, yeast, or certain algaes) (Friends of the Earth, 2018). Consumers concerned with the health and safety risks posed by industrial processing techniques may also be wary of highly processed plant-based meats (Smetana, Mathys, Knoch, & Heinz, 2015). Emerging public health research indicates that meat alternatives may be higher in salt than whole plant-based foods and at least in one case may contain added sugars or sweeteners that are not contained in either whole plant foods or animal meat (Action on Salt, 2018; Environmental Working Group, 2018). Additional concerns include allergenic properties of some ingredients, such as soy proteins and whether companies should be required to disclose allergen information on the package label – an issue irrelevant for single ingredient protein sources (Joshi & Kumar, 2015).

Lastly, given the critical role of price in determining food choice (Andreyeva, Long, & Brownell, 2010), the relatively high cost of meat alternatives currently on the market may pose a barrier for those looking to substitute their animal meat consumption with novel plant-based meat alternatives (Kumar et al., 2017). However, research highlights the potential for public policy to reduce the price of meat substitutes to expand market access for lower income consumers in Western countries. For instance, Ritchie, Reay, and Higgins (2018) tested five scenarios in which reduced prices for meat alternatives avoided between 8,500 and 52,000 premature deaths annually, as well as declines in greenhouse gas emissions (GHGE) by 3 to 583 MtCO2e/year.

Environmental sustainability

In 2018, the United Nations Environment Program (2018) presented two plant-based meat alternative companies – Impossible Food and Beyond Meat – with the Champion of the Earth award for their environmentally friendly products, reflecting a mounting body of evidence on the positive substitution effects of replacing animal protein with meat alternatives. For instance, Eshel et al. (2016) found that "replacement diets" that substitute plant-based meat alternatives for beef consumption use only 10% of the land, 4% of the GHGE, and 6% of the reactive nitrogen traditionally required by diets high in beef consumption. Direct substitution of beef for plant-based meat alternatives also significantly reduced annual GHGE and land use linked to diets, but with mixed results on water use (Goldstein, Moses, Sammons, & Birkved, 2017; Smetana, Aganovic, Irmscher, & Heinz, 2018; Van Mierlo, Rohmer, & Gerdessen, 2017). However, there may be notable distinctions in the environmental footprints of different brands of plant-based meat alternatives depending on their use of renewable energy sources in production and the types of farms from which they source their ingredients. For example, organic farms have been shown to provide more ecosystems services and produce fewer greenhouse gas emissions per acre than conventional farms (Squalli & Adamkiewicz, 2018).

However, some researchers have begun to question if reductions in animal meat in Western diets actually need to be fully replaced with meat alternatives. For instance, Aiking and de Boer (2018) found that *reducing* overconsumption of animal protein was more efficient than *replacing* animal protein with plant-based meat alternatives because Westerners are, in large part already, over-consuming protein and any reduction would decrease reliance on production inputs. On the other hand, replacements still require inputs, albeit fewer than that required to produce animal meats (Aiking & de Boer, 2018). However, for individuals shifting entirely to a plant-based diet, the need for plant-based protein sources to maintain health is obvious.

As the plant-based meat alternative industry continues to grow, and as cultured meat products approach market release, the differing environmental impacts of the two product categories will become an increasingly important dimension for environmentally conscious consumers. One recent life-cycle assessment compared the resource use of novel proteins with traditional livestock production, finding that cultured meats had similarly high reliance on electricity, water, and transportation, while plant-based meat alternatives demanded less of agricultural land, marine and freshwater sources, and ozone depletion (Smetana et al., 2015).

Food safety

Cultured meat holds distinct food safety risks due to the novel methods of its production. In fact, both its risks and benefits have yet to be assessed due to its innovative stature in the spectrum of plant-based meat alternatives. In the laboratory, producers have greater control over the product's environment and exposure to disease (i.e. cells are unaffected by the changes in weather, feed, or land availability that can lead to zoonotic diseases in animals) (Arshad, Javaid, Sohaib, Saeed, & Imran, 2017; Ravensdale, Coorey, & Dykes, 2018), while human producers within the laboratory may also unknowingly contribute to the contamination of the cell culture itself (e.g. bacteria, parasites, viruses, and other animal cells) (Pauwels et al., 2007). For plant-based meat alternatives, concerns have been raised that the combination of a neutral pH and high moisture content heightens susceptibility to spoilage and endospore-forming bacteria (Wild et al., 2014).

Antimicrobial resistance is a major concern in global agriculture, both in animal meat production and new meat alternatives. The use of antibiotics to eliminate bacterial or fungal infections within a cell culture raises similar concerns to those posed by the systemic, non-therapeutic uses of antibiotics in current animal-protein production (Bhat, Kumar, & Fayaz, 2015). Several cultured meat companies and their proponents have publicly stated that they do not use antibiotics, but some scientists are concerned about the stability of the sterile environment once these products reach the marketplace (Watson, 2018).

It may be possible for producers to genetically engineer plant-based ingredients that are invulnerable to antimicrobial resistance as one particularly salient example of a technofix that could mitigate the food safety concerns posed by both meat alternatives and animal meat production. But limited consumer acceptance of genetic engineering techniques could also stymie scientific efforts to improve the quality and safety within both markets (Wunderlich & Gatto, 2015). Slow regulatory approval processes on the safety of genetically modified ingredients may also confuse consumers while placing companies at risk. For example, Impossible Foods began selling its magic ingredient *heme* months before the FDA confirmed the company's voluntary request to affirm that the ingredient was generally recognized as safe (GRAS). Impossible Foods marketed its burger as *bleeding*, as it appeared pink in the middle due to the presence of the genetically engineered heme protein (i.e. a strain of soy leghemoglobin) (Devenyns, 2018). But the FDA did not finalize Impossible Foods' GRAS determination until July 2018, ending a six-month-long regulatory indeterminant state during which the burger was already available for mass market consumption (D. M. Keefe, 2018).

Farmed animals

Plant-based meat alternatives have no animal inputs, thus eliminating harms to farmed animals. However, several meat alternatives continue to use dairy and egg ingredients, preventing complete independence from large-scale animal farming. Furthermore, at least one of the novel ingredients in plant-based meat alternatives have been tested on animals: the previously mentioned heme in the Impossible Burger was tested on rats to provide additional safety data to the FDA (Impossible Foods, 2019).

Cultured meat presents a more complex situation. Although cells could theoretically be sourced from cell lines programmed to proliferate indefinitely, harvesting cells directly from living animals is currently more feasible (Stephens et al., 2018). Further, the media used for culturing cells often include fetal calf or horse serum, though animal-free media are currently being studied (Stephens et al., 2018). These processes remain so novel that it is unclear what production methods will be viable, profitable, and in use once production is scaled up for the commercial market.

Finally, the emphasis on meat alternatives may also contribute to a widespread assumption that a whole-food, plant-based diet is insufficient to meet dietary needs. Some researchers have raised concerns that the development of meat alternatives that closely resemble or identically replicate the composition of conventional animal meats perpetuates carnism, the cultural norm that animals are a foodstuff ethically appropriate for human consumption (Joy, 2011; Laestadius, Deckers, & Baran, 2018).

Business practices

Industry profit motives underlie many of the aforementioned concerns. Several cultured meat and plant-based meat alternative companies have obtained funding from venture capitalists, with the assumption of receiving a return on investment. While meat alternatives may be mutually beneficial for both business owners and public health, the profit-seeking nature of these industries subjects them to the same incentives for legal and ethical food crimes as the conventional animal meat industry (Laestadius et al., 2018). Food crimes, which also include "lawful but awful" practices, can include mislabelled or adulterated foods; misleading advertising; price fixing; exploitation of workers, animals, and the environment; and "mass processing of unhealthy foods" (Croall, 2012). Put simply, a different product and technology does not inherently result in an ethical production process when companies continue to operate within the same criminogenic environment (Croall, 2013). For example, JUST foods, previously known as Hampton Creek, was at the centre of several controversies regarding production and business practices (Kowitt, 2016). As companies continue to grow in both operations and market share, the need to meet shareholder profit expectations may have unintended consequences on workers, the environment, and public health.

To date, large agribusinesses with poor environmental and labour practices have invested significant funding in plant-based meat alternative and cultured meat start-up companies. Rather than putting large agricultural interests out of business, meat alternative companies are becoming increasingly intertwined with them. For example, Tyson Foods now holds stakes in both plant-based meat alternative company Beyond Meat and cultured meat company Memphis Meats (Trotter, 2018). Tyson Foods, the world's largest processor and marketer of many animal meats, is known to have engaged in multiple environmental and occupational health violations, resulting in millions of dollars of penalties by federal authorities (US Department of Justice, 2017; US Environmental Protection Agency, 2013). Plant-based meat alternative producer Field Roast was fully acquired by Maple Leaf Foods (2018), one of the largest farmed animal processors in Canada. As small companies shift from start-ups to large enterprises, the original, often ethically grounded, intent of their founders may be obscured. This deviation may also inadvertently diminish appeal to the public, which increasingly seeks food industry transparency alongside commitments to environmental sustainability.

Recommendations and conclusion

Meat alternatives offer choice to consumers who wish to mitigate harmful, unintended consequences of conventional animal agriculture. But environmentally and nutritionally conscious consumers and producers alike must recognize the inherent limitations of trying to forge systematic change in a profit-driven system. As these markets expand, so will claims of products' environmental and health benefits. Consumers must both question the evidence underlying any product's apparent halo and push for structural policy changes to ensure that producers are held to appropriate standards. Ethical trade-offs will continue to abound within the meat alternative market, leaving consumers to make choices that reflect their individual values.

Ultimately, meat alternatives are not cruelty-free if they are produced in a way that causes harm to the environment, human health, or animal or human well-being (White, 2017). While the perfect should not be the enemy of the good, it is also critical not to allow a halo effect or a technofix mentality to obscure harms that need to be addressed through more significant food system reforms. Consumers and interest groups must continue to interrogate the practices and inputs to production of the companies that make their foods, whether it be conventional animal meat or meat alternatives. Federal agencies should exercise regulatory authority to ensure fair wages for workers, ethical sourcing of inputs to production, fair and accurate labelling claims, and the safety of innovative processing techniques. Businesses themselves should ensure that they engage in ethical sourcing and labour practices, and consider applying for status as a Certified B Corporation. B Corporation status requires businesses to receive a minimum verified score on an "assessment of a company's impact on its workers, customers, community, and environment" (Certified B Corporation, 2019).

This chapter has illustrated a substantial opportunity for greater transparency in the meat alternatives sector. While meat alternatives are without a doubt an improvement on large-scale animal agriculture, they are not without risks and harms of their own. Further, the merging of interests between meat alternative start-ups and large-scale agribusiness requires interrogation of both sectors' commitments to transparency, food system equity, environmental sustainability, and public health as central goals of business.

The low carbon footprint of a product does not guarantee ethical labour practices or nutritious ingredients, nor can these products engineer away the myriad ethical issues throughout the modern food system. Achieving the vision outlined in this collection – to be fed, nurtured, and loved – cannot be fulfilled by merely consuming a different protein source. Meat alternatives have the potential to make a contribution along the way, with the recognition that a change to sustainable food systems will ultimately require societies to rethink more than the meat on their plates.

References

Action on Salt. (2018). *2018 meat alternatives survey*. Retrieved from www.action-onsalt.org.uk/media/action-on-salt/Meat-Alternatives-Oct-18-Report.pdf

Aiking, H. (2011). Future protein supply. *Trends in Food Science & Technology*, 22(2–3), 112–120.

Aiking, H., & de Boer, J. (2018, in press). The next protein transition. *Trends in Food Science & Technology*. https://doi.org/10.1016/j.tifs.2018.07.008

Andreyeva, T., Long, M. W., & Brownell, K. D. (2010). The impact of food prices on consumption: A systematic review of research on the price elasticity of demand for food. *American Journal of Public Health*, 100(2), 216–222.

Arshad, M. S., Javaid, M., Sohaib, M., Saeed, F., & Imran, A. (2017). Tissue engineering approaches to develop cultured meat from cells: A mini review. *Cogent Food & Agriculture*, 3(1). doi:10.1080/23311932.2017.1320814

Bhat, Z. F., Kumar, S., & Fayaz, H. (2015). In vitro meat production: Challenges and benefits over conventional meat production. *Journal of Integrative Agriculture*, 14(2), 241–248.

Bloch, S. (2019). Following Missouri's lead, other states take on cell-cultured meat. *The New Food Economy*. Retrieved from https://newfoodeconomy.org/missouri-nebraska-cell-cultured-plant-based-meat-labeling/

Certified B Corporation. (2019). *About*. Retrieved from https://bcorporation.net/about-b-corps

Croall, H. (2012). Food, crime, harm and regulation. *Criminal Justice Matters*, 90(1), 16–17. doi:10.1080/09627251.2012.751218

Croall, H. (2013). Food crime: A green criminology perspective. In N. South & A. Brisman (Eds.), *Routledge international handbook of green criminology* (pp. 167–183). New York, NY: Routledge.

Devenyns, J. (2018). Impossible Burger's 'bleeding' ingredient gets FDA approval. *Food Dive*. Retrieved from www.fooddive.com/news/impossible-burgers-bleeding-ingredient-gets-fda-approval/528577/

Environmental Working Group (EWG). (2018). Beyond meat plant protein beast burger patties. *EWG's Food Scores*. Retrieved from www.ewg.org/foodscores/products/852629004231-BeyondMeatPlantProteinBeastBurgerPatties+

Eshel, G., Shepon, A., Noor, E., & Milo, R. (2016). Environmentally optimal, nutritionally aware beef replacement plant-based diets. *Environmental Science & Technology, 50*(15), 8164–8168.

Friends of the Earth. (2018). *From lab to fork: Critical questions on laboratory-created animal product alternatives*. Retrieved from https://1bps6437gg8c169i0y1drtgz-wpengine.netdna-ssl.com/wp-content/uploads/2018/06/From-Lab-to-Fork-1.pdf

Go Clean Label. (2019). *About*. Retrieved from https://gocleanlabel.com/about

Good Food Institute. (2018). *Plant-based market overview*. Retrieved from www.gfi.org/marketresearch

Goldstein, B., Moses, R., Sammons, N., & Birkved, M. (2017). Potential to curb the environmental burdens of American beef consumption using a novel plant-based beef substitute. *PLoS One, 12*(12), e0189029.

Hocquette, J. F. (2016). Is in vitro meat the solution for the future? *Meat Science, 120*, 167–176.

Husemann, J., & Husemann, M. (2011). *Techno-fix: Why technology won't save us or the environment*. Canada: New Society Publishers. ISBN: 9780865717046.

Impossible Foods. (2019). *The agonizing dilemma of animal testing*. Retrieved from https://impossiblefoods.com/if-pr/the-agonizing-dilemma-of-animal-testing/

Joshi, V. K., & Kumar, S. (2015). Meat analogues: Plant based alternatives to meat products – A review. *International Journal of Food and Fermentation Technology, 5*(2), 107.

Joy, M. (2011). *Why we love dogs, eat pigs, and wear cows: An introduction to carnism*. San Francisco, CA: Conari Press.

Keefe, D. M. (2018). *Letter to Gary Yingling on GRAS Notice No. GRN 000737*. Office of Food Additive Safety, Center for Food Safety and Applied Nutrition of the Food and Drug Administration. Retrieved from www.fda.gov/downloads/Food/IngredientsPackagingLabeling/GRAS/NoticeInventory/UCM620362.pdf

Keefe, L. M. (2018). #FakeMeat: How big a deal will animal meat analogs ultimately be? *Animal Frontiers, 8*(3), 30–37.

Kowitt, B. (2016). Hampton Creek: The history of a mayo startup in 5 controversies. *Fortune*. Retrieved from http://fortune.com/2016/09/23/hampton-creek-controversies/

Kumar, P., Chatli, M. K., Mehta, N., Singh, P., Malav, O. P., & Verma, A. K. (2017). Meat analogues: Health promising sustainable meat substitutes. *Critical Reviews in Food Science and Nutrition, 57*(5), 923–932.

Laestadius, L., Deckers, J., & Baran, S. (2018). Food crimes, harms and carnist technologies. In R. Hinch & A. Gray (Eds.), *A handbook of food crime: Immoral and illegal practices in the food industry and what to do about them* (pp. 295–312). Bristol, UK: Policy Press.

Leathwood, P. D., Richardson, D. P., Sträter, P., Todd, P. M., & van Trijp, H. C. (2007). Consumer understanding of nutrition and health claims: Sources of evidence. *British Journal of Nutrition, 98*(3), 474–484.

Maple Leaf Foods. (2018). *Maple leaf foods closes acquisition of Field Roast Grain Meat Co*. Retrieved from www.mapleleaffoods.com/news/maple-leaf-foods-closes-acquisition-of-field-roast-grain-meat-co/

Pauwels, K., Herman, P., Van Vaerenbergh, B., Dai Do Thi, C., Berghmans, L., Waeterloos, G., . . . Sneyers, M. (2007). Animal cell cultures: Risk assessment and biosafety recommendations. *Applied Biosafety, 12*(1), 26–38.

Prichep, D. (2017). The rise of mock meat: How its story reflects America's ever-changing values. *National Public Radio.* Retrieved from www.npr. org/sections/thesalt/2017/09/02/547899191/the-rise-of-mock-meat-how-its-story-reflects-americas-ever-changing-values

Ravensdale, J. T., Coorey, R., & Dykes, G. A. (2018). Integration of emerging bio-medical technologies in meat processing to improve meat safety and quality. *Comprehensive Reviews in Food Science and Food Safety, 17*(3), 615–632.

Ritchie, H., Reay, D. S., & Higgins, P. (2018). Potential of meat substitutes for climate change mitigation and improved human health in high-income markets. *Frontiers in Sustainable Food Systems, 2,* 16.

Rowland, M. P. (2018). Beyond meat continues to sizzle, announces IPO. *Forbes.* Retrieved from www.forbes.com/sites/michaelpellmanrowland/2018/11/18/ vegan-ipo-beyond-meat/#7081c96a314c

Scott, D. (2011). The technological fix criticisms and the agricultural biotechnology debate. *Journal of Agricultural and Environmental Ethics, 24*(3), 207–226.

Smetana, S., Aganovic, K., Irmscher, S., & Heinz, V. (2018). Agri-food waste streams utilization for development of more sustainable food substitutes. In E. Benetto, K. Gericke, & M. Guiton (Eds.), *Designing sustainable technologies, products and policies: From science to innovation* (pp. 145–155). Cham, Switzerland: Springer International. https://doi.org/10.1007/978-3-319-66981-6

Smetana, S., Mathys, A., Knoch, A., & Heinz, V. (2015). Meat alternatives: Life cycle assessment of most known meat substitutes. *The International Journal of Life Cycle Assessment, 20*(9), 1254–1267.

Squalli, J., & Adamkiewicz, G. (2018). Organic farming and greenhouse gas emissions: A longitudinal U.S. state-level study. *Journal of Cleaner Production, 192,* 30–42. doi:10.1016/j.jclepro.2018.04.160

Stephens, N., Dunsford, I., Di Silvio, L., Ellis, M., Glencross, A., & Sexton, A. (2018). Bringing cultured meat to market: Technical, socio-political, and regulatory challenges in cellular agriculture. *Trends in Food Science & Technology, 78,* 155–166.

Trotter, G. (2018). Why Tyson, the largest meat processor in the U.S., is investing in fake meat. *Chicago Tribune.* Retrieved from www.chicagotribune.com/business/ ct-biz-tyson-ventures-beyond-meat-20180419-story.html

United Nations Environment Programme. (2018). *Tackling the world's most urgent problem: Meat.* Retrieved from www.unenvironment.org/news-and-stories/story/ tackling-worlds-most-urgent-problem-meat

US Department of Agriculture. (2018). *Statement from USDA Secretary Perdue and FDA Commissioner Gottlieb on the regulation of cell-cultured food products from cell lines of livestock and poultry* (Release No. 0248.18). Retrieved from www.usda.gov/media/press-releases/2018/11/16/statement-usda-secretary-perdue-and-fda-commissioner-gottlieb

US Department of Justice. (2017). *Tyson poultry pleads guilty to clean water act violations in connection with discharge of acidic feed supplement.* Retrieved from www.justice.gov/opa/pr/tyson-poultry-pleads-guilty-clean-water-act-violations-connection-discharge-acidic-feed

US Environmental Protection Agency. (2013). *Tyson Foods, Inc. Clean air act (CAA) settlement*. Retrieved from www.epa.gov/enforcement/tyson-foods-inc

Valeti, U., & Carpenter, B. (2018). *Letter to the Trump administration from Memphis Meats and the North American Meat Institute*. Retrieved January 30, 2019, from www.meatinstitute.org/index.php?ht=a/GetDocumentAction/i/148176

Van Mierlo, K., Rohmer, S., & Gerdessen, J. C. (2017). A model for composing meat replacers: Reducing the environmental impact of our food consumption pattern while retaining its nutritional value. *Journal of Cleaner Production, 165,* 930–950.

Watson, E. (2018). Cell-based meat cos: Please stop calling us 'lab-grown' meat . . . and we don't use antibiotics in full-scale production. *Food Navigator-USA.com*. Retrieved from www.foodnavigator-usa.com/Article/2018/10/25/Cell-based-meat-cos-Please-stop-calling-us-lab-grown-meat-and-we-don-t-use-antibiotics-in-full-scale-production#

White, R. (2017). Capitalism and the commodification of animals: The need for critical vegan praxis, animated by anarchism! In D. Nibert (Ed.), *Animal oppression and capitalism: The oppression of nonhuman animals as sources of food* (pp. 1–26). Santa Barbara, CA: Praeger.

Wild, F., Czerny, M., Janssen, A. M., Kole, A. P., Zunabovic, M., & Domig, K. J. (2014). The evolution of a plant-based alternative to meat. From niche markets to widely accepted meat alternatives. *Agro Food Industry Hi-Tech, 25*(1), 45–49

Williams, P. (2005). Consumer understanding and use of health claims for foods. *Nutrition Reviews, 63*(7), 256–264.

Wunderlich, S., & Gatto, K. A. (2015). Consumer perception of genetically modified organisms and sources of information. *Advances in Nutrition* (Bethesda, Md.), *6*(6), 842–851. doi:10.3945/an.115.008870

Part II

Nourishing humans, health, and well-being

5   Going back for the future? Learning from the past to support a fair, affordable, sustainable, and healthy food system

Sara F. L. Kirk

Introduction

In 2010, Olivier de Schutter, the UN special rapporteur on the Right to Food made the following statement, "Measured against the requirement that they should contribute to the realization of the right to food, the food systems we have inherited from the twentieth century have failed" (de Schutter, 2010). This premise underpins the following chapter because a food system that supports the health of populations and our planet requires us to critically reflect on the factors influencing our current food supply, sustainability, and consumption. Some of these factors have been introduced in earlier chapters or will be explored in ones to follow. In this chapter, the ways that food production and procurement can be modified to better support health and well-being across the life course will be explored. This chapter will also include reflections on the power of food to transform our lives for the better, in ways that are sensitive to the challenges we collectively face. It will explore what it means to build a fair, affordable, sustainable, and healthy food system: where there is social and economic value for all, available and accessible nourishing food, alignment with societal goals for sustainable development, and support for individual and planetary health. Innovation in this regard does not mean ignoring what has been done in the past but building on it for our present and future.

The complex evolution of our modern food system

If there was ever a simple food rule that could make a huge difference to the health of people globally, it is Michael Pollan's oft-cited nutritional wisdom "eat foods, not too much, mostly plants" (Pollan, 2009). Featured in his 2009 book *Food Rules*, it represents a simple, understandable, and achievable goal for most people (Pollan, 2009). While this simple rule could, on its own, have a significant impact on population health, it sharply contrasts with the reality of our modern food system, which is mind-boggling in its complexity. Indeed, the 20th and 21st centuries have been defined by transformative technological shifts in the way that our food is produced and consumed that are not only impacting the health of people but also the health of our planet, as earlier chapters have outlined. While there is no doubt that many of these advances have been positive, there are downsides too. Food, long considered a basic human right, as defined by Maslow's (1943) hierarchy of needs (Maslow, 1943) and the United Nations (United Nations, n.d.), is now widely regarded as a commodity rather than a necessity. As food production has been concentrated in a smaller number of large agri-businesses, so has society become more and more disconnected from how food is raised, grown, processed, distributed, and marketed (Vivero Pol, 2013).

This scenario of disconnection plays out across many countries and cultures and is typically viewed as a natural, indeed inevitable, progression as societies advance and prosper. The corporatization and commodification of our food supply are lauded as desirable by-products of progress, yet our modern food environment, with its reliance on non-renewable energy to produce heavily processed convenience foods, is contributing to a range of chronic diseases, including obesity, heart disease, and cancer (Kickbusch, 2010). Ironically, therefore, we have made significant advances in the management and eradication of communicable diseases, only to replace them with non-communicable diseases (NCDs). Layer on shifting demographics, time pressures, and the desire for convenience, and we can see a complex web of factors that, when viewed together, have created a modern food environment that is not reflective of optimal health, but instead undermines it. As a result of the focus on energy-dense, nutrient-poor food, healthy behaviours, like consuming sufficient fruit and vegetable servings, are abnormal within our modern food environment. To illustrate, the World Health Organization suggests consuming more than 400 grams of fruits and vegetables per day to improve overall health and reduce the risk of certain NCDs (World Health Organization, 2019), which translates into at least five servings per day. Yet global estimates suggest that more than three-quarters of adults do not achieve this benchmark (Hall, Moore, Harper, & Lynch, 2009). More concerning, a recent analysis found that global production of fruits and vegetables is not sufficient to meet the nutritional needs of the current population (Kc et al., 2018). In other words, the world is not producing enough fruits and vegetables, pulses, nuts, and seeds for good health, even if people were shifting to a higher level of consumption. The authors go on to note that achieving the global sustainable development goals will require us to consume and produce more fruits and vegetables, as well as transition to diets higher in plant-based protein (Kc et al., 2018), demonstrating the wide chasm between knowledge and action.

So how did we get to this point, whereby the food that we eat is harming rather than helping our health and the health of our planet? More importantly, what can we do, as individuals and collectively, to address these complex challenges and ensure a healthier, more sustainable food system? To be able to answer these questions, we first need to reflect on our current system and how it differs from the diet of our ancestors. Over the course of evolution, survival of the human species has been dependent on the ability to adapt to the available food supply. Without this ability, the human species would not have survived when food was scarce. Anthropological studies have shown that, for most of its history, the human species existed on a limited diet consisting of meat, cereals, roots, fruits, nuts, and leafy vegetables (Garn, 1989). Such a diet has been calculated to be low in fat, high in fibre, and rich in micronutrients (Garn, 1989). The decline of hunter gathering in approximately 8500 BC was the start of what Lang (2009) has noted as a long history of transformations that have shaped food and health. These events changed the way that food was produced and preserved, with the industrial and agricultural revolutions of the mid-19th century onwards providing the blueprint for our modern food system. This model of food production is characterized by specialization, mechanization, and consolidation into a smaller number of large farms (Lang, 2009). A full review of these events is beyond the scope of this chapter; however, the ramifications have shaped our food system profoundly throughout the 20th century and underpin two of the challenges that we now face in the 21st century: the juxtaposition of hunger with overconsumption and the unsustainability of our food supply (Food and Agriculture Organization of the United Nations, 2017).

The typical diet of most people in industrialized countries is high in fat and sugar, and low in complex carbohydrates and fibre (Kickbusch, 2010). This comparatively rapid change in food intake experienced in industrialized societies over recent years has occurred so quickly in evolutionary terms that it has not been accompanied by evolutionary adaptation. The existence of an abundant supply of palatable, energy-dense food promotes overconsumption, which in turn leads to an increase in fat deposition linked to the development of diet-related disease (Lang, 2009), also discussed in Chapter 6. The mechanisms that drive overconsumption in the face of dietary excess can be explained in terms of the evolutionary response to an irregular food supply. For thousands of years, the biggest threat to the human species was starvation through food shortage. From an evolutionary perspective, therefore, it makes sense that when food is available, there will be a strong biological drive to overeat, hence preventing starvation, an essential survival mechanism for an unpredictable food supply. However, this process appears to work in one direction only, with no corresponding drive to under-consume in the presence of excess food. This hunter-gatherer existence required large amounts of daily physical activity to obtain food, such that physical activity was driven by the need to eat. Nowadays, eating drives the need to be physically active, but this is a much weaker feedback loop. Thus, the increasing prevalence of diet-related diseases, including obesity and diabetes, highlights a far more complex situation governing food intake than a response purely to physiological need (Foresight, 2011).

Food intake is also no longer reliant on food availability due to improvements in the processing and storage of foods that have eliminated the seasonal variations in food intake encountered before the industrial revolution. This means that the range of foods available has so rapidly expanded over recent years that the choices are now overwhelming. According to the Food Marketing Institute website, the average number of items carried in a supermarket in 2017 was over 30,000 (Food Marketing Institute, 2019). In addition, portion sizes of processed foods and drinks have greatly increased, and value-added items, like *meal deals*, where patrons can add additional items to their food choices at a subsidized price, can dramatically increase the energy content of meals (Young & Nestle, 2007). Thus, the trend towards providing consumers with healthier choices within restaurants is inadequate when considered alongside the proliferation of energy-dense, nutrient-poor foods (Kirk, Penney, & Freedhoff, 2010).

Going back to our roots

A paradigm shift is necessary to bring about the system-wide changes necessary to reduce the burden of chronic disease and improve the health of populations (Finegood, Karanfil, & Matteson, 2008; World Cancer Research Fund, 2009). Doing so requires coordinated action across multiple levels, from individual actions through to national and trans-national policies. This represents a socio-ecological approach, which takes into account interactions between individuals and their environments (Turner et al., 2018). It must be stressed, however, that socio-ecological approaches do not mean that individuals cannot take responsibility for their own health. Instead, they recognize that health is connected to other social and structural determinants and that individual behaviour change can be constrained in the context of the health-disrupting environments in which we live (Turner et al., 2018). It is also increasingly recognized that the substantial changes required by the food industry require some forms of government regulation, rather than an over-reliance on industry self-regulation (Lang, 2009, 2010).

The complexity of the food system can feel overwhelming to address when it comes to individual agency. While individuals have a role to support a fair, affordable, sustainable, and healthy food system, facing the complexity of our modern food system, as noted in this chapter, places formidable obstacles and often undermines citizens' desires to live by these principles. It is important to focus on actionable targets that have potential for the degree of system change we need. Three key actions that can be taken individually and collectively are as follows:

1) RECLAIM food as a basic human right;
2) RESTORE food as a common good; and
3) RECONNECT with where our food comes from and how it is produced.

Each of these three Rs is described in detail next.

RECLAIM food as a basic human right

The conclusion of the 20th century was credited as the first time in human history when the number of overfed people in the world equalled the number of underfed people, reinforcing how the juxtaposition of hunger and excess remains a significant challenge (Gardner, Halweil, & Peterson, 2000). In Canada, more than 4,000,000 Canadians, or 12% of households, faced food insecurity in 2014 (Tarasuk, Mitchel, & Dachner, 2016). Meanwhile, globally, around one-third of food produced is wasted, with Canadian consumers wasting 47% of food at the household level (Soma, n.d.). These statistics underpin a complex system of food production and supply that introduces inequities at multiple levels of the food system.

As previously noted, the right to adequate food is widely recognized in international law (United Nations, 1966). Since 2015, ending hunger is explicit as the second of 17 sustainable development goals (United Nations, n.d.). While some critics have questioned why this particular goal is not framed in the same way as the right to food, others note that hunger and food access are inextricably linked (Creating Better Futures, 2019). As Creating Better Futures eloquently notes, "Starvation is the characteristic of some people not having enough food to eat. It is not the characteristic of there not being enough food to eat" (Creating Better Futures, 2019). In other words, the concept of zero hunger is broader than food as a basic human right, although both are essential ingredients for a fairer and more sustainable food system. The aftermath of the global recession that began in 2008 highlighted the issue of food insecurity more starkly than ever before. Rising food prices during this time focused attention on both the availability and affordability of food, with the realization that countries lacked the capacity to adapt to food shortages at the level of the food system (de Schutter, 2010). As noted earlier, it also highlighted the challenges with food distribution, resulting in food shortages for some alongside food wastage for others. Addressing these challenges is not easy and requires a high degree of political will. Enshrining food as a basic human right into legal frameworks and national strategies is one way to address these challenges, and this approach has already been applied in some parts of the world, most notably in Africa, Latin America, and South Asia (de Schutter, 2010). However, much more needs to be done to engage other jurisdictions in such an approach, including North America and Europe (de Schutter, 2010). As noted by de Schutter (2010), embedding such a principle into constitutions, as Brazil has done, is no mean feat, but can be fostered through the formation of coalitions, nationally and internationally, allowing a consistent and coherent message to be shared across all levels of society. Action at the grassroots level can help to drive change by creating a sense of urgency and exposing the inconsistencies that perpetuate these challenges. One example of innovation in food distribution is The Real Junk Food Project (TRJFP) (The Real Junk Food Project, 2019). With its roots as an environmental initiative in the UK, the project intercepts discarded or out-of-date food from grocery stores, restaurants, and communities, and redistributes it through "Pay as You Feel" cafés, open to all, where people can get healthy, pre-cooked meals in return for donations of time, skills, material goods, or money. Though it only started in 2013, TRJFP has rapidly expanded into a global network, offering a model of food distribution that supports access to nutritious food in a way that maintains personal dignity and self-respect.

RESTORE food as a common good

Strongly aligned with reclaiming food as a basic human right is the need to restore food as a common good. If we reflect on the past, we can see how our hunter-gatherer ancestors worked collectively to secure food; it is only within the last century that food has become a commodity. The commodification of food now over-rides the long-standing principle of food established as a common good as practiced by our ancestors (Vivero Pol, 2013). The relatively short time frame in which this transformation took place – a mere 100 years versus the 10,000 or so years of history preceding it – should offer hope that this (over)commodification is reversible (Lang, 2009). In other words, returning to the notion of food as a common good is not out of our reach in the 21st century. However, doing so means challenging the prevailing neoliberal, free-market economy and recognizing the market failures that magnify inequities rather than reducing them (Alvaro et al., 2011). As Alvaro et al. (2011) noted, the neoliberal agenda is one that is committed to the dominance of the free market and providing the Departments of Finance, Industry, Trade and Economic Development greater power than the Departments or Ministries of Health, yet these non-health departments are not traditionally concerned with the health of populations. Further, the *health* values of a Department or Ministry of Health are typically quite different from the economic development and profit-oriented values of the Department of Industry, Trade, and Commerce (Alvaro et al., 2011). This difference holds true even when the products sold by businesses are contributing significantly to the poor health of the population as the operation and proliferation of fast-food restaurants demonstrates (Young & Nestle, 2007). There is, therefore, a need to influence public policy across a number of areas, including agriculture, manufacturing, retail, education, culture, trade, and economics (Lang, 2009).

A major factor that needs to be unpacked is the cost of food within the commodification paradigm. Not only are healthier foods typically less available to people, they are also more expensive (Monsivias, McLain, & Drewnowski, 2010). Indeed, the more processing a food receives, the cheaper it seems to become (Monsivias & Drewnowski, 2007). Furthermore, as purchasing and consuming food away from home becomes increasingly the norm, there has been an explosion in fast-food restaurants that provide energy-dense and nutrient-poor food that is highly accessible, inexpensive, and available in increasing portions (Young & Nestle, 2007). Key to this shift in thinking is the need to challenge the notion of *value-for-money* consumerism and adopt a paradigm of *values for money* that recognizes and celebrates food as a public good (Lang, 2010). We can see this shift already taking place in the increasing interest in plant-based eating, concerns for animal welfare, and demand for locally grown foods, as illustrated by the term "locavore", which was first used in 2005 to describe people who eat foods grown locally whenever possible (*Merriam-Webster*, 2019). Support for local food systems is also a key recommendation in the report of the UN special rapporteur, whose quote began this chapter (de Schutter, 2010).

Restoring food as a common good represents a philosophical shift in thinking about the food system that is translating into action across the world (Vivero Pol, 2013). In Scotland, for example, Common Good Food (2015) is working to build connections across local food systems as well as strengthen sustainability and resiliency through skills building, technology, and the arts. One component of this is the Farm Hack movement, a global community of farmers and growers developing appropriate tools for small-scale ecological farming and sharing these resources through open source technology (Farm Hack, n.d.). Farm Hack offers a wealth of examples to support small-scale farming, including repurposing old farm equipment and finding new uses in the 21st century. This leads us to the third R, which is to reconnect with where our food comes from and how it is produced.

RECONNECT *with where our food comes from and how it is produced*

A significant opportunity to support both population and planetary health exists through alignment with the environmental movement (Robinson, 2010). This movement represents a solution-oriented approach to identifying common goals that can achieve shared outcomes, known as *stealth interventions* (Robinson, 2010). Furthermore, if we accept the notion of *food* as a common good, as some have proposed, then by extension, we should view *nutritious food* as a common good as well (Vivero Pol, 2013). The reframing of food in this way can, therefore, be a means to encourage greater personal and societal investment in how our food is sourced and its impact on other resources, including land use, environment sustainability, and the economic viability of food producers. In other words, food as a common good becomes everyone's responsibility, and we owe it to each other to protect this societal resource. Similarly, it could be argued that protecting individual health is a common good, which aligns with the historical context of policies and practices, such as those that underpin Canada's dietary guidance first introduced in the 1940s (Health Canada, 2019). In this, the first food rules for Canada, the Nutrition Division, launched radio, newspaper, and school campaigns to disseminate information on not only the production but also the consumption of healthy foods using the slogan "Eat right, feel right – Canada needs you strong!" (GI Society, 2017).

Supporting local food systems can strengthen the regional economy and boost local communities, as noted in Chapter 11. Direct selling to customers and through local markets is not a new concept. Indeed, farmers' markets have long been a means for farmers to sell excess produce, and in many rural areas across the globe, they have retained this purpose (de Schutter, 2010). Other ways to connect farmers to consumers include community-supported (or shared) agriculture schemes, whereby consumers purchase shares in local farming enterprises in exchange for weekly baskets of local and seasonal produce. By reconnecting with the producers of our food, we can strengthen local economies and promote greater food literacy (Hernandez, Engler-Stringer, Kirk, Wittman, & McNicholl, 2018). The east coast province of Nova Scotia, Canada, has an interesting example of innovation to support healthy, local food programmes in schools called Nourish Nova Scotia. In 2015, Nourish Nova Scotia introduced the Nourish Your Roots farm-to-school fundraiser to help schools support their own healthy eating programmes and initiatives. This programme encourages students to sell boxes of fresh produce from local farms to their families and the broader community. This model has multiple benefits: farmers are paid fairly; families receive fresh local harvest and the opportunity to try new foods; children learn more about where food comes from and how to prepare food; finally, the sales generate revenue for the schools to support food programming (Nourish Nova Scotia, 2018). Evaluation of the programme noted that in its first year, the programme delivered over 1,500 farm boxes containing over 45,000 pounds of fresh produce. This resulted in $30,000 (Canadian dollars [CDN]) of revenue for the three participating farms and over $15,000 CDN to support health-promoting initiatives in schools (Stewart, 2016). Within two years, the fundraiser had expanded to 14,608 boxes of local produce, with $438,240 CDN in gross revenue. This fundraiser yielded $270,073 CDN for local farms, $124,268 CDN for schools, and $43,899 CDN for Nourish to reinvest into the program (Nourish Nova Scotia, 2018).

Reconnecting with our food also means having the confidence to grow food ourselves. This does not necessarily require a lot of space – even a balcony or window box can produce salad crops during the summer months. Such solutions are the focus of organizations like the Kitchen Gardeners International initiative that is reigniting interest in people harvesting, storing, preserving, and preparing their own food (Kitchen Gardeners International, 2017). School gardens provide another opportunity to connect with food and can engage the community in tending the garden throughout the year, even when students are not there. The role of schools is further explored in Chapter 13.

Conclusion

The three Rs described earlier offer a blueprint for a future food system that is fair, affordable, sustainable, and healthy. They represent actions that each of us can take, either individually or collectively, since they each build on the others. They also represent a paradigm shift that takes us back to our past, acknowledging the context of the 20th century as it relates to the industrial food system, while shaping our future – in a world where we support food as a basic human right, a common good, and a means to build resilient food systems in every community. Most of all, they acknowledge that we all have a role to play in building a fair, affordable, sustainable food system that enables us to enjoy succulence, health, and vitality.

References

Alvaro, C., Jackson, L. A., Kirk, S., McHugh, T. L., Hughes, J., Chircop, A., . . . Lyons, R. F. (2011). Moving Canadian governmental policies beyond a focus on individual lifestyle: Some insights from complexity and critical theories. *Health Promotion International*, 26(1), 91–99.

Common Good Food. (2015). *Food commons*. Retrieved March 13, 2017, from www.commongoodfood.org/food-commons

Creating Better Futures. (2019). *5 Reasons to end world hunger*. Retrieved from http://creatingbetterfutures.org.uk/5-reasons-to-end-world-hunger

de Schutter, O. (2010). *Countries tackling hunger with a right to food approach* (Briefing Note 01). United Nations Human Rights. Retrieved from https://www2.ohchr.org/english/issues/food/docs/briefing_note_01_may_2010_en.pdf

Farm Hack. (n.d.). Retrieved March 19, 2019, from http://farmhack.org/wiki/getting-started

Finegood, D. T., Karanfil, O., & Matteson, C. L. (2008). Getting from analysis to action: Framing obesity research, policy and practice with a solution-oriented complex systems lens. *Healthcare Papers*, 9(1), 36–84.

Food and Agriculture Organization of the United Nations (FAO). (2017). *The future of food and agriculture – Trends and challenges*. Retrieved from www.fao.org/3/a-i6583e.pdf

Food Marketing Institute. (2019). *Supermarket facts*. Retrieved from www.fmi.org/our-research/supermarket-facts

Foresight. (2011). *The future of food and farming: Final project report* [PDF file]. The Government Office for Science. Retrieved from https://assets.publishing.service.gov.uk/government/uploads/system/uploads/attachment_data/file/288329/11-546-future-of-food-and-farming-report.pdf

Gardner, G. T., Halweil, B., & Peterson, J. A. (2000). *Underfed and overfed: The global epidemic of malnutrition*. Washington, DC: Worldwatch Institute. Retrieved from www.worldwatch.org/system/files/EWP150.pdf

Garn, S. M. (1989). What did our ancestors eat? *Nutrition Reviews*, 47(11), 337.

GI Society. (2017). *Looking to the future and understanding the past*. Retrieved March 30, 2019, from www.badgut.org/information-centre/health-nutrition/canadas-food-guide-2018-updates/

Hall, J. N., Moore, S., Harper, S. B., & Lynch, J. W. (2009). Global variability in fruit and vegetable consumption. *American Journal of Preventive Medicine*, 36(5), 402–409.e5.

Health Canada. (2019). *History of Canada's food guide from 1942 to 2007*. Retrieved from www.canada.ca/en/health-canada/services/canada-food-guide/about/history-food-guide.html

Hernandez, K., Engler-Stringer, R., Kirk, S., Wittman, H., & McNicholl, S. (2018). The case for a Canadian national school food program. *Canadian Food Studies/ La Revue canadienne des etudes sur l'alimentation, 5*(3), 208–229.

Kc, K. B., Dias, G. M., Veeramani, A., Swanton, C. J., Fraser, D., Steinke, D., . . . Fraser, E. D. G. (2018). When too much isn't enough: Does current food production meet global nutritional needs? *PLoS One, 13*(10), e0205683.

Kickbusch, I. (2010). *The food system: A prism of present and future challenges for health promotion and sustainable development.* Retrieved from www.popline.org/node/210655

Kirk, S. F. L., Penney, T. L., & Freedhoff, Y. (2010). Running away with the facts on food and fatness. *Public Health Nutrition, 13*(1), 147–148.

Kitchen Gardeners International. (2017). *Nutrients for all: Vitality for people and the planet.* Retrieved March 14, 2019, from www.changemakers.com/nutrientsforall/competition/entries/kitchen-gardeners-international

Lang, T. (2009). Reshaping the food system for ecological public health. *Journal of Hunger & Environmental Nutrition, 4*(3–4), 315–335.

Lang, T. (2010). From 'value-for-money' to 'values-for-money'? Ethical food and policy in Europe. *Environment and Planning A: Economy and Space, 42*(8), 1814–1832.

Maslow, A. H. (1943). A theory of human motivation. *Psychological Review, 50*(4), 370–396.

Merriam-Webster. (2019). *Locavore.* Merriam-Webster's Collegiate Dictionary. Retrieved from www.merriam-webster.com/dictionary/locavore

Monsivias, P., & Drewnowski, A. (2007). The rising cost of low-energy-density-foods. *Journal of the American Dietetic Association, 107*(12), 2071–2076.

Monsivias, P., McLain, J., & Drewnowski, A. (2010). The rising disparity in the price of healthful foods: 2004–2008. *Food Policy, 35*(6), 514–520.

Nourish Nova Scotia. (2018). *Nourish your roots evaluation report.* Retrieved from https://static1.squarespace.com/static/5b5b5824f2e6b10639fdaf09/t/5ba236d58 98583e2106ee032/1537357529549/NYR_2017_Evaluation_Report_20180403_FINAL.pdf

Pollan, M. (2009). *Food rules: An eater's manual.* New York, NY: Penguin Books.

Robinson, T. N. (2010). Save the world, prevent obesity: Piggybacking on existing social and ideological movements. *Obesity, 18*(Suppl. 1), S17–S22.

Soma, T. (n.d.). *National food policy briefing note: Addressing food waste in Canada.* Food Secure Canada. Retrieved from https://foodsecurecanada.org/sites/foodsecurecanada.org/files/files/food_waste_briefing_note_soma1.pdf

Tarasuk, V., Mitchel, A., & Dachner, N. (2016). *Household food insecurity in Canada, 2014.* Retrieved from https://proof.utoronto.ca/wp-content/uploads/2016/04/Household-Food-Insecurity-in-Canada-2014.pdf

The Real Junk Food Project. (2019). Retrieved from https://trjfp.com/

Turner, C., Aggarwal, A., Walls, H., Herforth, A., Drewnowski, A., Coates, J., . . . Kadiyala, S. (2018). Concepts and critical perspectives for food environment research: A global framework with implications for action in low-and middle-income countries. *Global Food Security, 83*, 93–101.

United Nations. (1966). *International covenant on economic, social and cultural rights.* Human Rights Office of the High Commissioner. Retrieved from www.ohchr.org/EN/ProfessionalInterest/Pages/CESCR.aspx

United Nations. (n.d). *Sustainable development goals.* Retrieved from https://sustainabledevelopment.un.org/?menu=1300

Vivero Pol, J. L. (2013). Food as a commons: Reframing the narrative of the food system. *SSRN Electronic Journal.* http://dx.doi.org/10.2139/ssrn.2255447

World Cancer Research Fund. (2009). *Policy and action for cancer prevention.* Washington, DC: American Institute for Cancer Research.

World Health Organization. (2019). *Increasing fruit and vegetable consumption to reduce the risk of noncommunicable diseases.* E-Library of Evidence for Nutrition Actions (eLENA). Retrieved from www.who.int/elena/titles/fruit_vegetables_ncds/en/

Young, L. R., & Nestle, M. (2007). Portion sizes and obesity: Responses of fast-food companies. *Journal of Public Health Policy, 28*(2), 238–248.

6 Let thy food be thy medicine

Health professionals' recommendations for food

Tushar Mehta, Pamela Fergusson, and Zeeshan Ali

Introduction

Plant foods can be sustainable, succulent, and nutritious. Healthy food can taste satisfying and delicious, and the current boom in plant-based restaurants, food bloggers, cookbooks, and food products show that there is a large and growing appetite for plant-based foods. Most cultures have some plant-based traditional recipes, so we can draw on techniques and flavours from a range of cultures to meet the preferences and nutritional needs of people from pregnancy through to old age. In their paper titled "Position of the Academy of Nutrition and Dietetics: Vegetarian Diets", the Academy of Nutrition and Dietetics (2015) states that appropriately planned vegetarian, including vegan, diets can be healthful, nutritionally adequate, and provide health benefits for the prevention and treatment of certain diseases. These diets can be made appropriate for all stages of the life cycle, including pregnancy, lactation, infancy, childhood, adolescence, and older adulthood, as well as for athletes.

In this chapter, we review the scientific evidence for the nutritional benefits of a plant-based diet and discuss how to optimize that diet to deliver the best results. As authors, we want to first acknowledge that there are controversies in the field of nutrition. There are many interest groups, large industries, and zealots peddling a myriad of diets. These groups have extreme biases. This includes plant-based advocates who may be on the right track but have exaggerated beliefs. As responsible plant-based health professionals, we intend to bring clarity by sharing balanced nutrition recommendations based on the highest quality evidence.

Vegan versus plant-based: defining our terms

It is helpful to define our terminology and review subtle distinctions, though we often use words like *vegan* and *plant-based* interchangeably. A *plant-based diet* means it consists *mostly* or *exclusively* of plant foods. Unfortunately, there is not enough research available on exclusively plant-based populations. The research reporting on the plant-based diet often includes pescatarians, semi-vegetarians, vegetarians who include dairy or eggs, and vegans. What these diets have in common is that they predominantly get protein and calories from plant foods. These studies of exclusively or predominantly plant-based populations inform our recommendations in this chapter. Even with the inclusion of a small amount of animal products, we still are able to see the benefits of a high-plant diet.

Plant-based foods are foods that are created from the plant kingdom, and include mushrooms and even micro-organisms involved in processes like fermentation. A *vegan diet* means exclusively eating plant foods. In this chapter, we are referring to *diet* as a long-term pattern of eating, as opposed to short-term diets for quick fixes.

The cornerstone of the message of this chapter is the importance of eating a *whole-food, plant-based* (WFPB) diet. Whole foods are foods that are unprocessed or minimally processed. Processing is not always a negative thing: slicing an apple or baking a squash are both forms of processing. Processing reduces the health value of a food when too many important nutrients are removed or too many additives such as salt, sugar, unhealthy fats, or other chemicals are added.

Some examples of plant foods that are highly processed include white bread, white rice and white pasta, sugar, salt, oil, ramen noodles, sugar-sweetened peanut butter, some veggie meats, potato chips, soda pop, cookies and cakes, ice creams, some cheeses, and fruit juices. Of course, many animal-based foods are also overly processed, but here we will focus on the plant foods.

Examples of whole or minimally processed plant foods include whole grain breads and pasta, fruits and vegetables, tofu and soya milk, baked potato with minimal fat, lentils and beans, nuts, seeds, and natural nut and seed butters. When we say WFPB in this chapter, we mean *whole or minimally processed foods*.

The research: why do animal foods have a negative health impact?

Animal foods contain higher levels of saturated fat than healthy plant fats, and they contain cholesterol, which plant foods do not contain at all. Despite various controversies, the balance of evidence concludes that saturated fat and cholesterol are not healthy. So, butter is back? No! In 2017, the American Heart Association (AHA) published its scientific review to squash the controversy created by interest groups and research funded by the meat and dairy industries. In their study of research on cardiovascular disease (CVD), trials that lowered intake of dietary saturated fat reduced CVD around 30% when it was replaced with polyunsaturated and monounsaturated fat. Replacing saturated fat with mostly refined carbohydrates and sugars is not associated with lower rates of CVD (Sacks et al., 2017). Other aspects of animal foods that are thought to cause harmful effects include the animal protein itself, higher choline levels, residual hormones in animal foods (including the natural hormones of animals raised in "organic" settings), and more. All of these components of animal foods act in concert to increase certain important chronic diseases. The mechanisms by which animal foods cause disease is not the thrust of this chapter; here, we focus on scientific studies and findings that reveal dietary patterns offering the greatest health advantages with the least amount of harm.

Methods: the importance of clinical nutrition research

Where do we get our research, and what studies are we to believe? Our review of the literature reveals thousands of studies that are often contradictory. We filter the studies with the following principles:

1   We consider only clinical studies that look at the real-world outcomes of disease and death in humans (clinical studies).
2   We avoid studies reporting results only from test tubes, animals, or biomarkers and blood test (except for standard cholesterol, diabetes, and blood pressure tests).
3   We only include studies with appropriate comparison groups to answer research questions, and that do not state conclusions beyond the parameters of their study design.
4   We do not include studies that are funded by industries that would profit from findings in their own favour or researchers with significant industry attachments. We have also avoided studies whose study design is flawed or biased, such as those which fail to distinguish between whole grains and refined carbohydrates, or cholesterol studies which lack comparison groups who have zero or near zero intake of cholesterol (Barnard, Willett, & Ding, 2017; Collier, 2016; Greger, 2018).

While reviewing these details may seem dry, they demonstrate the intellectual integrity and critical criteria we have used to guide the writing of this chapter. And although research is dynamic and new studies are published each year, we have selected what we feel is the highest quality and most important information for this overview.

Balanced and realistic advice

At the outset, we, the authors, declared that we do prefer and promote a completely plant-based diet. Based on compelling scientific evidence from an array of studies, we can see the multiple benefits for all plant-based diets, not only vegans. Some studies do show additional benefits for vegans, yet such results may vary depending on the actual quality of the food consumed. For example, these studies include a smaller number of *early vegans* who were some of the first adopters of this diet and would not have had access to the evolving insights and array of foods of today (i.e. affordable fortified soy milk). More data are still needed on vegan diets, and we keep learning from new studies.

We urge readers to remember that following a plant-based diet does not guarantee the absence of chronic diseases. Rather, a WFPB diet increases an individual's or population's chance of avoiding certain diseases. In this chapter, we review the evidence for cardiovascular disease, diabetes, obesity, hypertension, and cancer. These are our most prevalent and deadly chronic diseases, and a WFPB diet is useful in terms of preventing and even treating each of them. This is important in understanding population health: if there were to be 100,000 new cases of a cancer and a certain diet or test could reduce this by 10%, it means that 10,000 people would be spared. These numbers add up. In addition to individuals being spared from suffering, their families would also suffer less stress and cost, and government budgets would benefit.

On the other hand, while not all people who eat meat or highly processed foods will suffer from the diseases in question, they will have increased risk. Studies show that people who move towards a WFPB diet access incremental benefits: it's not all or nothing, and step-by-step changes offer protective effects as well (Orlich et al., 2013; Sabate, Harwatt, & Soret, 2015).

In addition to diet, the major factors for long-term health are proving to be engaging in exercise, not smoking, and maintaining a healthy body weight (Ford et al., 2009). This is discussed more in the chapter that follows. Such health behaviours offer additional benefits for social, emotional, and spiritual health. While these other aspects of health are also critical, our focus here is to shine a light on the evidence steering us all towards a plant-based diet for greater overall vitality. Next, we examine which diseases have strong evidence of prevention from a whole-food diet.

Literature review

Cardiovascular disease

One of the strongest areas of evidence for WFPB eating is the prevention of cardiovascular disease, which is the leading cause of death worldwide. Cardiovascular disease includes all diseases of the circulatory system, including, but not limited to, hypertension, stroke, and peripheral artery diseases (PAD). It is projected that by 2030, 43.9% of the US adult population will have some form of CVD (American Heart Association, 2017). Large cohort studies, such as Adventist Health Study-2, show that people who consume animal proteins have 60% higher cardiovascular mortality rates compared with people who eat plant proteins (Tharrey et al., 2018). Death rates from heart disease have dropped steadily since they peaked in the late 1960s, mostly due to reductions in the risk factors, including high blood pressure, high cholesterol, and smoking.

In 1998, a groundbreaking study by Dean Ornish, MD, demonstrated for the first time in history that coronary artery atherosclerotic disease could actually be reversed with exclusive low fat, plant-based whole foods, regular exercises, and stress management (Ornish et al., 1998). Then in 2014, another landmark study by Caldwell Esselstyn Jr., MD, showed that exclusive low fat plant-based whole food nutrition could prevent, halt, and reverse heart disease. Over 99% of the patients who followed the dietary recommendations from Esselstyn avoided further atherosclerotic events (Esselstyn, Gendy, Doyle, Golubic, & Roizen, 2014). Both Esselstyn et al. (2014) and Ornish et al. (1998) demonstrated that food is a potent lifestyle factor in heart disease prevention and reversal. Note that the fat content in both studies was extremely low, and included nearly zero added fats to achieve these goals.

Plant-based diets have zero cholesterol and have very little saturated fat with added benefits of soluble fibre, which helps lower cholesterol. Animal-based products such as meat, dairy, and eggs have significant cholesterol and saturated fats, and cause plaque build-up in the arteries of the heart and subsequently increase rates of heart attacks. Further to the cholesterol and saturated fat issues, well-planned studies with appropriate comparison groups show that people with high cholesterol levels have a 50%–80% increased risk of heart disease (Abdullah et al., 2018).

In 2017, the American Heart Association published an article entitled "Dietary Fats and Cardiovascular Disease: A Presidential Advisory from the American Heart Association". In this paper, they reported a randomized control trial that replaced saturated fats from both plant and animal sources with polyunsaturated vegetable oil. The experimental group reduced cardiovascular disease occurrence by 30%. The authors also emphasized that when saturated fats were replaced with refined carbohydrates and sugars, there was no reduction in CVD rates. However, if they were replaced by whole grains, benefits were noted. The message was to keep dietary saturated fats and sugars low, and to consume whole grains and vegetable fats instead (Sacks et al., 2017). The *Journal of the American College of Cardiology* published a powerful study of 127,500 men and women followed over 24–30 years, showing that every 5% of calories from saturated fat replaced by plant fats resulted in 15%–25% decrease in heart disease and 9% decrease if replaced by whole grains (Li et al., 2015).

More on cholesterol and saturated fat

Related to cardiovascular disease is peripheral vascular disease (PVD), which can lead to amputations in extreme cases. A 2017 study published in the *Journal of Vascular Surgery* showed that people consuming the most meat over a 20 year time frame had 60% higher PVD rates than those consuming the least (Ogilvie, Lutsey, Heiss, Folsom, & Steffen, 2017). Despite these excellent studies, the controversy created by industry-sponsored studies and hyped by media, as well as particular books and celebrities, have intention-ally caused confusion about the role of cholesterol and saturated fat in caus-ing coronary heart disease. The Canadian College of Cardiology published a scathing critique of the media and animal food lobby groups, again stat-ing the devastating effects of cholesterol and saturated fat on heart health (Spence, Jenkins, & Davignon, 2010). Reduced cholesterol and saturated fat intake not only improve blood tests but can also prevent cardiovascular disease.

Fish and the heart are yesterday's news on omega-3s

There has been substantial fanfare about fish and omega-3 being some type of panacea for heart disease and beyond. Some small and early stud-ies showed a benefit, perhaps since pescatarians ate less meat in general. However, a larger systematic review including 79 randomized controlled tri-als suggested no benefit of increasing omega-3 on cardiovascular mortality and other cardiovascular events (Abdelhamid et al., 2018). Should we still eat them for other reasons? There is weak evidence of omega-3 oils being beneficial for brain health and during pregnancy for the brain development of children. At the same time, ocean fish contain methyl mercury, dioxins, furans, PCBs, and other toxins. Mercury is shown to cause prenatal neu-rodevelopmental defects. Depending on the quantity of fish consumed dur-ing pregnancy, there could be some loss in IQ score of children (Zeilmaker et al., 2013). Thankfully, the same long-chain marine omega-3 oils are available through toxin-free algae, which are now easily available. We must also take note that the world's oceans are being devastated by the massive amount of fishing (Jones et al., 2018). There are also good sources of plant-based omega-3, including flax seeds, walnuts, and canola oil, in addition to many more plant sources. Popular belief often considers them as lacking, but in truth, there has been little research done on their long-term benefits. Small amounts of these plant omega-3s are converted into the longer-chain marine type, but since these plant sources contain large amounts of shorter plant omega-3s, our bodies may achieve the good quantities of the long-chain Omega-3 fatty acids just by converting a small percentage (Welch, Shakya-Shrestha, Lentjes, Wareham, & Khaw, 2010).

So what to do?

At present, there is not conclusive evidence for supplementing with the marine omega-3 oils. Pregnant women and others concerned about child brain development may use a supplement, but should stick to the toxin-free algae oils. Flaxseeds, walnuts, hemp seeds, flax oil, soya-bean oil, and canola oil all contain large amounts of the shorter plant omega-3s. These are great foods for more than just omega-3s, especially when consumed as whole foods, rather than oils, as part of a diverse plant-based diet.

Type 2 diabetes

Type 2 diabetes is a worldwide epidemic. In 2016, the World Health Organization (WHO) estimated that there are 422 million adults with diabetes, and there will be over 640 million by 2040. It is a scourge, with severe health consequences from cardiovascular disease and stroke, blindness, loss of limbs, and kidney failure. It also can impact the mental health of a person, as well as the quality of life for the extended family. Diabetes is a growing global economic disaster, with medications alone costing billions of dollars. Randomized trials show dramatic improvement in blood sugars and mental well-being with a WFPB diet compared to standard diabetes meal plans (Toumpanakis, Turnbull, & Alba-Barba, 2018). Large cohort trials show that people following plant-based diets have roughly a *50% less* chance for type 2 diabetes occurrence and as such suggests a significant pathway to improve health and well-being. Data from Adventist Health Study-2 show a stepwise reduction in type 2 diabetes prevalence with the reduction of animal products in the diet (McMacken & Shah, 2017). Studies also show a reduction in weight and cholesterol levels. In addition to avoiding animal products, the key here is to avoid refined grains, added sugar and oils, sweet fruit juices, sweets, French fries, and other junk foods, which, despite being vegan, are still disease promoting (Satija et al., 2016).

Obesity

Obesity rates, in many countries, including the USA, show no sign of decline. Obesity is another epidemic linked to increased cardiovascular disease, diabetes and cancer rates, and shorter lifespan (Steele et al., 2017). We are seeing an increasing prevalence of obesity in young children. Weight-loss intervention studies indicate that plant-based diets can reduce obesity in childhood and into adult life (Sabaté & Wien, 2010). As mentioned earlier, plant-based diets are associated with decreased obesity, and those following a plant-based diet have the lowest body mass index compared to other types of dietary patterns (Rizzo, Jaceldo-Siegl, Sabate, & Fraser, 2013).

Hypertension

High blood pressure or hypertension can cause serious problems for heart and kidney function. Hypertension is also associated with stroke, diabetes, and other cardiovascular diseases. Both randomized controlled trials and observational studies show that a plant-based diet decreases blood pressure (Pettersen, Anousheh, Fan, Jaceldo-Siegl, & Fraser, 2012; Yokoyama et al., 2014).

Cancers

The effect of a plant-based diet on cancer is more moderate, since cancer cells develop over many decades, eventually causing disease. Also, the causes of the many types of cancer are more multifactorial and complex compared to metabolic syndrome and cardiovascular disease. Studying cancer (and even cardiovascular disease) and diet is also challenging because many people switch to a WFPB diet after receiving a diagnosis. Despite this, multiple studies do show a modest decrease in an array of cancers There have been a few studies showing that those consuming a plant-based-diet have 8%–10% lower cancer rates, and vegans have 15% lower cancer rates. Some of these studies show no mortality difference (Dinu, Abbate, Gensini, Casini, & Sofi, 2017; Key et al., 2014). Other studies indicate decreased mortality through choosing to consume plant-based foods (Huang et al., 2012).

Breast cancer

Some studies do show an association between increased animal product consumption and increased incidence of breast cancer. These studies did not, however, have a fully vegan subgroup or assess diet quality. Overall, these studies show a roughly 20% increase rate of breast cancer in women who eat more animal products and a 10%–15% reduction in rates for those who eat plant based (Farvid, Cho, Chen, Eliassen, & Willett, 2014; Link et al., 2013; Sieri et al., 2014; Taylor, Burley, Greenwood, & Cade, 2007).

One topic of great interest is the effect of consumption of soy foods on breast cancer. A study of women in Asian countries showed those consuming a higher proportion of soy had approximately 40% decreased rates of breast cancer. In Western countries there was no benefit or harm, but this was probably because Western women only consumed miniscule amounts compared to Asian counterparts (Messina & Wu, 2009). Of further interest are studies showing a modest decrease of breast cancer recurrence with soy consumption in women who were treated for breast cancer. One of the studies also shows that the soy consumption does not interfere with concurrent treatment using standard chemotherapy medications (Dong & Qin, 2011; Magee & Rowland, 2012).

On the topic of ovarian cancers, there are studies showing a significant decrease in ovarian cancer in women whose diet are more plant based and those who eat more soy foods. These studies showed a roughly twofold difference, but we do require more studies to see how pronounced the benefits really are (Chang et al., 2007; Kolahdooz, Ibiebele, van der Pols, & Webb, 2008).

Prostate cancer

Another common cancer, prostate cancer, can be reduced through a plant-based diet. One study showed that the vegan subgroup fared the best, with a 35% reduction in prostate cancer risk (Tantamango-Bartley et al., 2015). The authors hypothesize the benefit is due to reducing the harmful properties of meats while also getting more beneficial effects of plants. Similar to the breast and ovarian studies, a 2009 study found Asian men who ate higher quantities of soy throughout life developed 50% less prostate cancer (Yan & Spitznagel, 2009). Again, Western men ate very small amounts of soy, and no benefit or harm was found.

Interesting data exists for dairy consumption. One study showed men consuming a serving a day of whole milk had about 50% more mortality from prostate cancer than those who did not. Those already treated for prostate cancer and who consumed whole milk had double the rates of recurrence (Song et al., 2012). Other studies also showed dairy as a risk for prostate cancer, to a greater or lesser extent (Torfadottir et al., 2011; Sacks et al., 2017).

Also of interest is one article showing that men with the highest marine omega-3 consumption, likely from fish sources, had a 40% greater chance of low-grade prostate cancer (more common but lower risk of death), 70% higher incidence of high-grade prostate cancer (which is less common but higher risk of death) after an average of seven years of monitoring (Brasky et al., 2013).

Pancreatic cancer

There are a group of studies regarding this less common but devastating cancer, including a 2009 study that showed a 40% increase in pancreatic cancer for those consuming high amounts of animal fats (Thiébaut et al., 2009). Others studies show varying risk, depending on meat and processed meat consumption (Larsson & Wolk, 2012). Refined sugars and starches also are found to be harmful, while vegetables and nuts decrease one's risk (Bosetti et al., 2013). Up to 80% of pancreatic cancer patients present with either new onset type 2 diabetes or with an impaired glucose tolerance test at the time of diagnosis (De Souza, Irfan, Masud, & Saif, 2016).

Colon cancer

World headlines were made when WHO published that red meat was classified as a 2A carcinogen and processed meat a 1A carcinogen, particularly for colorectal cancer. Red and processed meat were shown to be causal for cancer: eating a 50 gram portion of processed meat increases the risk of colorectal cancer by about 18%, while eating 100g of red meat daily increases the risk by 17% (Flood et al., 2008; World Health Organization, 2015).

There are those who believe that a vegan diet would protect or even cure most cancers, but this is simplistic and dangerous thinking regarding a complex set of diseases. Despite the greater complexities, when observing cancer rates, we can conclude that there are at least modest benefits of a plant-based diet in cancer prevention overall, with some types of cancer showing stronger effects. With longer study duration and larger populations following a WFPB diet, we are hopeful that future research may show increased benefits. Cancers are many and complex, and can be devastating to an individual and family. Even a modest decrease in cancer rates is a welcome effect of plant diets.

Dementia

Dementia is also a devastating disease. There is some evidence that strongly suggests that vascular disease of the brain is one of its major factors (Lathe, Sapronova, & Kotelevtsev, 2014). As such, WFPB is proposed as one of the major preventative approaches. Although further research is needed to confirm this, there are some emerging and promising data. Studies show that midlife cholesterol levels correlated with Alzheimer's dementia in later years (Solomon, Kivipelto, Wolozin, Zhou, & Whitmer, 2009). Higher saturated fat intake is linked to cognitive impairment in later life (Eskelinen et al., 2008). Fruits and vegetables were found to be protective of dementia and mild cognitive impairment (Chen, Huang, & Cheng, 2012; Eskelinen et al., 2008).

Diverticulitis

Diverticulitis is inflammation or infection occurring in pouches in the lining of the intestines, which may lead to severe bleeding, blockage of the intestine, or even death. Eating a plant-based diet can help to prevent it. Those eating plant-based diets and increased fibre had significantly less hospitalization and death from diverticulitis; those who were vegan had the best results, with 70% less hospitalization and death (Crowe, Appleby, Allen, & Key, 2011).

Conclusions from the literature review

A multitude of robust studies show the benefits of plant-based eating patterns. However, considering that most of these studies do not specifically look at subjects with an optimally planned WFPB diet, it is very likely that such an optimized diet would provide an even stronger benefit. Furthermore, looking at the data as a whole, it is quite possible that a purely WFPB vegan diet, or coming very close, would be most optimal. We look forward to more studies every year on the subject. In the meantime, a landmark publication released in January 2019 in the *Lancet*, one of the world's most respected medical journals, was called *Food in the Anthropocene: The EAT – Lancet Commission on Healthy Diets from Sustainable Food Systems* (Willett et al., 2019), which advocates for a higher proportion of WFPB eating. It cites the strong evidence for disease and mortality reduction on a global scale. The EAT-Lancet Commission also emphasizes that a plant-based eating pattern would have worldwide ecological benefits. Interestingly, Canada's latest food guide published also in 2019 (Government of Canada, 2019) and the EAT-Lancet Commission arrive at similar conclusions from their extensive review of global research and make similar recommendations. It is commendable that these organizations are strongly science based. The EAT-Lancet Commission goes further towards multidisciplinary and cross-sectoral solutions. This report recommends fully integrated solutions focused on simultaneously improving health, reducing food waste, increasing production of fruits and vegetables, nuts and seeds, and creatively incorporating technologies to improve agricultural productivity and sustainability (Willett et al., 2019). These ideas, along with others, are discussed further in the final chapter of this collection.

How to optimize a plant-based or vegan diet

Now that we have seen much of the research, our next question is, how do we optimize a WFPB or healthy vegan diet?

One of our favourite authors and vegan registered dietitians, Ginny Messina, says we should *eat the rainbow*. This idea goes well with the concepts of succulence and sustainability, that is to get a good variety in our diet from the broad world of healthy plant-based foods. Plant-based food groups include five main groups: whole grains, pulses and protein foods, fruits and vegetables, nuts and seeds, and oils and margarine.

Whole grains

Grains are a cornerstone of diets all over the world. There are many varieties – including wheat, oats, rice, teff, millet, and so many more – and each has a different flavour, culinary attributes, and nutritional benefits. Grains are often maligned in Western society by low-carb or gluten-free diet promoters, which we will discuss later in the chapter. But for now, we should know that there is consistent evidence that whole grains are found to moderately reduce cardiovascular disease and colorectal cancer (Li et al., 2015; Reynolds et al., 2019), and aid in reducing overall cancer rates (Aune et al., 2016; Ogimoto, Shibata, & Fukuda, 2000) and reduce diabetes (Ericson et al., 2013). Not all high carbohydrate foods are as beneficial to our health as whole grains. Refined grains increase diabetes, cardiovascular disease, cancer, and overall mortality (Li et al., 2015; Satija et al., 2016).

So as medical professionals, we advise people to avoid refined grains such as white bread, white rice, and white pasta; sweets and sugar-sweetened drinks; ramen noodles; refined crackers; snack foods; and so forth. This extremely important concept was reviewed earlier in the chapter. Consumers and professionals who guide others are reminded to look for the *whole grain* description on breads since even *whole wheat* means it is partly refined. One tip: the more complex and coarse the grains, the healthier they may be. Complex starches absorb even more slowly after we eat them, and they remain available to us for more lasting energy access. Look for multigrain breads, cereals, and other products that look coarse and, as a result, require more chewing.

It is important also to note that whole grains can be detrimental when people overeat beyond their daily calorie needs. Plant-based or vegan consumers may still eat far more calories than they burn and become overweight. In modern society, even those of us who exercise in the gym or go for a run or our daily walk still need fewer calories than we may realize. Simply put, eat whole grains but mind your portions!

Pulses and other high-protein foods

When people say they are vegan, vegetarian, or plant-based, inevitably, someone is going to ask how it is possible to get enough protein. In truth, it is not difficult: as long as people are consuming a variety of plant-based foods from across the food groups, and they get enough calories, they will consume enough protein. It is, however, possible to eat too little protein, usually if avoiding plant-based food groups such as pulses, whole grains, nuts, and seeds.

How much protein do you need?

Protein is important for metabolic needs, growth, healthy bones, and more. A commonly accepted protein intake, according to human studies, is 0.8 g per kg of body weight (roughly 0.4 g per pound of body weight). Often, we round up to 1 g per kg of body weight (British Nutrition Foundation, 2018; US Department of Agriculture, n.d.; see also Vegan Health, 2018). Children, pregnant or breastfeeding women, and elderly people have increased protein needs, meaning that they should reach the 0.8 to 1.0 g/kg body requirement. Vegan athletes and bodybuilders may need 1.2 g per kg to 2.0 g per kg per day depending on their type of activity (Dietitians of Canada, 2016).

A common myth is that plant proteins are incomplete and need to be complemented. This is not true, and in fact, all plant foods contain a complete protein. Meanwhile, animal foods have an amino acid composition that closely resembles the amino acid composition of the human body. As plant-protein composition differs somewhat compared to the human body, they may be deemed as *less efficient*. However, it should be noted, foods like pulses (beans and lentils), hemp, quinoa, and pumpkin seeds are high-protein foods that are much closer to the human physiological proportion of amino acids. Soy, a bean we will discuss in greater detail, very closely resembles the same amino acid combination as proteins in the human body and in this case is more similar to animal products. However, the slight discrepancies of plant proteins may be good for us. By comparison, our body burns glucose for fuel. However, if we eat glucose or sugars that are easily broken down to glucose, it may promote diabetes and other diseases. Simple sugars are easily absorbed, processed, and deemed unhealthy. Similarly, proteins that are too easily absorbed and processed could also be a reason that animal foods increase diabetes, heart disease, and cancer. Our bodies will rearrange some amino acids in plant foods according to our needs, and this integration process may be beneficial.

What are the best high-protein plant foods?

Pulses – are dried edible seeds of legumes – like dry peas, lentils, beans, and chickpeas are the chief protein foods for humans. They also happen to be some of the most sustainable and efficient food crops. Different pulses are grown all over the world using less water and land than any other form of protein; they fix nitrogen from the air, thus requiring far less fertilizer than most crops, and enrich the soil while consuming fewer resources than required for equivalent animal food production. Pulses are widely present in most traditional cultures around the world (Food and Agriculture Organization of the United Nations, 2016). The United Nations General Assembly recognized 2016 as International Year of Pulses due to their generally low cost, accessibility, sustainability, and health benefits. Beans and lentils are about 20% protein by weight, but varieties with higher protein are being developed. They also have iron, which is better absorbed in the presence of vitamin C, so beans and lentils are best eaten in combination with vegetables such as tomatoes and red peppers, or with a good squeeze of lemon or lime. Compared to animal products, legumes simultaneously protect from chronic diseases, extend longevity, and reduce climate change, water, and land use. Pulses also increase bone health, decrease diabetes, and improve brain health (Grant, 2016; Lousuebsakul-Matthews et al., 2014; Mollard et al., 2012).

Various diet gurus might say we should not eat beans and lentils due to their carbohydrates or lectins. But it is prudent to recognize that pulses have complex, slow-release carbs and high fibre. Lectins are certain proteins found in pulses, but also many other fruits and vegetables. The lectins in kidney beans, and some other beans, can have some gastrointestinal and other toxic effects if eaten raw, but there is no evidence that they are harmful when cooked. In fact, we have a preponderance of evidence about the benefits of eating pulses, and there is some evidence that lectins may have anticancer properties (Amidor, 2017; Sarup Singh, Preet Kaur, & Rakesh Kanwar, 2016).

Tips with pulses

Sprouting beans and lentils can make them easier to digest. Sprouted mung beans and lentils can be eaten raw or cooked. Use a pressure cooker or electric pressure cooker to prepare dried beans more quickly. Canned beans are convenient, but dry beans are tastier, cheaper, and contain less sodium. We advise people to experiment with Indian and Middle Eastern soups made from lentils and bean dishes from around the world. Try recipes from Forks over Knives www.forksoverknives.com/, Vegan Richa www.veganri cha.com/, the Minimalist Baker https://minimalistbaker.com/, and Oh She Glows https://ohsheglows.com/. Learn the great variety of interesting pulses from around the world, each having slightly different flavours and traditional recipes (Pulses, n.d.).

Soybeans

Soy is a special bean that seems almost too good to be true: it is a protein powerhouse with over 30% protein by mass. It can be made into a wide variety of foods, including soy milk, tofu, miso, and tempeh. Soy has health benefits, including decreasing the risk of prostate and breast cancer, as mentioned earlier. Soy intake can increase bone health and decrease fracture risk in old age, reduce cardiovascular risk, and even lessen the severity of menopause symptoms (Ramdath, Padhi, Sarfaraz, Renwick, & Duncan, 2017).

There is a great deal of false propaganda and myth about the phytoestrogens in soy. Soy isoflavones do not have true estrogen-like effects in the human body. Hence there is no increased risk of breast cancer, prostate cancer, ovarian cancer, or the abnormal sexual development of children, men, or women. In fact, meat, dairy, and eggs all contain real animal estrogen, which has a direct effect in the human body and may be one of the mechanisms by which they increase various diseases (Hartmann, Lacorn, & Steinhart, 1998). The notion that soy causes harm to humans originates from the anti-soy marketing of the meat, dairy, and egg industries' misinformation efforts to offset the possible threats increased soy consumption may pose to their businesses (Cheng et al., 2010; Dai et al., 2014; Hamilton-Reeves et al., 2010; Kalman, Feldman, Martinez, Krieger, & Tallon, 2007; Messina, 2010). The myth that soy is bad for the thyroid is often propagated, but also untrue (Messina & Redmond, 2006). Finally, there is no evidence that soy should only be eaten in fermented form. Nonfermented soy is just fine.

Soy is not required as part of a vegan diet but is an excellent food that can be eaten in combination with other plant protein foods. We can benefit from two to three servings of soy foods per day. Edamame, the whole soybeans, are a fantastic food taken with any meal: they are a whole soy food that can be found in the frozen section of the grocery store; either in pods or shelled. Soy milk fortified with calcium, vitamin D, and B12 is a convenient replacement for dairy milk. Soy milk is preferred over almond, coconut, and other plant-based milks, which do not have any significant protein compared to soy.

The vast majority of the world's soy is grown to feed animals, and a very small percentage is used for direct human consumption. When used for human consumption, soy is an efficient and ecological food, and can be grown in climates all over the world. Concerns have been raised by some about (genetically modified organisms) GMO soy, and efforts to select foods with less spray, inputs, and modifications may be more beneficial and appealing. Fortunately, almost all soy products in Western countries that are made for direct human consumption are organic and non-GMO. Hence soy is one of the most ecological and affordable organic products you can find.

Other vegan foods with protein

Whole grains are also a good source of protein, with about 10% protein by mass. Many people around the world depend on grains as a major source of their protein and energy, along with beans and lentils. Quinoa, a grain-like seed, is nutrient-dense and an excellent source of protein. It is fantastic to add into our cuisine in many ways: in salads, in place of rice in pilaf, or in power bowls as a morning porridge. Originally grown in South America, it is also grown in other parts of the world since it has become more popular. The ubiquitous peanut is also a great source of protein and grown in many parts of the world. However, we should avoid the processed peanut butter that contains sugar and hydrogenated fats and eat the natural peanut butter (the kind where the oil separates). Those healthy fats are good to eat. Flaxseeds, hemp seeds, sunflower seeds, chia seeds, and pumpkin seeds are all good sources of protein and dense with other nutrients. There are also many new developments in the field of plant-based proteins, such as water lentils, a new crop with exciting potential. Driven by the growing need to feed the global population, foods are being sought that are economical, healthy, and environmentally sound, and sustainable foods, and particularly succulent plant-based proteins, are the key to achieving these goals.

Protein powders

There are many types of vegan protein powders available. Many ask us, "Are these a highly processed food or healthy?" Our view is that these can be part of a healthy diet as long as we also consume a variety of plant foods from across the vegan food groups. For example, if you make a smoothie using protein powder and include berries or greens, nut butter, dates, hemp and chia seeds, and other goodies, it makes for a powerhouse healthy meal! Avoid protein powders with too much sugar or artificial sugars: it's important to avoid making your smoothie too sweet. Vegan protein powders are convenient in our busy lifestyles, and they can be excellent options for athletes who are eating more plant based. There are many varieties, including hemp, soy, pea, etc., and they can all be beneficial as part of a balanced diet.

Meat alternatives, aka transition foods

Finally, we must discuss meat alternatives, or *transition foods*, meaning foods that emulate meat products but are made from vegan ingredients, such as soy, pea, or wheat protein. Are these highly processed foods adverse for health, high-protein alternatives that are beneficial, or perhaps something in between?

The drawback of meat alternatives is that they are not whole foods. Much of the original soy, pea, or wheat component may have been removed, stripping away some of the nutritional value. They often have a moderate to high sodium content, and some have high fat content. Meat alternatives are highly variable in terms of nutritional value. We recommend becoming familiar with product contents by making a habit of reading food labels.

Positive aspects of meat alternatives include convenience, high-protein quantity, plant-based protein, moderate polyunsaturated fat content, low saturated fat, zero cholesterol, and many are organic. Many also contain key nutrients such as B12 and iron, and some have high fibre content. One of the biggest advantages is that meat alternatives can help people who are used to eating meat transition to a plant-based diet. There are also people who continue to consume meat alternatives as part of their plant-based diet. Meat alternatives are a great option for people who are attached to the familiar taste and texture they grew up with, and one can remake many cultural recipes that originally involved meat. When on the go in our busy lives, they are a fast way to get a substantial protein meal, so long as we choose the less-processed options that contain more whole-food ingredients more often.

Tips for these transition foods include reading the ingredients and nutritional value; choosing products that are organic, higher in fibre and protein, and relatively lower in fat and sodium; and comparing products by calculating the amount of fat and sodium per 10 grams of protein. The Tofurky sausage is a good benchmark (note that we are not endorsed by any brand, but this is a practical pointer). Transition foods provide the most value on a once-in-a-while basis; enjoy them, but they should not be your main protein source. Instead, keep focused on whole and minimally processed protein sources and experiment and enjoy new tastes and textures by learning to prepare pulses. Table 6.1 shows some of the better transition meat products, but even they are somewhat high in sodium. If you cook with them – for example, by adding vegan sausage chunks to a stew – then avoid adding extra salt. Also, be aware of the additional sodium in ketchup and other condiments.

Table 6.1 Comparing protein and sodium in transition meat products

Brand	Fat per 10g Protein	Sodium per 10g Protein
Tofurky Italian Sausage	4.7 g	206.7 g
Gardien Chick'n Strips	4.6 g	215.4 g
Yves Good Veggie Burger	2.7 g	246.2 g
Gusta Seitan	5.8g	308.3 g

Source: Authors own work, created for this volume.

Fruits and vegetables

This will be a simple section, as we should eat as many fruits and veggies as we can, and include a broad variety. Fresh fruits are healthier than canned, which are not fresh and often packed in syrup or juice, increasing their sugar content. Frozen fruits are also a good option, particularly for smoothies. Diabetics should be careful of too much fruit consumption at once, depending on their blood sugar response. Eat whole fruit: fruit juices contain concentrated sugars with all of the fibre removed. Vegetables with low sugar content are best for juicing.

Vegetables can be eaten raw and cooked: there is a benefit to both. When sautéing or steaming vegetables, avoid overcooking. Instead, cook them briefly to preserve colours and nutrients. Rather than draining the cooking water, use it in cooking recipes to capture the nutrients. Brightly coloured vegetables are nutrition powerhouses, especially green vegetables. Kale and broccoli are superfoods, as they contain iron and calcium, as well as the vitamin C that helps with absorption. Potatoes and sweet potatoes are an excellent source of complex carbohydrates and fibre.

Nuts and seeds

Nuts and seeds are great in snacks, salads, sauces, cereals, soups, and smoothies. Nuts are also a good source of protein, especially peanuts. Peanuts are actually a legume, botanically; however, we have grouped them with nuts because they have a similar fat content and texture. Nuts and seeds are high in fat, but consumed as whole foods, they have great health protective effects. They reduce CVD and are thought to be a key ingredient in the Mediterranean diet, which extends lifespan (Estruch et al., 2013; Luu et al., 2015).

Oils and margarine

In the Internet and media world, there is a wide range of controversy and opinion about oils, often based on misinformation driven by interest groups. Nutritional science has less controversy. It is clear that animal fats and cholesterol are unhealthy, and lead to more atherosclerosis, which can progress to cardiac and peripheral vascular disease, and even dementia. Plant-based fat sources are mostly monounsaturated and polyunsaturated, and are superior nutritionally to animal sources of fat (Baer et al., 2010; Li et al., 2015). As discussed in the cardiovascular disease section, larger trials of omega-3 supplementation turned out not to have significant benefit for cardiovascular disease. At the same time, people became worried about having a high intake of omega-6, which was thought to compromise omega-3 levels in the body. However, it turns out that oils with high levels of omega-6 are protective against cardiac disease when compared with animal fats; perhaps there is no need for concern, and we await more data (Abdelhamid et al., 2018; Wang et al., 2016).

Lower fat WFPB diets

The one controversy that nutritional experts often have is over added fats in a WFPB diet. Is any amount of oil healthy? Should a WFPB diet contain zero added oil, or are some oils actually healthy? The answer is context dependant. Most of the studies showing the benefits of polyunsaturated and monounsaturated fats are when plant-based fats are compared to animal fat consumption: there is consistent benefit shown. But we also know that whole foods are beneficial, and obesity is detrimental. So fats should be consumed in smaller amounts since overconsumption will contribute to obesity. Sounds familiar? This is just like what we mentioned with whole grains. Healthy plant-based fats can be good for you, but most of us must consume them modestly, since most people's caloric needs are low. However, having some fat in our foods can lead to increased food satisfaction, and many people have problems on a vegan diet when they become too strict. Some can be so strict as to be in a calorie deficit, so it's important not to over- or under-consume.

In the context of reversing cardiovascular disease and severe type 2 diabetes or obesity, the zero added oils diet may be of use in these specific circumstances. As mentioned earlier, the studies of Ornish et al. (1998) and Esselstyn et al. (2014) showed reversal of atherosclerosis with an ultra-low-fat diet. As authors, we recommend diets ultra-low in fat, with no added oils, only under these conditions, and we recommend that people discuss their diets with their physicians. For example, if a person suddenly goes to an ultra-low-fat vegan WFPB diet and has diabetes type 2 and is on insulin, it should only be done under medical supervision, as the diet may be so effective that the insulin dose may become too high, which could be dangerous. Some insulin-dependent type 2 diabetics can actually get off their insulin on such a diet, but only under medical supervision. This is a wonderful example of a WFPB diet as disease treatment, not just prevention: it can be life changing.

Healthier plant fats

Try to get your whole-food fat sources as much as possible from nuts and nut butters, seeds and seed butters, tahini, edamame, and avocado, which are all good choices. When choosing an oil, look for one that is high in polyunsaturated or monounsaturated fats like canola oil, olive oil, flax oil, sunflower oil, grape seed oils, or soybean oil. All of us are reminded to consume oil in moderation.

Plant fats to limit or avoid

As mentioned earlier, it's important to ignore the fad diets concerning coconut oil and palm oil, and limit or avoid these fats, which are both high in saturated fat. Trans-fats are created when polyunsaturated fats are heated to high temperatures for prolonged times, such as when frying foods. Hydrogenated margarine or shortening and some snack foods contain trans-fats, which are consistently shown to increase cancer and heart disease, and should be avoided; though these are less common now in North America, they are likely worse than animal fats for our health. Fried foods are extremely high in fat and contribute to obesity and other metabolic problems. Many foods are fried in palm oil, which reduces the trans-fats, but the saturated fat of palm oil is not much better, even if the label says, "No Trans-Fats!" Also, palm oil cultivation and harvesting can cause significant environmental destruction.

Further nutritional considerations

Calcium and bone health

Maintaining strong bones and preventing osteoporosis and fractures are important. The causes of osteoporosis are multifactorial. Calcium is an important factor, though there is some discrepancy about intake requirements. The recommended intake of calcium in the USA is higher than the UK, but may also be too high (National Institutes of Health, 2018). In the EPIC study, where vegans had increased fractures compared with the general population, vegans who did not get at least 525 mg of calcium per day sustained more fractures than the general population, but those exceeding that amount did not have more fractures than the general population (Appleby, Roddam, Allen, & Key, 2007). Other dietary factors that decrease fracture risk due to osteoporosis include good protein intake, high fruit and vegetable intake, and increased intake of pulses and soy foods (Butler, van Dam, Ang, Yuan, & Koh, 2014; Dai et al., 2014; Lousuebsakul-Matthews et al., 2014). Again, we remind readers that exercising, including in elderly age, and never smoking are important for healthy bones. One practical tip we suggest is including at least one to two glasses of fortified soy milk per day – this is an excellent way to get calcium, protein, and other long-term benefits of soy. The Canadian and the USA recommended daily allowance (RDA) of calcium is 1,000 mg/day, with increased requirements for adolescents, older adults, and during pregnancy, and two glasses of fortified soy milk provides 600 mg of calcium.

Vitamin B12

Vitamin B12 is a supplement that all vegans should be taking. B12 is produced by bacteria. Evolutionarily, when our ancestors lived in jungles and ate mainly plants, they would get B12 through the food and water contamination by bacteria that were everywhere. Since we are purifying our water, washing our hands, and washing our foods, our plant foods do not contain B12. Hence it is very useful that our commercial plant-based milks and some other vegan foods are fortified with B12. But one challenge is that our absorption of B12 is variable from person to person. In fact, many people who eat meat, dairy, and eggs have low B12, and vegans are more at risk. Therefore, we suggest a 1,000 mcg supplement twice per week, though many are fine with even once per week. It's important to test B12 levels once a year, and if normal two years in a row, then test every two years. B12 absorption worsens with age, so it's important to be diligent after the age of 55 and speak to your doctor about how often you should be tested.

B12 is an important nutrient during pregnancy, and women considering pregnancy should ensure that their B12 levels are adequate before pregnancy. During pregnancy and lactation, it is important to be tested as well as to take supplements. For a pregnant or lactating woman, if personal B12 levels are adequate, the baby will get enough in the uterus or during breastfeeding. If a child is weaned, then formula should be used, and it will contain B12. After the age of one, if not breastfeeding, use a commercially available B12 supplement. A liquid B12 supplement will be easier for a child to take, and he or she can take it off the breast or sprayed directly into the mouth. However, it is critical that a child's B12 supplements are reviewed with a doctor. Low levels of B12 can potentially increase cancer and heart disease, and cancel out the benefits of a WFPB diet. Low B12 during pregnancy and breastfeeding can affect the baby's developing brain; at worst, very low B12 levels can be fatal in children. See Table 6.2 as follows with levels recommended for B12.

For older people, B12 deficiency may lead to anemia, nerve dysfunction, depression, paranoia, and memory loss. Some effects may be permanent.

Table 6.2 Recommended vitamin B12 supplements for maintaining already normal B12 levels in pregnant and lactating women, infants, and children

Population	Daily Single Dose	Daily Multiple Dose	Weekly Dose
Pregnant and lactating women	50 μg[1]	2 μg × 3	1,000 μg × 2
Children aged 6 months to 3 years	5 μg	1 μg × 2	-
Children aged 4 to 10 years	25 μg	2 μg × 2	-
Children aged 11 years and above	50 μg	2 μg × 3	1,000 μg × 2

Source: Baroni, L., Goggi, S., Battaglino, R., Berveglieri, M., Fasan, I., Filippin, D., . . . & Battino, M. (2019). Vegan nutrition for mothers and children: Practical tools for healthcare providers. *Nutrients*, *11*(1), 5 (used with permission).

[1] During pregnancy, taking this dose in two separate halves can increase B12 bioavailability.

We highly recommend making the inclusion of B12 a regular habit. It is important, and it is easy.

Some people worry that B12 supplements are not *natural*, compared to B12 from animal products. But livestock animals, in large part from factory farms, are not getting B12 naturally through their food. Therefore, B12 powder is added to their feed. Hence, there is nothing more or less natural about B12 in most animal products than in the supplements for a plant-based diet.

Iron containing foods

Good sources of iron in vegan diet include molasses, beans, lentils, raisins, soy milk, peas, tofu, tempeh, and kale, and there are many more (vegan health.org – iron). Eat a variety of vegan iron sources and remember that foods containing vitamin C will increase iron absorption. During blood tests, note that ferritin levels on the low side are acceptable, as long as they are within the normal range, and hemoglobin levels are normal. There is some evidence that high iron levels may increase diabetes, heart disease, and cancer, so normal levels on the low end may be a good thing (while iron deficiency anemia or below normal ferritin is not okay). Some studies indicate that it may be heme iron, meaning iron from animal foods, that may be a greater cause of these ailments than iron from plant foods (Geissler & Singh, 2011; Hunnicutt, He, & Xun, 2014; Talaei, Wang, Yuan, Pan, & Koh, 2017). Some women will need to take iron supplements to prevent or correct iron deficiency anemia, even if their diets are optimized. This is particularly true of athletic women who have high menstrual blood losses.

A word about salt

Canadian and US guidelines warn adults to take less than 2,300 mg of sodium, which is the amount present in 6 g, or one teaspoon, of table salt, which is technically sodium plus chloride. A healthier amount would be even less, at 1,500 mg of sodium. The average American male consumes 4,000 mg of sodium and woman 3,000 mg. Read labels and be mindful of canned and processed foods, even vegan ones. We all have some treats . . . but watch your sodium intake. One little tip: most veggie meats have higher sodium. When adding veggie meat to dishes, little to zero table salt is needed. Some salt from the veggie meat will flavour the rest of the dish. For those who are prefer salty foods, it is helpful to note that tastes do readjust after cutting salt for a couple of weeks. Changes throughout a diet are possible. For those with blood pressure well below the normal range and others with symptoms of feeling faint, it is important to discuss these issues with a doctor. Some people may have sodium intake that is too low (Government of Canada, 2017; Healthy Eating, 2018).

Other supplements to consider

People living in the northern climates may benefit from a vitamin D supplement, especially in the winter months. Omega-3 fats were discussed earlier in this chapter. Readers are advised to eat plenty of the plant omega-3 sources (flax, hemp, chia, and so many more) since they are healthy for many reasons. Adding marine omega-3 supplements from sea vegetables is optional, and the evidence is variable.

Different stages of life

The American Academy of Nutrition and Dietetics (2015) states that vegan and vegetarian diets are healthful at all stages of life. Pregnancy and lactation and elderly age are times where good nutrition are particularly important; during these periods, ensure calcium, B12, and folate supplementation. It is also very important to get adequate protein: about 1 g per kg of body mass. Children can thrive on a WFPB diet. They should eat a variety of foods from across the plant food groups, and it is important to ensure that they are meeting the RDAs of key nutrients, such as calcium, iron, B12, and protein. A WFPB diet is an excellent way to start a long-term healthy eating pattern.

Failing vegan diets . . . oops!

There are many people who proudly become vegan, and after some time, long or short, they feel that something is missing. If a person is experiencing low energy or excessive weight loss, he or she should do the following:

- Check B12 levels, protein intake, and see doctor to check for anemia or thyroid issues
- Increase energy- and protein-dense foods if needed
- Include nut butters, pulses, and transition foods, as they can help
- While the scientific evidence shows benefits from plant-based, people making the transition may seek the emotional satisfaction of familiar former diets and may wish to temporarily incorporate small amounts of organic animal-based foods

For others who may be experiencing weight gain:

- Decrease fats
- Decrease carbohydrate intake
- Guard against eating junk foods, refined carbohydrates, sugary juices, or drinks.

Conclusion

Evolving eating patterns can be a long process with some ups and downs, but they should not involve judgemental or guilt-ridden emotions: they should be happy endeavours. Transitioning to a plant-based or vegan diet should be enjoyable and involve some fun with friends and family. There will be the exploration and experimentation, trial and error, and over time, new habits become strong, taste buds adjust, and new menus become full of succulent options. These elements help to maintain and improve food choices, health habits, and lifestyles. For some people, it may come easier, but the accumulated evidence suggests that the most protective diet is a plant-based one, although people may embrace it gradually.

We encourage everyone to undertake taste adventures and increase food options by exploring many tastes from worldwide recipes. We consider it imperative to find amazing and tasty ways to incorporate beans and lentils, which are under-consumed in our Western world. Relish the opportunity to eat mindfully, as the Canada Food Guide suggests: eat with friends and family, prepare more meals at home, and enjoy a broad variety from all the food groups. Explore interesting restaurants and share experiences with friends; explore the Internet for WFPB dishes of many varieties and get savvy at your staple meals that are nutritious, delicious, and efficient. Keep learning and applying new skills in food preparation. Over time, the majority of us can enjoy the excellent taste and health benefits of a well planned whole food plant-based diet.

References

Abdelhamid, A. S., Brown, T. J., Brainard, J. S., Biswas, P., Thorpe, G. C., Moore, H. J., . . . Song, F. (2018). Omega-3 fatty acids for the primary and secondary prevention of cardiovascular disease. *Cochrane Database of Systematic Reviews* (7). doi:10.1002/14651858.CD003177.pub3.

Abdullah, S. M., Defina, L. F., Leonard, D., Barlow, C. E., Radford, N. B., Willis, B. L., . . . Berry, J. D. (2018). Long-term association of low-density lipoprotein cholesterol with cardiovascular mortality in individuals at low 10-year risk of atherosclerotic cardiovascular disease: Results from the Cooper center longitudinal study. *Circulation*, 138(21), 2315–2325.

Academy of Nutrition and Dietetics. (2015). Position of the academy of nutrition and dietetics: Vegetarian diets. *Journal of the Academy of Nutrition and Dietetics*, 116(12), 1970–1980.

American Heart Association. (2017). Heart disease and stroke statistics – 2017 update. *Circulation*, 135(10), e146–e603. doi:10.1161/CIR.0000000000000485

Amidor, T. (2017). Ask the expert: Clearing up lectin misconceptions. *Today's Dietitian*, 19(10), 10. Retrieved from www.todaysdietitian.com/newarchives/1017p10.shtml

Appleby, P., Roddam, A., Allen, N., & Key, T. (2007). Comparative fracture risk in vegetarians and nonvegetarians in EPIC-Oxford. *European Journal of Clinical Nutrition*, 61(12), 1400.

Aune, D., Keum, N., Giovannucci, E., Fadnes, L. T., Boffetta, P., Greenwood, D. C., . . . Norat, T. (2016). Whole grain consumption and risk of cardiovascular disease, cancer, and all cause and cause specific mortality: Systematic review and dose-response meta-analysis of prospective studies. *BMJ*, *353*, i2716.

Baer, H. J., Glynn, R. J., Hu, F. B., Hankinson, S. E., Willett, W. C., Colditz, G. A., . . . Rosner, B. (2010). Risk factors for mortality in the nurses' health study: A competing risks analysis. *American Journal of Epidemiology*, *173*(3), 319–329.

Barnard, N. D., Willett, W. C., & Ding, E. L. (2017). The misuse of meta-analysis in nutrition research. *JAMA*, *318*(15), 1435–1436.

Baroni, L., Goggi, S., Battaglino, R., Berveglieri, M., Fasan, I., Filippin, D., . . . Battino, M. (2019). Vegan nutrition for mothers and children: Practical tools for healthcare providers. *Nutrients*, *11*(1), 5.

Bosetti, C., Bravi, F., Turati, F., Edefonti, V., Polesel, J., Decarli, A., . . . Zeegers, M. P. (2013). Nutrient-based dietary patterns and pancreatic cancer risk. *Annals of Epidemiology*, *23*(3), 124–128.

Brasky, T. M., Darke, A. K., Song, X., Tangen, C. M., Goodman, P. J., Thompson, I. M., . . . Klein, E. A. (2013). Plasma phospholipid fatty acids and prostate cancer risk in the SELECT trial. *Journal of the National Cancer Institute*, *105*(15), 1132–1141.

British Nutrition Foundation. (2018). *Protein*. Retrieved from www.nutrition.org. uk/nutritionscience/nutrients-food-and-ingredients/protein.html

Chang, E. T., Lee, V. S., Canchola, A. J., Clarke, C. A., Purdie, D. M., Reynolds, P., . . . Pinder, R. (2007). Diet and risk of ovarian cancer in the California Teachers Study cohort. *American Journal of Epidemiology*, *165*(7), 802–813.

Chen, X., Huang, Y., & Cheng, H. G. (2012). Lower intake of vegetables and legumes associated with cognitive decline among illiterate elderly Chinese: A 3-year cohort study. *The Journal of Nutrition, Health & Aging*, *16*(6), 549–552.

Cheng, G., Remer, T., Prinz-Langenohl, R., Blaszkewicz, M., Degen, G. H., & Buyken, A. E. (2010). Relation of isoflavones and fiber intake in childhood to the timing of puberty. *The American Journal of Clinical Nutrition*, *92*(3), 556–564.

Collier, R. (2016). Dairy research: "Real" science or marketing? *Canadian Medical Association Journal/Journal de l'Association Medicale Canadienne*, *188*(10), 715–716. https://doi.org/10.1503/cmaj.109-5278

Crowe, F. L., Appleby, P. N., Allen, N. E., & Key, T. J. (2011). Diet and risk of diverticular disease in Oxford cohort of European prospective investigation into cancer and nutrition (EPIC): Prospective study of British vegetarians and non-vegetarians. *BMJ*, *343*, d4131.

Dai, Z., Butler, L. M., van Dam, R. M., Ang, L. W., Yuan, J. M., & Koh, W. P. (2014). Adherence to a vegetable-fruit-soy dietary pattern or the Alternative Healthy Eating Index is associated with lower hip fracture risk among Singapore Chinese. *The Journal of Nutrition*, *144*(4), 511–518.

De Souza, A., Irfan, K., Masud, F., & Saif, M. W. (2016). Diabetes type 2 and pancreatic cancer: A history unfolding. *Journal of the Pancreas*, *17*(2), 144.

Dietitians of Canada. (2016). *Nutrition and athletic performance*. Retrieved from www.dietitians.ca/Downloads/Public/noap-position-paper.aspx

Dinu, M., Abbate, R., Gensini, G. F., Casini, A., & Sofi, F. (2017). Vegetarian, vegan diets and multiple health outcomes: A systematic review with meta-analysis of observational studies. *Critical Reviews in Food Science and Nutrition*, *57*(17), 3640–3649.

Dong, J. Y., & Qin, L. Q. (2011). Soy isoflavones consumption and risk of breast cancer incidence or recurrence: A meta-analysis of prospective studies. *Breast Cancer Research and Treatment, 125*(2), 315–323.

Ericson, U., Sonestedt, E., Gullberg, B., Hellstrand, S., Hindy, G., Wirfält, E., . . . Orho-Melander, M. (2013). High intakes of protein and processed meat associate with increased incidence of type 2 diabetes. *British Journal of Nutrition, 109*(6), 1143–1153.

Eskelinen, M. H., Ngandu, T., Helkala, E. L., Tuomilehto, J., Nissinen, A., Soininen, H., . . . Kivipelto, M. (2008). Fat intake at midlife and cognitive impairment later in life: A population-based CAIDE study. *International Journal of Geriatric Psychiatry, 23*(7), 741–747.

Esselstyn, C. B., Jr., Gendy, G., Doyle, J., Golubic, M., & Roizen, M. F. (2014). A way to reverse CAD? *Journal of Family Practice, 63*(7), 356–364.

Estruch, R., Ros, E., Salas-Salvadó, J., Covas, M. I., Corella, D., Arós, F., . . . Lamuela-Raventos, R. M. (2013). Primary prevention of cardiovascular disease with a Mediterranean diet. *New England Journal of Medicine, 368*(14), 1279–1290.

Farvid, M. S., Cho, E., Chen, W. Y., Eliassen, A. H., & Willett, W. C. (2014). Premenopausal dietary fat in relation to pre-and post-menopausal breast cancer. *Breast Cancer Research and Treatment, 145*(1), 255–265.

Food and Agriculture Organization of the United Nations (FAO). (2016). *2016 International year of pulses.* Retrieved from www.fao.org/pulses-2016/en/

Flood, A., Rastogi, T., Wirfält, E., Mitrou, P. N., Reedy, J., Subar, A. F., . . . Schatzkin, A. (2008). Dietary patterns as identified by factor analysis and colorectal cancer among middle-aged Americans. *The American Journal of Clinical Nutrition, 88*(1), 176–184.

Ford, E. S., Bergmann, M. M., Kröger, J., Schienkiewitz, A., Weikert, C., & Boeing, H. (2009). Healthy living is the best revenge: Findings from the European prospective investigation into cancer and nutrition-potsdam study. *Archives of Internal Medicine, 169*(15), 1355–1362.

Geissler, C., & Singh, M. (2011). Iron, meat and health. *Nutrients, 3*(3), 283–316. doi:10.3390/nu3030283

Government of Canada. (2017). *Sodium in Canada.* Retrieved from www.canada.ca/en/health-canada/services/food-nutrition/healthy-eating/sodium.html#a2

Government of Canada. (2019). *Canada's food guide.* Retrieved from https://foodguide.canada.ca/en/

Grant, W. B. (2016). Using multicountry ecological and observational studies to determine dietary risk factors for Alzheimer's disease. *Journal of the American College of Nutrition, 35*(5), 476–489.

Greger, M. (2018). *How the dairy industry designs misleading studies.* Retrieved from https://nutritionfacts.org/video/how-the-dairy-industry-designs-misleading-studies/

Hamilton-Reeves, J. M., Vazquez, G., Duval, S. J., Phipps, W. R., Kurzer, M. S., & Messina, M. J. (2010). Clinical studies show no effects of soy protein or isoflavones on reproductive hormones in men: Results of a meta-analysis. *Fertility and Sterility, 94*(3), 997–1007.

Hartmann, S., Lacorn, M., & Steinhart, H. (1998). Natural occurrence of steroid hormones in food. *Food Chemistry, 62*(1), 7–20.

Healthy Eating. (2018). *USDA guidelines for sodium intake.* Retrieved from https://healthyeating.sfgate.com/usda-guidelines-sodium-intake-7839.html

Huang, T., Yang, B., Zheng, J., Li, G., Wahlqvist, M. L., & Li, D. (2012). Cardiovascular disease mortality and cancer incidence in vegetarians: A meta-analysis and systematic review. *Annals of Nutrition and Metabolism, 60*(4), 233–240.

Hunnicutt, J., He, K., & Xun, P. (2014). Dietary iron intake and body iron stores are associated with risk of coronary heart disease in a meta-analysis of prospective cohort studies. *The Journal of Nutrition, 144*(3), 359–366.

Jones, K. R., Klein, C. J., Halpern, B. S., Venter, O., Grantham, H., Kuempel, C. D., . . . Watson, J. E. (2018). The location and protection status of Earth's diminishing marine wilderness. *Current Biology, 28*(15), 2506–2512.

Kalman, D., Feldman, S., Martinez, M., Krieger, D. R., & Tallon, M. J. (2007). Effect of protein source and resistance training on body composition and sex hormones. *Journal of the International Society of Sports Nutrition, 4*(1), 4.

Key, T. J., Appleby, P. N., Crowe, F. L., Bradbury, K. E., Schmidt, J. A., & Travis, R. C. (2014). Cancer in British vegetarians: Updated analyses of 4998 incident cancers in a cohort of 32,491 meat eaters, 8612 fish eaters, 18,298 vegetarians, and 2246 vegans. *The American Journal of Clinical Nutrition, 100*(Suppl. 1), 378S–385S.

Kolahdooz, F., Ibiebele, T. I., van der Pols, J. C., & Webb, P. M. (2008). Dietary patterns and ovarian cancer risk. *The American Journal of Clinical Nutrition, 89*(1), 297–304.

Larsson, S. C., & Wolk, A. (2012). Red and processed meat consumption and risk of pancreatic cancer: Meta-analysis of prospective studies. *British Journal of Cancer, 106*(3), 603.

Lathe, R., Sapronova, A., & Kotelevtsev, Y. (2014). Atherosclerosis and Alzheimer-diseases with a common cause? Inflammation, oxysterols, vasculature. *BMC Geriatrics, 14*(1), 36.

Li, Y., Hruby, A., Bernstein, A. M., Ley, S. H., Wang, D. D., Chiuve, S. E., . . . Hu, F. B. (2015). Saturated fats compared with unsaturated fats and sources of carbohydrates in relation to risk of coronary heart disease: A prospective cohort study. *Journal of the American College of Cardiology, 66*(14), 1538–1548.

Link, L. B., Canchola, A. J., Bernstein, L., Clarke, C. A., Stram, D. O., Ursin, G., . . . Horn-Ross, P. L. (2013). Dietary patterns and breast cancer risk in the California Teachers Study cohort. *The American Journal of Clinical Nutrition, 98*(6), 1524–1532.

Lousuebsakul-Matthews, V., Thorpe, D. L., Knutsen, R., Beeson, W. L., Fraser, G. E., & Knutsen, S. F. (2014). Legumes and meat analogues consumption are associated with hip fracture risk independently of meat intake among Caucasian men and women: The adventist health study-2. *Public Health Nutrition, 17*(10), 2333–2343.

Luu, H. N., Blot, W. J., Xiang, Y. B., Cai, H., Hargreaves, M. K., Li, H., . . . Shu, X. O. (2015). Prospective evaluation of the association of nut/peanut consumption with total and cause-specific mortality. *JAMA Internal Medicine, 175*(5), 755–766.

Magee, P. J., & Rowland, I. (2012). Soy products in the management of breast cancer. *Current Opinion in Clinical Nutrition & Metabolic Care, 15*(6), 586–591.

McMacken, M., & Shah, S. (2017). A plant-based diet for the prevention and treatment of type 2 diabetes. *Journal of Geriatric Cardiology, 14*(5), 342.

Messina, M. (2010). Soybean isoflavone exposure does not have feminizing effects on men: A critical examination of the clinical evidence. *Fertility and Sterility, 93*(7), 2095–2104.

Messina, M., & Redmond, G. (2006). Effects of soy protein and soybean isoflavones on thyroid function in healthy adults and hypothyroid patients: A review of the relevant literature. *Thyroid, 16*(3), 249–258.

Messina, M., & Wu, A. H. (2009). Perspectives on the soy – Breast cancer relation. *The American Journal of Clinical Nutrition, 89*(5), 1673S–1679S.

Mollard, R. C., Luhovyy, B. L., Panahi, S., Nunez, M., Hanley, A., & Anderson, G. H. (2012). Regular consumption of pulses for 8 weeks reduces metabolic syndrome risk factors in overweight and obese adults. *British Journal of Nutrition, 108*(Suppl. 1), S111–S122.

National Institutes of Health. (2018). *Calcium*. Retrieved from https://ods.od.nih.gov/factsheets/Calcium-HealthProfessional/

Ogilvie, R. P., Lutsey, P. L., Heiss, G., Folsom, A. R., & Steffen, L. M. (2017). Dietary intake and peripheral arterial disease incidence in middle-aged adults: The atherosclerosis risk in communities (ARIC) study. *The American Journal of Clinical Nutrition, 105*(3), 651–659.

Ogimoto, I., Shibata, A., & Fukuda, K. (2000). World Cancer Research Fund/American Institute of Cancer Research 1997 recommendations: Applicability to digestive tract cancer in Japan. *Cancer Causes & Control, 11*(1), 9–23.

Orlich, M. J., Singh, P. N., Sabaté, J., Jaceldo-Siegl, K., Fan, J., Knutsen, S., . . . Fraser, G. E. (2013). Vegetarian dietary patterns and mortality in adventist health study-2. *JAMA Internal Medicine, 173*(13), 1230–1238.

Ornish, D., Scherwitz, L. W., Billings, J. H., Gould, K. L., Merritt, T. A., Sparler, S., . . . Brand, R. J. (1998). Intensive lifestyle changes for reversal of coronary heart disease. *JAMA, 280*(23), 2001–2007.

Pettersen, B. J., Anousheh, R., Fan, J., Jaceldo-Siegl, K., & Fraser, G. E. (2012). Vegetarian diets and blood pressure among white subjects: Results from the adventist health study-2 (AHS-2). *Public Health Nutrition, 15*(10), 1909–1916.

Pulses. (n.d.). *A visual guide to pulses*. Retrieved from https://pulses.org/what-are-pulses/visual-guide-to-pulses

Ramdath, D., Padhi, E., Sarfaraz, S., Renwick, S., & Duncan, A. (2017). Beyond the cholesterol-lowering effect of soy protein: A review of the effects of dietary soy and its constituents on risk factors for cardiovascular disease. *Nutrients, 9*(4), 324.

Reynolds, A., Mann, J., Cummings, J., Winter, N., Mete, E., & Te Morenga, L. (2019). Carbohydrate quality and human health: A series of systematic reviews and meta-analyses. *The Lancet, 393*(10170), 434–445.

Rizzo, N. S., Jaceldo-Siegl, K., Sabate, J., & Fraser, G. E. (2013). Nutrient profiles of vegetarian and nonvegetarian dietary patterns. *Journal of the Academy of Nutrition and Dietetics, 113*(12), 1610–1619.

Sabate, J., Harwatt, H., & Soret, S. (2015). Health outcomes and greenhouse gas emissions from varied dietary patterns – Is there a relationship? *Annals of Nutrition and Metabolism, 67*, 547–548.

Sabaté, J., & Wien, M. (2010). Vegetarian diets and childhood obesity prevention. *The American Journal of Clinical Nutrition, 91*(5), 1525S–1529S.

Sacks, F. M., Lichtenstein, A. H., Wu, J. H., Appel, L. J., Creager, M. A., Kris-Etherton, P. M., . . . Stone, N. J. (2017). Dietary fats and cardiovascular disease: A presidential advisory from the American Heart Association. *Circulation, 136*(3), e1–e23.

Sarup Singh, R., Preet Kaur, H., & Rakesh Kanwar, J. (2016). Mushroom lectins as promising anticancer substances. *Current Protein and Peptide Science, 17*(8), 797–807.

Satija, A., Bhupathiraju, S. N., Rimm, E. B., Spiegelman, D., Chiuve, S. E., Borgi, L., . . . Hu, F. B. (2016). Plant-based dietary patterns and incidence of type 2 diabetes in US men and women: Results from three prospective cohort studies. *PLoS Medicine, 13*(6), e1002039.

Sieri, S., Chiodini, P., Agnoli, C., Pala, V., Berrino, F., Trichopoulou, A., . . . Amiano, P. (2014). Dietary fat intake and development of specific breast cancer subtypes. *JNCI: Journal of the National Cancer Institute, 106*(5), dju068. https://doi.org/10.1093/jnci/dju068

Solomon, A., Kivipelto, M., Wolozin, B., Zhou, J., & Whitmer, R. A. (2009). Midlife serum cholesterol and increased risk of Alzheimer's and vascular dementia three decades later. *Dementia and Geriatric Cognitive Disorders, 28*(1), 75.

Song, Y., Chavarro, J. E., Cao, Y., Qiu, W., Mucci, L., Sesso, H. D., . . . Ma, J. (2012). Whole milk intake is associated with prostate cancer-specific mortality among US male physicians. *The Journal of Nutrition, 143*(2), 189–196.

Spence, J. D., Jenkins, D. J., & Davignon, J. (2010). Dietary cholesterol and egg yolks: Not for patients at risk of vascular disease. *Canadian Journal of Cardiology, 26*(9), e336–e339.

Steele, C. B., Thomas, C. C., Henley, S. J., Massetti, G. M., Galuska, D. A., Agurs-Collins, T., . . . Richardson, L. C. (2017). Vital signs: Trends in incidence of cancers associated with overweight and obesity – United States, 2005–2014. *Morbidity and Mortality Weekly Report, 66*(39), 1052.

Talaei, M., Wang, Y. L., Yuan, J. M., Pan, A., & Koh, W.-P. (2017). Meat, dietary heme iron, and risk of type 2 diabetes mellitus: The Singapore Chinese health study. *American Journal of Epidemiology, 186*(7), 824–833.

Tantamango-Bartley, Y., Knutsen, S. F., Knutsen, R., Jacobsen, B. K., Fan, J., Beeson, W. L., . . . Herring, P. (2015). Are strict vegetarians protected against prostate cancer? *The American Journal of Clinical Nutrition, 103*(1), 153–160.

Taylor, E. F., Burley, V. J., Greenwood, D. C., & Cade, J. E. (2007). Meat consumption and risk of breast cancer in the UK women's cohort study. *British Journal of Cancer, 96*(7), 1139.

Tharrey, M., Mariotti, F., Mashchak, A., Barbillon, P., Delattre, M., & Fraser, G. E. (2018). Patterns of plant and animal protein intake are strongly associated with cardiovascular mortality: The adventist health study-2 cohort. *International Journal of Epidemiology, 47*(5), 1603–1612.

Thiébaut, A. C., Jiao, L., Silverman, D. T., Cross, A. J., Thompson, F. E., Subar, A. F., . . . Stolzenberg-Solomon, R. Z. (2009). Dietary fatty acids and pancreatic cancer in the NIH-AARP diet and health study. *Journal of the National Cancer Institute, 101*(14), 1001–1011.

Torfadottir, J. E., Steingrimsdottir, L., Mucci, L., Aspelund, T., Kasperzyk, J. L., Olafsson, O., . . . Jonsson, E. (2011). Milk intake in early life and risk of advanced prostate cancer. *American Journal of Epidemiology, 175*(2), 144–153.

Toumpanakis, A., Turnbull, T., & Alba-Barba, I. (2018). Effectiveness of plant-based diets in promoting well-being in the management of type 2 diabetes: A systematic review. *BMJ Open Diabetes Research & Care, 6*(1), e000534. doi:10.1136/bmjdrc-2018-000534

United States Department of Agriculture. (n.d.). *Protein and amino acids.* Retrieved from www.nal.usda.gov/fnic/protein-and-amino-acids

Vegan Health. (2018). *Protein and amino acids.* Retrieved from https://veganhealth. org/protein/

Wang, D. D., Li, Y., Chiuve, S. E., Stampfer, M. J., Manson, J. E., Rimm, E. B., . . . Hu, F. B. (2016). Association of specific dietary fats with total and cause-specific mortality. *JAMA Internal Medicine, 176*(8), 1134–1145.

Welch, A. A., Shakya-Shrestha, S., Lentjes, M. A., Wareham, N. J., & Khaw, K. T. (2010). Dietary intake and status of n – 3 polyunsaturated fatty acids in a population of fish-eating and non-fish-eating meat-eaters, vegetarians, and vegans and the precursor-product ratio of α-linolenic acid to long-chain n – 3 polyunsaturated fatty acids: Results from the EPIC-Norfolk cohort. *The American Journal of Clinical Nutrition, 92*(5), 1040–1051.

Willett, W., Rockström, J., Loken, B., Springmann, M., Lang, T., Vermeulen, S., . . . Jonell, M. (2019). Food in the Anthropocene: The EAT – Lancet Commission on healthy diets from sustainable food systems. *The Lancet, 393*(10170), 447–492.

World Health Organization. (2015). *Q&A on the carcinogenicity of the consumption of red meat and processed meat.* Retrieved from www.cancer.ie/content/ qa-carcinogenicityconsumption-red-meat-and-processed-meat

Yan, L., & Spitznagel, E. L. (2009). Soy consumption and prostate cancer risk in men: A revisit of a meta-analysis. *The American Journal of Clinical Nutrition, 89*(4), 1155–1163.

Yokoyama, Y., Nishimura, K., Barnard, N. D., Takegami, M., Watanabe, M., Sekikawa, A., . . . Miyamoto, Y. (2014). Vegetarian diets and blood pressure: A meta-analysis. *JAMA Internal Medicine, 174*(4), 577–587.

Zeilmaker, M. J., Hoekstra, J., van Eijkeren, J. C., de Jong, N., Hart, A., Kennedy, M., . . . Gunnlaugsdottir, H. (2013). Fish consumption during child bearing age: A quantitative risk – Benefit analysis on neurodevelopment. *Food and Chemical Toxicology, 54*, 30–34.

7 Healthy eating and active living in healthy environments – HEAL

Kathleen May Kevany and Chinweoke Asagwara

Introduction

In the widespread culture of neoliberalism, economic policies are sought after to reduce impediments and increase access to markets for "free trade" of industrial food products. This laissez-faire environment fosters conditions in Canada, like many other countries in the world, of seemingly intractable health, environmental, and social problems. Outcomes like inequity, ill health, and environmental contamination are predictable from market economies predicated on consumption-based growth where profitability is the primary litmus test of success (Swinburn et al., 2011). In this chapter, while considering various examples from Canada and the US, lessons and insights may be applied to inform practices in other countries as well, given the global phenomena of climate change and epidemics of noncommunicable diseases. This chapter clarifies some of the predominant beliefs, policies, and practices contributing to obesogenic environments that lead to social suffering of citizens across all socio-economic groups, but further disadvantage, lower income communities. As the health literature suggests, socio-economic and environmental determinants impact obesity along with a combination of factors: including dietary patterns, levels of physical (in)activity, along with social resources and networks (Bauer, Briss, Goodman, & Bowman, 2014).

Food systems are harbingers for neoliberalism, as noted in the opening chapter. Governmental subsidy and regulatory regimes that support agro-industrial food systems have assisted with increasing yields of commodity crops and flooding global markets with a dizzying array of ultra-processed food products. Along with a growing middle class, the ubiquitous influence of agro-industrial food products is leading to increases in meat and dairy production, as well as ensuring foods high in fat, sugar, and salt remain affordable, accessible, and desirable. Other results also are troubling. Full-cost accounting of food production is not adequately factored into the price, and the external costs often are left for local communities and concerned consumers to address through their food choices in opaque food systems (Apostolidis & McLeay, 2016). Intensive concentration and centralization of global food businesses make it challenging for small farm operations to survive in free markets (Ackerman-Leist, 2013). Agri-food corporations control farmers through requiring particular agricultural inputs as well as determining their compensation (Scrinis, 2007). Over the last half century, we have seen the reversal of household expenditures; now less is spent on food and more spent on illness care (Walsh, 2009).

Currently, chronic, non-communicable diseases, often described as life-style diseases, such as diabetes, obesity, and cardiovascular disease, have surpassed infectious diseases in prevalence; both drive worldwide poor health, disability, and premature death (Bauer et al., 2014). Investments in treating, rather than preventing, these diseases generate excessive economic burdens on health-care costs with widespread physical and emotional pain. To generate adequate solutions and preventative strategies, we must work together across sectors and disciplines to calculate and then recalibrate the complex network of interconnected systems of health, economics, politics, and agriculture, along with natural and built environments that drive individual well-being and population health. As might be said for many arenas of human endeavour, significant gaps remain between what science knows may be optimal and how humans operate. Fast, nutrient-poor, tasty foods are made readily available in the opaque, corporatized food environments that busy and ill-informed consumers must navigate daily. As more light is shone on food systems, this opacity is replaced with more clarity and responsibility, and different actions can be taken throughout the network of interconnected systems. This could be our time when the norm of being lethargic, overweight, and undernourished can be supplanted by the human aspiration for vitality, health, and happiness. When fuelled with nutrient-dense whole foods and regular movement, the human body is able to operate more optimally, think more strategically, and live more compassionately.

Public health

As described in Chapter 6, global increases in obesity are driven predominantly by changes in the consumption of sub-optimal foods emerging from the industrial food system. The mission of corporate marketing is to seek and secure markets for their products and to maximize profit through taking advantage of all options in the food environment. What is most profitable becomes most prolific. This availability breeds obesogenic environments that citizens are subject to living near, working in, and interacting with. As Alvaro and colleagues (2010) describe, these obesogenic environments promote obesity in individuals and populations through public policies and their corresponding practices, such as zoning and planning that determine surroundings, opportunities, and conditions of life with which citizens must contend. When combined with modern technology use, and dependence on vehicles and machines, these environments contribute to widespread sedentary lifestyles and physical inactivity (Swinburn et al., 2011). Yet in our democratic societies, the supply of goods, such as fast food, cigarettes, alcohol, and legalized drugs, must be understood as public and political. Consequently, individual habits and personal preferences, such as eating the standard meat-centric diet, smoking cigarettes, drinking alcohol, or leading a sedentary lifestyle, cannot be viewed as being made in isolation. Consumers cannot consume what is not there. Viewing individual habits solely as acts of individuals with "free will" would overlook the reality that citizens face a range of forces that actively undermine individual health and community well-being. These habits are heavily influenced by neoliberal policies, the marketplace, and the food environment. For example, smoking use is amplified by the design and addictive chemicals of cigarette products, the marketing campaigns, and the wide availability, attractive images in media, tobacco sponsorship of sport events, and the sex-appeal promoted by cultural icons (Cunningham, 1996). Public health campaigns and budgets around smoking cessation are dwarfed when compared to financing available through multinational corporations. In this climate, in spite of what is known about the perils of smoking, tobacco-attributable mortality worldwide is projected to increase from 30 million deaths in 1990 to 8.4 million deaths in 2020 (Yasin & Helms, 2010). How can public health be promoted and environments protected under such well-crafted and masterfully marketed campaigns?

Free-market food environments

The relationship between one's diet, disease, obesity, and local food environments are well established (Morland & Evenson, 2009). Food environments include households, or domestic spaces of all types, sharing of food amongst personal and social networks, and foods purchased for consumption at home or away. Food environments also include the policies and practices that support places, spaces, and types of foods available in surrounding environments, including government-controlled environments such as schools, day cares, nursing homes, hospitals, penitentiaries, community programmes, and others. Often, when thinking of *food environments*, one might envision roadways of commercial areas with a range of fast-food outlets. However, all food establishments contribute to the food environment. Private-sector and community food agencies contribute through food production businesses, grocery stores, restaurants, cafes. workplace cafeterias, and farmers' markets, along with other sites where food is available for consumption.

Research, unsurprisingly, shows that higher proximity to certain foods within an environment leads to an increased consumption of those foods. A study done by Laxer and Janssen (2014) explored this relationship between proximity of fast-food restaurants and fast-food consumption in youth. The study found that having fast food close to the subjects' environments contributed to a higher intake of fast, ultra-processed foods that are heavy in fats, salt, and sugars, contributing to less healthy youth. The study results suggest that the fast-food environments frequented by youths have an influence on their eating behaviours and health, both at the individual and population levels. Consequently, fast-food outlets situated close to secondary schools, for example, may be ideal locations for businesses to sell their goods to a steady flow of customers. However, the construction of such environments, based on municipal zoning by-laws, provincial business supports and incentives, and federal priorities and investments all feed into undesirable health outcomes through sub-optimal food environments. Consequently, various economic, zoning, or international trade policies inadvertently become health policies. Even with sound science, governments are criticized for not providing adequate warnings against preventable illnesses or adequately devising policies to address the obesogenic environments (Alvaro et al., 2010; Raphael, 2008).

Decades of epidemiological studies reveal two-thirds of deaths are from chronic diseases associated with modifiable behaviours, such as dietary intake, smoking, and physical activity (The Secretariat for the Intersectoral Healthy Living Network, 2005). It is sobering to recognize that, in Canada, the growing percentage of coronary heart disease is largely preventable (McGill, McMahan, & Gidding, 2008). Additionally, one in five Canadian children ages 2 to 5 are considered overweight or obese, and many are insufficiently active (McKay & Nigro, 2016). With such child and youth obesity statistics predicted to increase (Twells, Gregory, Reddigan, & Midodzi, 2014), quality of life will be compromised and health-care pressures compounded.

To reduce risk factors such as poor diet, inactivity, hypertension, high cholesterol, stroke, smoking, and the effects of alcohol and drugs, public education campaigns that include innovative and multi-prong strategies are critical, but insufficient on their own (Yasin & Helms, 2010). Marketplace shifts, along with lifestyle improvements, will be difficult to achieve without political will, financial incentives, and effective advocates from all sectors. This insufficiency leads us to the role of health promotion in reducing preventable diseases and guarding against emotional, environmental, and economic burdens from damaging food systems and lifestyle practices.

Health promotion

The World Health Organization (WHO) defines health promotion as the process of helping people to have control over and improve their health (2019). Health promotion focuses beyond individual behaviour towards a wide range of social determinants and environmental interventions (World Health Organization, 2019). The social determinants of health are the conditions in which people are born, grow, live, work, and age. Yet, as noted earlier, an array of interests and priorities, beyond the individual, influence health policies, planning, and health outcomes. Health promotion seeks to integrate the *best available evidence* to design policy and practice, and increase access to environments and programmes to afford people increasing control over their health and well-being.

Yet the growing levels of preventable disease reveal structural and political mechanisms impeding public health. More citizens and organizations are calling for preventative strategies and urge governments to calculate the multiple impacts from industrial food systems and food environments, and the impact of policies seemingly unrelated to health. To counter significant forces, wide collaboration becomes paramount. Successful examples might include the ubiquity of seat belt use, reduction of drinking and driving, reductions in smoking, zoning for healthy food outlets near schools, and removal of sugary drinks from some school campuses (Apostolidis & McLeay, 2016).

Governmental mechanisms to promote health

To prompt desired behaviours, governments have a multitude of tools they may use, including fiscal policy initiatives, such as subsidies or taxes, as well as incentives. Lower taxes could be levied, for example, to reduce the financial barriers for consumers who purchase and consume health-promoting products or foods. The Provincial Government of Nova Scotia, Canada, is applying such a reduced tax incentive for the emerging micro-distilleries to keep the price lower than imported products. This acts as an incentive for consumers to purchase provincially produced products. If such strategies can be deployed for alcohol products, surely creative taxation and incentives can be applied to foods that are linked to better health. Government can also apply taxes on food items shown to adversely affect human and environmental health, such as meat (Campbell & Campbell, 2006), cigarettes, and alcohol (Nugent & Knaul, 2006). Specific food subsidies or subsidies in conjunction with food campaigns can be explored specifically for promoting healthy eating and active living. Some jurisdictions financially support preventative strategies, such as *social prescriptions* provided by physicians and health-care professionals, yet the efficacy of these methods are not well substantiated (Bickerdike, Booth, Wilson, Farley, & Wright, 2017). Such social investments seek to increase the mental and physical health of community members through subsidizing access to recreation facilities and social activities, supporting engagement in social relationships, and mentoring opportunities (Sallis et al., 2006).

Unlike the well-known benefits arising from social relations and physical recreation, many physicians and other health-care professionals often lack knowledge of or personal experience with coaching on active lifestyles or the benefits of a whole-food, plant-based diet. This lack of knowledge reduces the awareness and confidence of physicians, and this may lead to misguiding patients considering these lifestyles. Subratty, Heesambee, Jowaheer, and Doreemiah (2002) reported that more physicians would discuss and prescribe the role of nutrition with their patients if they had more knowledge, time, and patient compliance. Training for many physicians has been inadequate in nutrition and holistic lifestyle medicine (Campbell & Jacobson, 2013). Increasing the knowledge of physicians, nurses, kinesiologists, registered dietitians, and other professionals in holistic approaches inclusive of physical activity, nutrition, and lifestyle counselling (Subratty et al., 2002) could help increase patient adoption of healthier dietary patterns. Studies such as Morley and Cashell (2017) suggest that providing medical care within an inter-professional team setting results in high-quality patient care and improved health outcomes. Currently, several medical schools are making such shifts. Some examples of which are shared in the success stories that follow. But first, strategies to shape greater policy coherence and promote national food guides will be discussed.

Policy coherence

As earlier suggested, government policies, at all levels, and from all departments, by their influence become de facto policies for health and well-being (Story, Hamm, & Wallinga, 2009). When governments are promoting more plant-based consumption, then these policies should also be matched by increased investments in plant-based production. In this sense, agricultural policy purposefully becomes and aligns with public health policy. Governments may feel pressured to support food production with the greatest revenue generation and job creation, which, when described in this way, seems politically and economically sound. To enable citizens to access healthy diets, suitable government policies across all departments are called to foster healthy food environments, from healthy production, healthy communities, to healthy consumption. Consequently, policies and practices that promote obesogenic environments need to be scrutinized and revised (Morland & Evenson, 2009).

National food guides

Governments, and particularly health departments, are mandated with the responsibility for health promotion and guiding citizens on healthy eating and active living through food guides and health policies. Developing and implementing a national food policy may pose significant challenges, as food policy lies at the intersection of agriculture, health, trade, environment, and economics, along with other policy areas. As Steier notes in Chapter 10, prudent food policies go beyond nutrition and environment to also include economic and sociocultural dimensions. The 2019 Canada Food Guide places emphasis on diet variety through reducing animal products and increasing whole, minimally processed plant-based foods, such as beans, nuts, whole grains, fruits, and vegetables. This new food guide also strongly advises citizens to reduce sodium, sugar, and saturated fats, which aligns well with plant-based eating. Such dietary guidelines that emphasize plant-based foods also help to reduce climate change and lifestyle diseases, and their associated costs (Lang, 2009; Mason & Lang, 2017). Meanwhile, most Canadians do not eat enough fruits and vegetables, and if Canadians ate more fruits and vegetables one or two days a week and, similarly, eat less meat and dairy, significant improvements could be realized in health, reduced body weight, and enhanced vitality, along with associated environmental improvements. If Canadians were to seek to meet their daily recommended amounts of plant-based foods, production levels in Canada would not be sufficient to meet these requirements (Henchion, Hayes, Mullen, Fenelon, & Tiwari, 2017). Again, a sign of the need for greater coherence and perhaps clairvoyance.

Food guides and other health promotion materials are designed to help individuals and families examine their beliefs and habits around food and lifestyle, and help them modify habits to prevent detrimental outcomes. Bacon and colleagues (2019) noted how policies and guidelines for healthier eating and improvements in where, with whom, and how citizens eat may help reduce health-care costs by millions. More governments are taking note of the evidence for health improvements that can lead to reduced health-care costs (Schepers & Annemans, 2018). By integrating the best available evidence, dietary guidelines that are high in whole plant foods are being promoted in the UK, Germany, Brazil, Sweden, and Qatar (Fischer & Garnett, 2016). As Greger (2016) reminds us, the best diet for health just so happens to also be the best environmentally and ethically. For example, the 2015 US Dietary Guidelines Advisory Committee noted remarkable consistency in a wide range of disease outcomes through a healthy dietary pattern that is higher in vegetables, fruits, whole grains, low- or nonfat dairy, seafood, legumes, and nuts; moderate in alcohol (amongst adults); lower in red and processed meat; and low in sugar-sweetened foods and drinks, and refined grains (Cespedes & Hu, 2015). The EatWell Guide by Public Health England (NHS, 2016) recommends a variety of foods and places greater emphasis on whole plant foods. They advise citizens to "get active and be a healthy weight" based on their findings that over 60% of adults in the UK are overweight or obese, which increases the risk of getting type 2 diabetes, heart disease, and some cancers. Physical activity can reduce the risk of type 2 diabetes, heart disease, and stroke, and help maintain a healthy weight. The government recommends 150 minutes of moderate intensity or 75 minutes vigorous intensity physical activity for adults 19–64 years of age and muscle strength training on at least two days per week (NHS, 2019).

Healthy eating

To live well on a whole-foods, plant-based diet, beans, seeds, and nuts are foundational ingredients. The production, promotion, and inclusion of legumes, such as beans, soya beans, and dry peas, are efficient and economical approaches to bolster global protein supply while addressing the issues of climate change, soil health, and human health. Worldwide, pulses are significant sources of plant protein and are economically important crops for farmers in developing and developed countries. Canadian farmers, for example, contribute significantly to world pea and lentil production, along with other beans. World trade in beans is worth billions and growing (Global Pulse Confederation, n.d.). Despite their immense health benefits and low impact on our planet, North Americans are not big consumers of legumes. A study conducted by Desrochers and Brauer (2001) revealed that in Canada, a lack of familiarity and inexperience in cooking plant foods (specifically legumes) was found to be a barrier for consuming plant-based foods and meals. This opens the door for tremendous business opportunities by introducing the bulk of the population to the succulence to be enjoyed when serving up a variety of bean-based dishes.

Assistance with understanding and overcoming barriers to the adoption of a plant-based diet can also be helpful in guiding consumers in healthier eating patterns. With the guidance of registered dietitians, consumers can be supported to achieve adequate nutritional intake while following a plant-based diet. Lynch, Johnston, and Wharton (2018) reviewed literature that revealed the impact of whole-food, plant-based diets on human health, environmental sustainability, and exercise performance capacity compared to meat-based diets. This review reveals exercise performance did not differ between these two dietary groups across multiple measures and types of activities (Lynch et al., 2018). These findings can then supplant the misinformation or assumption that an exercising or active body requires meat-based protein. Clearly, adequate nutrition can be achieved through a plant-based diet with no compromise to performance, while offering consumers the added benefits of health improvement, environment protection, and respect for animals and ecosystems. Guidance to encourage healthier eating should consider past routines around food, particularly meat consumption frequency, and understanding of factors influencing one's health. Meat consumption is often associated with family traditions as a favoured source of nutrients, as well as a sign of economic progress or prosperity (Pohjolainen, Vinnari, & Jokinen, 2015).

Active living

Logically, national health strategies for well-being often promote the importance of active living in addition to guidelines for healthy eating, and health professionals are encouraged to recommend that individuals and families include physical activity in their daily routines and to regularly make use of outdoor greenspaces. Research shows that having nearby access to outdoor greenspace, such as parks, forests, sports fields, and open space, is a critical factor in increasing physical health (Ward & Aspinall, 2011). Perhaps unsurprisingly, the closer a greenspace is to residents of a community, the more likely they will access it (Coombes, Jones, & Hillsdon, 2010; LeBras-seur, 2018; Nielsen & Hansen, 2007). Mansor, Harun, and Zakariya (2015) noted that active living using greenspaces provides multiple health benefits in addition to the physical, such as increased mental health and social bonding. Active living researchers, like Kohl and colleagues (2012), remind policymakers that the lack of sidewalks, pedestrian pathways, and cycling lanes are detrimental to the physical and social health of a community. Other research shines light on the tragic loss of life through poor community planning when pedestrians and cyclists are injured or killed by speeding traffic and when physical inactivity due to lack of public facilities contributes to obesity and lifestyle diseases (Pollack, 2014). The design of our communities and the availability of recreation spaces matter. Collaboration amongst researchers, policy advocates, designing companies, and government officials is essential to facilitate community designs that foster access to natural spaces and green infrastructure for greater ease and frequency of use.

Ideally, it would be common for registered dietitians to make physical activity suggestions to the clients they work with (McKenna, Henderson, & Baic, 2004). However, specific exercise recommendations call for referral to clinicians trained in exercise science. Johnson and colleagues (2007) completed a survey study amongst Canadian dietitians on their promotion of physical activity, and over half of respondents (54.9%) indicated they "some of the time" or "never" refer clients to physical activity experts, such as coaches or kinesiologists. This lack of referral suggests that a gap remains in the holistic health-care approach. Like healthy eating, regular physical activity needs to become the "standard operating procedure" for citizens to live long, disease-free lives. As people most highly trust nurses and physicians, along with pharmacists, as rated from a list of professions (Brenan, 2017), it would be prudent to ensure that these key actors, as well as registered dietitians, coaches, and kinesiologists, are equipped with this knowledge. With what we know about the power of diet and lifestyle in influencing health outcomes, it makes sense to establish policies and funding to support citizens to access health-care professionals, such as kinesiologists, therapists, and registered dietitians. As Morley and Cashell (2017) suggest funding inter-professional medical care teams leads to care of the whole person. Such diverse care would enable citizens to pursue holistic care and obtain professional guidance in physical activity, nutrition, and mindful eating, and benefit from social support as well as lifestyle counselling.

HEAL policy strategies

Citizens are also called upon to exercise their freedom and self-directedness to manage their own health. While self-directedness and self-efficacy, along with shared responsibility are important principles, citizens alone should not have to shoulder the burden of their families' health, as argued by Alvaro and colleagues (2010). Achieving desirable health outcomes requires that healthy foods be available in healthy food environments or made accessible through government policies and supports. With diverse government policies focused on public health, a number of benefits could accrue lower health-care costs, reductions in workdays missed, and increased citizen well-being, including mobility and independence. Government departments can undertake full-cost accounting to ensure externalities are not off-loaded to individuals and environmental damage or illness costs are accounted for. With full-cost accounting, governments are equipped with stronger rationale for investments in infrastructure, such as active transportation systems, financing of nutrition counselling, and implementation of policies like the Canadian Food Guide. To advance health policies such as Healthy Eating Active Living (HEAL), integrative and cross-sectoral collaboration are needed to instruct areas like community planning, social welfare, transportation practices, and park and recreation priorities (Sallis et al., 2006). The resulting reductions in the burden of disease and costs saved through preventing lifestyle and diet-related illnesses could be significant, as has been shown in cases in Belgium and UK (Schepers & Annemans, 2018). Mechanisms for data collection will enable informed public policies for community planning and land protection, zoning for healthy food outlets near schools, and living wages that make healthy diets affordable, amongst other policies. Other strategies include reorienting local policies to support healthy living and healthy food environments through incentives and infrastructure to increase local food production (Apostolidis & McLeay, 2016; Viviano, 2017), along with expanding access to greenspaces infrastructure, which encourage physical activity, mental health, and enhance community interaction (LeBrasseur, 2018; Mansor et al., 2015).

Case study in municipal early childhood education

Some stories of policies encouraging healthy living and healthy food environments briefly profiled in this chapter are from childcare facilities and medical schools. The following example highlights a collaborative, interdisciplinary project group mandated to develop HEAL guidelines and strategies for implementation in municipal childcare settings. This working group included specialists from Ottawa Public Health and Ottawa Municipal Child Care, and was supported by two project advisory groups of actively engaged cooks, early childcare educators and supervisors, public health nurses, and registered dietitians, along with observations of and input from the children themselves. Some staff educators received physical activity training and certification. Including this novel approach of coaching and certification opportunities for education staff was well received (McKay & Nigro, 2016). Further study is forthcoming on the impact of healthy eating on food costs. Other successes in early childcare centres point to the merit of such coaching for staff as they benefit the students and the families through learning and integrating various healthy living strategies (Hancock, 2016).

National campaign for fruit and vegetable consumption

The publication *5 A Day Works!* is a collection of programme descriptions and success stories of creative approaches to increasing fruit and vegetable consumption in all 50 states, two US cities, and two branches of the US Armed Forces (Centers for Disease Control and Prevention [CDCP], 2005). Case studies in the publication highlight how they accomplished these objectives through specific interventions. In Arkansas, participants were encouraged to obtain and consume more fruit and vegetables, along with other plant-based food, and, for example, were treated to healthy snacks, including "salad on a stick" prepared by staff members from the state's 5 A Day Program, and to increase activity levels, they encouraged people to walk at lunch, which was demonstrated by employees of Blue Cross Blue Shield and the Arkansas Department of Health who got out together to walk (CDCP, 2005, p. 4). In Alabama, leaders like Doris Smith and her team worked to bring together local growers, cooperative extension agents, community leaders, and local residents, along with a cadre of trained community health advisors, to establish a farmers' market. Public education campaigns were developed to encourage residents to purchase fresh, locally grown produce and to eat "their veggies" (CDCP, 2005, p. 11). This initiative provides practical ideas and shows what can be accomplished in diverse settings, often with little money.

Medical training enhancements

We also offer examples of some medical schools updating and modernizing their curricula and programmes to integrate the benefits of plant-based diets. Their innovations range from providing physicians greater education on nutrition, exercise/physical activity, behaviour change, and student self-care, including increasing stress management and resiliency. A first illustration comes from *Live Healthy Appalachia*, a non-profit that found success with their Complete Health Improvement Program with medical students. Over their noon-hour, several medical students attend sessions to learn more about plant-based nutrition and short informative presentations such as "Where Do I Get My Protein?" Students also present cooking demos, teach short segments, and lead the class in relaxation techniques. These experiences present medical students with opportunities to evaluate the efficacy of such lifestyle medicine. With the positive uptake by medical students of these learning opportunities, the administrations of some medical schools are modifying curriculum and including more lifestyle medicine as a core or optional part of their programmes (Muscato, Phillips, & Trilk, 2018).

Faculty at the University of Toledo College of Medicine saw enrolment for their lifestyle medicine elective grow from four students in 2015 to 27 students in the spring semester of 2017. In this course, students review patient case studies on eating habits, physical activity, and stress management under the supervision of primary care physicians and become practised in assessing and prescribing physical activity and resources on diet. After monitoring these new interventions over a few years, the curriculum committee at the University of Toledo's College of Medicine incorporated lifestyle medicine components across the four years of medical school training (Muscato et al., 2018). They redesigned curricula to help improve medical students' competencies and perceptions around care of persons with obesity. Part of the curriculum re-design included active forms of learning, such as students' role-playing in case studies of patients, along with personal fitness challenges. Faculty also incorporate taste tests and experiments with food from a Mediterranean diet, along with demonstrations of sugar-sweetened beverages. By teaching more culinary and lifestyle knowledge and skills, faculty are able to underscore how such guidance can translate into the lives of patients and help to improve their quality of life (Muscato et al., 2018). Additionally, through evaluating these educational and experiential enhancements to medical students' training, findings showed significant improvements to student confidence in interacting with patients with obesity and feelings of competency with prescribing weight loss programmes (Muscato et al., 2018). Findings of the study of programming changes at Virginia Tech Carilion also revealed that physicians who were deemed more credible and effective at obesity counselling were those who maintain a normal weight, eat healthy, and stay fit (Muscato et al., 2018). The Kaiser Permanente School of Medicine incorporates teaching about relationships between lifestyle risk factors and health outcomes in preventative, acute, and chronic care. And like the findings at Virginia Tech, studies of Kaiser Permanente's lifestyle medical programmes found pronounced relationships between a physician's own health habits and patient outcomes (Muscato et al., 2018). Currently, more physicians are being trained in assessment of lifestyle risk factors and intervention techniques that may include counselling and skills-building opportunities for patients in areas of nutrition, physical activity, sleep, tobacco, alcohol/drugs, stress/emotional well-being, and behaviour change (Muscato et al., 2018). While these changes in some institutes for physician education reveal promising results, they are insufficiently widespread and need to become more integrated into medical training.

Producing and promoting more plant foods

Clearly, implementing effective strategies for increasing consumption of fruits and vegetables, along with educating medical students and the public on lifestyle and dietary habits, are proving successful. Now, more investment is also needed to accelerate the production, availability, and affordability of fruits and vegetables, along with other plant-based foods. An example from the Netherlands includes how the country, with partnerships across governments, businesses, academics, and community organizations, is turning around health and environmental challenges by making a national commitment to sustainable agriculture. With their crop production strategies, Dutch farmers, researchers, and innovators have reduced their dependence on water for key crops by as much as 90%, and many have almost completely eliminated the use of chemical pesticides on plants in greenhouses (Viviano, 2017). Their motto? "Twice as much food using half as many resources" (Viviano, 2017). Through this strategy, the Netherlands is the second-largest producer and exporter in the world of largely sustainable, plant-based foods. As Ernst van den Ende indicated, in the next four decades, more food will have to be produced than in the past 8,000 years to feed 10 billion people, while using less water and fossil fuels (as cited by Viviano, 2017). In many countries, we can also find numerous innovative enterprises; some innovations include significant expansion of greenhouse developments and creative use of composts from greenhouse wastes that offer high nutrient values in comparison to other growing medium, which generated slightly greater yields (Cheuk, Lo, & Fraser, 2003). A multi-generational family business purports to provide sustainable nourishment for healthier lifestyles (Pure Flavor, 2018). Rooftop farms on industrial buildings require little-to-no warehousing, and they use smart analytics and offer a short delivery chain that provides loyal customers with scheduled supplies of plant foods (Elton, 2010). Producing and making available affordable, high-quality produce with a lower ecological footprint and higher health benefits are responsibilities that need to be taken up by visionaries in all sectors. Next, we look at future research directions and our recommendations.

Further research

As plant-based diets are proving to offer the highest protective effects (Bauer et al., 2014; Hu, 2003) and are being promoted by more governments (Cespedes & Hu, 2015; Health Canada, 2019; NHS, 2016), further inquiry may identify expeditious pathways to implementation and research on the cost/benefit analysis of plant-based approaches. Those promoting the science behind and benefits arising from plant-based diets may wish to inquire further into whether multi-sector actors are working in parallel, in partnership, or in opposition. As well, research into whether the threats to health and lifestyle are widely understood and credible in the minds of the public and scientific community (Nathanson, 1999) needs attention, along with approaches that help re-orient mind-sets around food systems and facilitate more plant-based production and consumption. Chiolero (2018) also calls for further research into the efficacy of prevention around obesity through diet and physical activity. Lastly, continued critical review is needed of how policies, including those outside of health disciplines, such as agriculture and trade, prevent or, alternatively, promote obesogenic environments and unsustainable food systems.

Recommendations and conclusion

There are many avenues through which to support mental, physical, and environmental health. To achieve greater individual and collective well-being, we have argued for supports that HEAL through nutrition and physical activity. Prevention approaches are needed to integrate complex, multilevel, environmental, socio-economic, and life course approaches (Dietz as cited by Chiolero, 2018). As collaboration amongst multidisciplinary/cross-disciplinary health-care professionals is proving beneficial to behaviour change in patients, we highly recommend integral thinking and approaches to improve individual and population health arising from plant-based living. We encourage practitioners to become familiar with resources and community groups that support plant-based diets. Links to such organizations should be made available to individuals and communities moving towards more plant-based living, as having even a single vegetarian family member, friend, or support person can make a significant difference in shifting thinking and habits around plant-based living.

Given the preponderance of the omnivore diet, health professionals should also be prepared to discuss meat consumption. While different barriers are present for diverse meat-eating, socio-demographic groups, the focus should not only be on the group with the strongest barriers but also on those willing to consider the science around meat consumption and who want to make changes in their meat consumption patterns. We also suggest strategizing ways to increase the availability of vegetarian foods wherever feasible, such as in public cafeterias or school canteens, and to encourage consumers to decrease their meat consumption frequency. This availability of succulent, non-meat food choices is strongly correlated with the ability to change perceptions about the enjoyment and satiability from such alternative dishes (Pohjolainen et al., 2015).

We encourage policymakers, particularly those in agriculture, health, economics, social welfare, and environmental policy, to consider strategies for achieving desired outcomes through greater policy coherence. Indifference to, or ignorance of, the implications of various government policies on the types of foods produced and consumed and on food environments would not be sound.

> Policy makers should ensure policy coherence and coordination in the long-term by devising and implementing long-term approaches to achieve the food-related Sustainable Development Goals and implement the Paris Agreement by integrating the social, environmental, health and cultural impacts while enabling conducive environments to favor society action and response.
>
> (Sustainable Development Solutions Network, 2018, n.p.)

We join with many others cited in this chapter in noting that greater commitments are needed from all sectors to achieve healthy dietary and activity patterns, and to replace obesogenic food environments. Greater attention must be paid to environmental influences on individual well-being and public health through preventative government policy and practice, including setting standards for the food industry to provide nutritious low-cost food and place restrictions on the number of fast-food stores (Alvaro et al., 2010). Additionally, we consider it imperative, given the many benefits to be accrued, that policy measures be deployed to increase the quantity, quality, and accessibility to natural spaces, such as parks, public green infrastructure, and active transportation networks. The obesity epidemic and disparities in built environments urge us to more effectively translate this evidence into urgent action and policy. This combination of actions would thereby improve health equity and afford greater opportunities for healthy eating and active living for all.

References

Ackerman-Leist, P. (2013). *Rebuilding the foodshed: How to create local, sustainable, and secure food systems.* White River Junction, VT: Chelsea Green Publishing.

Alvaro, C., Jackson, L. A., Kirk, S., McHugh, T. L., Hughes, J., Chircop, A., & Lyons, R. F. (2010). Moving Canadian governmental policies beyond a focus on individual lifestyle: Some insights from complexity and critical theories. *Health Promotion International, 26*(1), 91–99.

Apostolidis, C., & McLeay, F. (2016). Should we stop meeting like this? Reducing meat consumption through substitution. *Food Policy, 65,* 74–89.

Bacon, S. L., Campbell, N. R., Raine, K. D., Tsuyuki, R. T., Khan, N. A., Arango, M., & Kaczorowski, J. (2019). Canada's new Healthy Eating Strategy: Implications for health care professionals and a call to action. *Canadian Pharmacists Journal/ Revue des Pharmaciens du Canada, 152*(3), 151–157.

Bauer, U. E., Briss, P. A., Goodman, R. A., & Bowman, B. A. (2014). Prevention of chronic disease in the 21st century: Elimination of the leading preventable causes of premature death and disability in the USA. *The Lancet, 384*(9937), 45–52.

Bickerdike, L., Booth, A., Wilson, P. M., Farley, K., & Wright, K. (2017). Social prescribing: Less rhetoric and more reality. A systematic review of the evidence. *BMJ Open Diabetes Research & Care, 7*(4), e013384. doi:10.1136/ bmjopen-2016-013384

Brenan, M. (2017). Nurses keep healthy lead as most honest, ethical profession. *Gallup.* Retrieved from https://news.gallup.com/

Campbell, T. C., & Campbell, T. M. (2006). *The China study: The most comprehensive study of nutrition ever conducted and the startling implications for diet, weight loss and long-term health.* Dallas, TX: BenBella Books Inc.

Campbell, T. C., & Jacobson, H. (2013). *Whole: Rethinking the science of nutrition.* Dallas, TX: BenBella Books.

Centers for Disease Control and Prevention (CDCP). (2005). *5 A Day Works!* Atlanta, GA: U.S. Department of Health and Human Services. Retrieved from www.cdc.gov/nccdphp/dnpa/nutrition/health_professionals/programs/5aday_works.pdf

Cespedes, E. M., & Hu, F. B. (2015). Dietary patterns: From nutritional epidemiologic analysis to national guidelines. *The American Journal of Clinical Nutrition, 101*(5), 899–900. https://doi.org/10.3945/ajcn.115.110213

Cheuk, W., Lo, K. V., & Fraser, B. (2003). Use of composted greenhouse waste as a growing medium component will contribute to a sustainable waste management solution for vegetable greenhouses. *Biological Agriculture & Horticulture, 21*(4), 321–335.

Chiolero, A. (2018). Why causality, and not prediction, should guide obesity prevention policy. *The Lancet Public Health, 3*(10), e461–e462.

Coombes, E., Jones, A. P., & Hillsdon, M. (2010). The relationship of physical activity and overweight to objectively measured green space accessibility and use. *Social Science & Medicine, 70*(6), 816–822.

Cunningham, R. (1996). *Smoke & mirrors: The Canadian tobacco war*. Ottawa, Canada: International Development Research Centre.

Desrochers, N., & Brauer, P. M. (2001). Legume promotion in counselling: An e-mail survey of dietitians. *Canadian Journal of Dietetic Practice and Research, 62*(4), 193–198. Retrieved from https://uwinnipeg.idm.oclc.org/login?url=https://search-proquest-com.uwinnipeg.idm.oclc.org/docview/220779298?accountid=15067

Elton, S. (2010). *Locavore: From farmers' fields to rooftop gardens. How Canadians are changing the way we eat*. Toronto, Canada: HarperCollins.

Fischer, C. G., & Garnett, T. (2016). *Plates, pyramids, and planets – Developments in national healthy and sustainable dietary guidelines: A state of play assessment*. Rome, Italy: Food and Agriculture Organization of the United Nations.

Global Pulse Confederation (GPC). (n.d). *Market access & stability*. Retrieved from https://iyp2016.org/themes/market-access-stability

Greger, M. (2016). *About NutritionFacts.org*. Retrieved from http://nutritionfacts.org/about

Hancock, T. (2016). Innovations in policy and practice: A work in progress/innovations dans les politiques et la pratique: Un travail en chantier. *Canadian Journal of Public Health, 107*(3), 220. Retrieved from http://ezproxy.library.dal.ca/login?url=https://search.proquest.com/docview/1837329059?accountid=10406

Health Canada. (2019). *Canada's dietary guidelines for health professionals and policy makers*. Retrieved from https://food-guide.canada.ca/static/assets/pdf/CDG-EN-2018.pdf

Henchion, M., Hayes, M., Mullen, A., Fenelon, M., & Tiwari, B. (2017). Future protein supply and demand: Strategies and factors influencing a sustainable equilibrium. *Foods, 6*(7), 53.

Hu, F. B. (2003). Plant-based foods and prevention of cardiovascular disease: An overview. *The American Journal of Clinical Nutrition, 78*(3), 544S–551S.

Johnson, S. T., Bates, H., Fitzpatrick, J., Marshall, J. D., Bell, R. C., & McCargar, L. (2007). Promotion of physical activity by Canadian Registered Dietitians in daily practice. *Journal of Human Nutrition and Dietetics, 20*, 37–40. doi:10.1111/j.1365-277X.2007.00744.x

Kohl, H. W., III, Craig, C. L., Lambert, E. V., Inoue, S., Alkandari, J. R., Leetongin, G., . . . Lancet Physical Activity Series Working Group. (2012). The pandemic of physical inactivity: Global action for public health. *The Lancet, 380*(9838), 294–305.

Lang, T. (2009). Reshaping the food system for ecological public health. *Journal of Hunger & Environmental Nutrition, 4*(3–4), 315–335.

Laxer, R. E., & Janssen, I. (2014). The proportion of excessive fast-food consumption attributable to the neighbourhood food environment among youth living within 1 km of their school. *Applied Physiology, Nutrition & Metabolism, 39*(4), 480–486. Retrieved from http://search.ebscohost.com.uwinnipeg.idm.oclc.org/login.aspx?direct=true&db=s3h&AN=95108092

LeBrasseur, R. (2018). *Transitional landscapes: Examining landscape fragmentation within peri urban green spaces and its impacts upon human wellbeing* (Unpublished doctoral dissertation). The University of Edinburgh, Edinburgh, UK. Retrieved from www.era.lib.ed.ac.uk/handle/1842/31257

Lynch, H., Johnston, C., & Wharton, C. (2018). Plant-based diets: Considerations for environmental impact, protein quality, and exercise performance. *Nutrients, 10*(12), 1841. doi:10.3390/nu10121841

Mansor, M., Harun, N. Z., & Zakariya, K. (2015). Residents' self-perceived health and its relationships with urban neighborhood green infrastructure. *Procedia Environmental Sciences, 28*, 433–442.

Mason, P., & Lang, T. (2017). *Sustainable diets: How ecological nutrition can transform consumption and the food system.* Taylor & Francis.

McGill, H. C., Jr., McMahan, C.A., & Gidding S. S. (2008). Preventing heart disease in the 21st century: Implications of the Pathobiological Determinants of Atherosclerosis in Youth (PDAY) study. *Circulation, 117*(9), 1216–1227.

McKinnon, J. (2008). Exploring the nexus between social work and the environment. *Australian Social Work, 61*(3), 256–268. doi:10.1080/03124070802178275

McKay, K., & Nigro, S. (2016). Policy at play: The implementation of healthy eating and active living guidelines in municipal child care settings. *Canadian Journal of Public Health, 107*(6), e556–e561. http://dx.doi.org/10.17269/CJPH.107.5561

McKenna, J., Henderson, L., & Baic, S. (2004). A survey to assess physical activity promotion by Registered Dietitians. *Journal of Human Nutrition and Dietetics, 17*, 63–69. doi:10.1046/j.1365-277X.2003.00495.x

Morland, K. B., & Evenson, K. R. (2009). Obesity prevalence and the local food environment. *Health & Place, 15*(2), 491–495.

Morley, L., & Cashell, A. (2017). Collaboration in health care. *Journal of Medical Imaging and Radiation Sciences, 48*(2), 207–216.

Muscato, D., Phillips, M., & Trilk, J. L. (2018). Lifestyle Medicine Education Collaborative (LMEd): "Champions of change" medical school leaders workshop. *American Journal of Lifestyle Medicine, 12*(5), 382–387.

Nathanson, C. A. (1999). Social movements as catalysts for policy change: The case of smoking and guns. *Journal of Health Politics, Policy and Law, 24*(3), 421–488.

NHS. (2016). *Eight tips for healthy eating.* Retrieved from www.nhs.uk/live-well/eat-well/eight-tips-for-healthy-eating/

Nielsen, T. S., & Hansen, K. B. (2007). Do green areas affect health? Results from a Danish survey on the use of green areas and health indicators. *Health & Place, 13*(4), 839–850.

Nugent, R., & Knaul, F. (2006). Fiscal policies for health promotion and disease prevention. In D. T. Jamison, J. G. Breman, A. R. Measham, G. Alleyne, M. Claeson, D. B. Evans . . . P. Jha (Eds.), *Disease control priorities in developing countries* (2nd ed., Chap. 11). Washington, DC: The International Bank for Reconstruction and Development/The World Bank; New York, NY: Oxford University Press. Retrieved from www.ncbi.nlm.nih.gov/books/NBK11714/

Pohjolainen, P., Vinnari, M., & Jokinen, P. (2015). Consumers' perceived barriers to following a plant-based diet. *British Food Journal, 117*(3), 1150–1167. https://doi.org/10.1108/BFJ-09-2013-0252

Pollack, K. (2014). The active living research 2014 conference: "Niche to norm". *Preventive Medicine, 69*, S1–S4.

Pure Flavor. (2018, March). *Live deliciously.* Retrieved from www.pure-flavor.com/about/

Raphael, D. (2008). Getting serious about the social determinants of health: New directions for public health workers. *Promotion & Education, 15*(3), 15–20.

Sallis, J. F., Cervero, R. B., Ascher, W., Henderson, K. A., Kraft, M. K., & Kerr, J. (2006). An ecological approach to creating active living communities. *Annual Review of Public Health, 27*, 297–322.

Schepers, J., & Annemans, L. (2018). The potential health and economic effects of plant-based food patterns in Belgium and the United Kingdom. *Nutrition, 48*, 24–32.

The Secretariat for the Intersectoral Healthy Living Network. (2005). *The integrated pan-Canadian healthy living strategy.* Ottawa, Canada: Minister of Health.

Story, M., Hamm, M. W., & Wallinga, D. (2009). Food systems and public health: Linkages to achieve healthier diets and healthier communities. *Journal of Hunger & Environmental Nutrition, 4*(3–4), 219–224.

Subratty, A. H., Heesambee, Y. B., Jowaheer, V., & Doreemiah, N. (2002). Nutritional knowledge of a heart-healthy diet among health care professionals and cardiac patients in Mauritius. *Nutrition & Food Science, 32*(5), 184–189. https://doi.org/10.1108/00346650210445749

Sustainable Development Solutions Network. (2018). *SDSN Networks.* Retrieved from https://networks.unsdsn.org/

Swinburn, B. A., Sacks, G., Hall, K. D., McPherson, K., Finegood, D. T., Moodie, M. L., . . . Gortmaker, S. L. (2011). The global obesity pandemic: Shaped by global drivers and local environments. *The Lancet, 378*(9793), 804–814.

Twells, L. K., Gregory, D. M., Reddigan, J., & Midodzi, W. K. (2014). Current and predicted prevalence of obesity in Canada: A trend analysis. *Canadian Medical Association Journal – CMAJ Open, 2*(1), E18.

Viviano, F. (2017, September 7). This small country feeds the world. *National Geographic.* Retrieved April 4, 2018, from www.nationalgeographic.com

Walsh, B. (2009, August 21). Getting real about the high price of cheap food. *Time Magazine.*

Ward, T. C., & Aspinall, P. A. (2011). Natural environments and their impact on activity, health, and quality of life. *Applied Psychology: Health and Well-Being, 3*(3), 230–260. https://doi.org/10.1111/j.1758-0854.2011.01053.x

World Health Organization. (2019). *Health promotion.* Retrieved from www.who.int/topics/health_promotion/en/

Yasin, J., & Helms, M. M. (2010). A comparison of health-related expenditures: A multi-country comparison. *Academy of Health Care Management Journal, 6*(2), 1–19.

Part III

Respecting animals and our shared well-being

8 Shifting perceptions through farm sanctuaries

Gene Baur and Kathleen May Kevany

Introduction

This chapter illuminates efforts to increase awareness and provide remedies to the deleterious impacts of industrial agriculture and the exploitation and slaughtering of animals. It describes the animal liberation movement, with an array of values, visions, and goals. In this chapter, we offer analyses of the animal rights movement with a more in-depth view of the world's first farm sanctuary, told in part by its leader, Gene Baur. We shed light on the process of social change used by Farm Sanctuary and its allies to examine how humans have institutionalized farm animals and animal products as food, and the consequences of such philosophies and practices. This work touches on ethical, economic, and spiritual perspectives of food production and consumption. The chapter ends with ideas for reforming modern food systems, which provide clear benefits to humans, the planet, and, particularly, to animals.

Method and analytical approach

Literature review

This chapter offers a review of the literature and considers some counter-narratives of animal rights and animal agriculture. This research includes an investigation into academic literature, online content, and lay materials that characterize the farm sanctuary model of animal welfare and animal liberation. As well, first-hand data from field research are made available through the co-author of the chapter, Gene Baur, who also is the founder of this animal rights movement. This chapter is also informed by attendance and participant observation at a number of animal rights and vegan conferences by the second author, Kathleen Kevany, a social-scientist examining plant-based food movements. The study duration unfolded from February 2015 to November 2018. The scope of this inquiry involves the historical context that ignited the launch of Farm Sanctuary, the issues that drove its formation, and the strategies that developed over time with significant successes and challenges identified. The following research questions framed this study: What are the implications of animal agriculture on the animals themselves? Why operate a farm sanctuary, and with what impact for humans and animals? What insights might we extract from this case study?

Case study and narrative storytelling

We selected the case study model as a bounded, integrated system for field research (Stake, 2000). The case study selected for this analysis was the first farm sanctuary established in the USA. This in-depth investigation becomes a form of storytelling. As Broad notes, narrative storytelling is central to the construction of individual and group identity, and the sharing of this narrative expands worldviews for self and others (Ellis & Bochner, 2000). The case may "tell its own story" (Carter, 1993 as cited by Stake, 2000, p. 441). In addition to the reader gleaning her/his own meaning, we offer an interpretative study of the data arising from the case. Data sources include first voice perspectives from the leader of the first sanctuary for rescued farm animals and participant observation of this leader in action. In addition, data are gathered around the context for, and history of, the animal rights movement. As such, our analysis includes critical reflection on this case study, interspersed with first-hand, narrative perspectives. Further corroboration is sought from the field of animal rights scholarship. Interactions between this research team also form part of the content wherein the researchers become "the researched". Findings in the literature and through the case study analyses are used to form the conclusions and recommendations.

Scientific foundations

Confinement and crowding

Far from the idyllic farms and spacious pastures that are used in advertisements to sell meat, milk, and eggs, most animals exploited for food are kept in factory farm warehouses where they are crowded by the thousands and denied basic humane consideration. Millions of animals are confined in cages and crates so tightly that they cannot walk, turn around, or extend their limbs. Large-scale operations, which have been designed to maximize agribusiness profits, dominate agriculture in North America, and are growing in numbers in other countries as well (Bai et al., 2018; MacDonald, 2009). While seeking profit may be a justifiable business goal, this narrow focus has come at the expense of animal welfare and human and environmental health. Each year, tens of billions of animals, in this industrial design of factory farms, are exploited as commodities; they face harsh living conditions that cause sickness and death to millions before reaching the slaughterhouse (Baur, 2008). On-site investigations have documented numerous systemic affronts to animal welfare in agriculture (Harris, 2017), including the extreme overcrowding and confinement; painful mutilations, such as debeaking, tail docking, and castration without pain killers; and genetic engineering, with little regard to animal suffering (Nibert, 2013; Rollin & Duncan, 2012).

Farm animals used for meat production have been genetically altered to grow faster and larger than their natural course to help these businesses accelerate their return on investments. Commercial chickens now grow four times faster than their predecessors, reaching slaughter weight at six weeks old. Their hearts and lungs strain to support this rapid growth rate, and their legs and joints struggle to support their abnormally large bodies (Rollin & Duncan, 2012). Turkeys have been genetically modified for fast growth and more breast meat, which is the most profitable cut, but this means that they cannot reproduce naturally. This inability requires the industry to now rely on artificial insemination as its sole means of reproduction. Just as animals exploited for meat are shaped for fast growth and profitable body parts, hens exploited for eggs and cows used for milk have been altered to produce ten times as many eggs and ten times more milk than they would in nature (Nibert, 2013). They are pushed to their biological limits, and their bodies wear out, which contributes to deformities, disease, and, for many, early death.

More animal production means more feed needed to feed them. Thus, more land is cleared of trees and other life forms to grow corn, soy, and other crops to feed confined and concentrated animals. Deforestation and the destruction of vast swaths of land and ecosystems then become integral elements of this burgeoning industrial-agricultural complex (Weis, 2015).

Antibiotic use

Animals confined to concentrated animal feeding operations (CAFOs) experience stressful, unsanitary living conditions, and agribusiness has come to rely on inordinate quantities of antibiotics and other drugs. The rapid growth of industrial agriculture and aquaculture industries around the world involve widespread, intensive, and insufficiently regulated use of antimicrobial agents (Heuer et al., 2009). Antibiotic use in agriculture and aquaculture is contributing to antibiotic resistance, and although identified decades ago as a public health crisis, inadequate attention has been paid to the causes and consequences (Landers, Cohen, Wittum, & Larson, 2012). If widespread antibiotic use is unmanaged, involving irresponsible applications, drug-resistant bacteria threatens to put human health at risk. Occurrence of resistance to antimicrobial agents in human pathogens may interfere with remedies for human infections (Heuer et al., 2009)

Excrement and waste management

With the high numbers of animals in confinement for production, industrial animal agriculture is producing extensive quantities of excrement and other waste. These wastes have to go somewhere. Lagoons and holding ponds are designed to capture or store these wastes, but these systems are connected to other systems, including the flow of water and the concentration and movement of animals. The high level of bacteria in these lagoons and pools is problematic for the spread of disease. Concentrated "waste can contain pathogens, heavy metals, and antibiotic-resistant bacteria, and the spray can reach nearby homes and drinking water sources. The odor plume, which often pervades nearby communities, contains respiratory and eye irritants including hydrogen sulfide and ammonia" (Nicole, 2013, p. 183). Posting signs in such farming regions with names like "Town of Perfect Water" does not make them impervious to, or inoculate them from, contamination in the event of an eruption of a waste lagoon that occurs too frequently (Mallin, 2000). These high volumes of manure and urine are contributing to significant pollution of air, water, and land. They disproportionately threaten the health and well-being of farm workers and residents in rural communities surrounding factory farms. Such industrial farms are located in rural areas where often people facing greater disadvantages live, and this has been described as a form of environmental racism (Nicole, 2013):

> Environmental racism both in North America and elsewhere, is the practice of viewing minority communities as a means to the majorities' ends, and of burdening the disempowered with what no one else is prepared to accept, or to further the economic success of some at the expense of the weak, the poor and the disempowered.
>
> (Westra, 1996, p. 63)

This array of unconscionable treatment of the environment, animals, and humans leads to substantial externalities – economic, social, and environmental costs – placed on society rather than as the responsibility of industrial animal agriculture. For decades, concerns have been raised about food industry research funding with industrial agriculture (Joy, 2011; Weis, 2015) and agricultural and nutrition programmes (Campbell & Jacobson, 2013). Productionistic and reductionistic food systems have been found to disconnect consumers from their citizenship and from each other (Levkoe, 2011; Scrinis, 2007), from their food and the healthy environments needed for foods to be produced.

Degrees of plant based

For Wrenn (2018a), advocating for a gradual transition away from consuming meat does not sufficiently reduce harm to animals or provide the associated environmental and health benefits. From her meta-study of vegan motivations, Wrenn indicated that most vegans go vegan out of altruistic concern for other animals, not health or environmental concerns (2018a). She posits that encouraging less meat consumption, or so-called *flexitarian* approaches, are not proving effective and that "the research indicates that flexitarians, in general, do not substantially cut back on their consumption of animal products. Some even consume *more* [italic in original] animal products than someone who does not identify as a flexitarian" (2018b, n.p.). Other research reveals that while vegans represent a very small segment of the population, their numbers are increasing. According to 2017 findings by GlobalData, US consumers identifying as vegan grew from 1% to 6% between 2014 and 2017, a 600% increase (Forgrieve, 2018). We see multiple drivers for changing to more plant-based foods and cutting down on meat consumption. HealthFocus International predicts greater growth in Americans eating a plant-based diet, as more than 60% surveyed indicated that they were cutting back on meat-based products (as cited by Gelski, 2017). Eating fewer or no animal products and more plants-based foods appears to be driven by a variety of concerns: ethical food production, environmental well-being, healthier lifestyles, weight management, muscle building, and increased energy (Gelski, 2017).

Animal rights campaigns

The campaigns promoting veganism or plant-rich living recommend members adopt the practices of consuming only foods that are plant-based and wearing or purchasing goods that involve little-to-no harm to animals or ecosystems. Early campaigners in the 1940s who were engaged in the personal practice of consuming no animal products sought to develop this into a society. They distinguished themselves from vegetarians, as persons not wanting to consume meat, but also excluded eggs and dairy. While veganism was promoted into the 1950s, it was challenging to generate resonance, as this was also the time of the launch of the fast-food movement and its corresponding media campaigns (Calvert, 2014 as cited in Mehl, 2017). Many social movements situated in the 1960s and 1970s often were associated with protest and rebellion. For many, veganism became associated with animal rights, extreme diets, and protest actions (Beverland, 2014; Greenebaum, 2012) designed to unsettle non-vegan lifestyles. The majority of the population continued to disregard vegan messaging and calls for reformation. In the 1990s and 2000s, more evidence was emerging about widespread industrial food systems, animal confinement, destruction to the environment, and adverse impacts on human health. For those choosing a vegan identity or a whole-foods plant-based diet, various factors may be involved. Many of the early vegans were motivated by ethical reasons and still avoid meat in solidarity with animal rights (Baur, 2008; Singer, 1975). Currently at 2019 and into 2020, veganism and plant based are becoming much more common place; more are demanding products without animal products or testing on or harm to animals. Plant based is not a fad but is becoming more and more mainstream (Infantino as cited by Stephenson, 2019).

The emergence of farm sanctuary

The harm being done to animals, humans, and the environment through industrial animal agriculture was not being addressed and was being ignored by many. So I, Gene Baur, and Lorri Houston were prompted to take action by our concerns about how factory farming institutionalizes animal commodification. We founded Farm Sanctuary in 1986, well before the advent of the Internet and the availability of social media. As the co-founder of a movement seeking animal liberation, I became known as an activist, advocate, champion, and author. To others, I may have been known as a menace or as an intruder on their freedoms to operate their businesses largely unimpeded or unexamined. I have dedicated my entire adult life to reducing the harm of animal agriculture and promoting vegan living through co-founding the farm animal protection organization Farm Sanctuary (FS). I was described by *Time* magazine as the "conscience of the food movement" (Walsh, 2011) and am a member of Oprah Winfrey's SuperSoul 100 dream team made up of "100 awakened leaders who are using their voices and talent to elevate humanity" (Oprah, n.d.). These references become data points in our inquiry as they illuminate how this crusade was launched when few were standing up to the unquestioned, ubiquitous adoption of the industrial animal agriculture model.

Our sanctuary, and the protection of animals, was a labour of love. As young social entrepreneurs testing this new concept, we assumed all of the financial and professional risk to develop this enterprise. We were part of an all-volunteer team that conducted risky undercover investigations, rescued animals, and were vigilant researchers documenting the treatment of animals on farms and in stockyards and slaughterhouses. At the time when we launched our initiative, the awareness of factory farming abuses was very low, as was general receptivity to our efforts. Over the decades, I led countless undercover investigations and animal rescues; these were critical to save animals from horrendous conditions. We also launched public education and advocacy work to help reform our food system. I actively sought to understand the motivations and pressures of the animal agriculture business by reading agribusiness journals and by obtaining a graduate degree in agricultural economics at Cornell University. To further extend the reach of our organization, I have also written two books (Baur, 2008; Baur & Stone, 2015) and undertaken international speaking tours. Sadly, the mission of FS continues, as animal exploitation and slaughter for human consumption have not been eliminated. More public awareness is needed to help orchestrate changes to regulations, laws, and business practices around the exploitation of animals. More recently, I have been involved in multidisciplinary research efforts that examine vegan lifestyles and plants-based diets free of all animal products (Kevany, Baur, & Wang, 2018, 2019).

By treating cows, pigs, chickens, and other farm animals as friends instead of a source of food, Farm Sanctuary is working to redefine our relationships with these animals while challenging the inconsistencies and contradictions between how we treat different species of animals. Our organization's first bumper sticker asked, *If you love animals called pets, why do you eat animals called dinner?* Farm sanctuaries, and the interactions with, and learning from, farm animals that they afford, serve to bridge the gap most people have in understanding and empathizing with farm animals. As these animals have been removed from most people's everyday lives, this disconnection gives rise to a profound lack of knowledge of and engagement with farm animals, except as food products. Rich Roll (2015) calls this "willful blindness" when it comes to many facets of how our world functions. Yet, morally, farm animals are similar to animals who share our homes. Cows, pigs, chickens, and other farm animals have the same range of personalities and interests as do cats and dogs. In the introduction to Hatkoff's (2009) *The Inner World of Farm Animals*, Dr. Jane Goodall says, "[F]arm animals feel pleasure and sadness, excitement and resentment, depression, fear, and pain. They are far more aware and intelligent than we ever imagined . . . they are individuals in their own right" (pp. 12–13).

Analyzing farm sanctuaries' roles in preventing harm and liberating animals

Exposing factory farms

Volunteers and staff at Farm Sanctuary have worked for decades to expose factory farming abuses and prevent animal suffering. Through his early pioneering efforts challenging the myths of the necessity of meat eating, Baur and his team helped to raise awareness about the harm to human, animal, and ecosystem health of meat production and consumption, and the benefits of plant-based eating (Cherian, 2016). Baur continues to operate working farm sanctuaries, guided by vegan ethics and by modelling non-exploitative relationships, where all are treated with respect and particularly farm animals are regarded as friends, not food (Baur, 2008). FS outreach is driven by a desire to increase people's understanding of the destructiveness of factory farming, the uniqueness of each farm animal, and the opportunities to sponsor animals through financially supporting the organization. Baur indicates that there are many unrealized opportunities to help animals through systemic reforms that could reshape our food industry.

Seeking animal protection

FS has been part of larger movements calling for humane laws and tougher animal protection standards (Walsh, 2011), while advocating for policies and incentives to bolster plant-based food production and consumption. Along with other food industry reformers, like Nelson Campbell (2015) or Will Tuttle (2005), Baur has confronted substantial obstacles in state capitals and in Washington, DC. As noted in the previous chapter, agribusiness operates within a neoliberal climate where governmental subsidy and regulatory regimes support industrial food systems to operate less encumbered (Levkoe, 2011; Weis, 2015). Over the decades, FS, along with its allies, has advocated for many changes, which could involve mandating changes to infrastructure and conditions on farms.

Changing consumer beliefs and behaviours

Other strategies advocated by FS and its allies include channelling citizen influence and economic power through the marketplace by shifting income and profits from the meat, dairy, and egg industries into plant-based businesses. By contributing to this chapter, Gene Baur aligns with his mandate to defend animal rights and encourage citizen-consumers to critically examine the impact of individual and collective food choices. In his second book, Baur emphasizes mindful choices around what is considered necessary and legitimate food. He seeks to help people align their ways of life driven by critical awareness, sustainable practices, joyful and mindful consumption, and humane values (Baur, 2015). This alignment involves reformulating cultural beliefs around food, as well as strategies to protect the environment that supports life.

FS has a long history of working to shift beliefs and practices in the marketplace. In the 1990s, they convinced a Burger King franchise in Watkins Glen, New York, to add a veggie burger to the menu. After testing it in upstate New York, the BK Veggie was distributed in Burger King restaurants across the country, enabling a plant-based burger to become an easy option for more consumers. The organization also engages in extensive public education in schools and through FS events, farm tours, and opportunities to develop personal connections with rescued farm animals. These and other FS programmes involve extensive media outreach and promotion, like Baur's (2015) appearance on *The Daily Show with Jon Stewart*, VegSource (2017), and *Now This News* (2018). FS is also able to leverage the support of many celebrities who advocate plant-based diets and kindness to animals. With celebrity support, FS can reach wider audiences and encourage them to rethink their view of animals as food (Cherian, 2016).

Respecting sentience of animals

Concerns about the harm being done to non-human animals, including those exploited for food, are increasingly being corroborated through scientific studies. Greater understanding of the sentience and sensitivity to the rights of animals have helped to bring about the termination of chimpanzee experimentation in the US and led to a declaration of rights for cetaceans (i.e. whales, dolphins, and porpoises) at the annual American Association for the Advancement of Science (Cherian, 2016). Baur suggests that more scientific inquiry into the sentience of farm animals will bring about more informed recommendations and may advance the protection of animals exploited in agriculture (Baur, 2008; Baur & Stone, 2015; Hatkoff, 2009). Scientific studies help us understand the cognitive and emotional capacities of other animals, as well as their uniqueness and individuality, which help people to see animals as worthy of respect (Cherian, 2016; Hatkoff, 2009) – as someone, not something.

Choosing not to eat animals is a fundamental way of acknowledging that they are living, feeling creatures who have interests that deserve to be respected (Be Fair Be Vegan, 2016). For Baur and other advocates, abstaining from animal products is the best option for the animals, as well as for humans and the environment. In promoting vegan eating, Baur asks people to consider, "If we can live well without causing unnecessary harm, why wouldn't we?" Central to his activism is the tenet of meeting people where they are on their own personal journeys and having patience with consumers who may transition to vegan lifestyles more gradually (Plant Based News, 2016).

Disparate views on animal rights

The complexity and diversity of food movements and, particularly, the animal rights movements, are notable. There are citizens arguing for their right to eat meat and those against the raising and slaughtering of animals for food. We see also anti-whistle-blower or "ag-gag" laws, while others call for more food labelling and the right to know where the food comes from. Amongst animal advocates, some argue for animal welfare, which may include notions like "humane meat" or "killing them kindly". Others seek to achieve full liberation as abolitionists, calling for the end of all forms of oppression or commodification of living beings (Tuttle, 2005). Those who are African American animal rights activists also may experience living within what Aph Ko calls "a white supremacist patriarchy" (Ko, 2016). Ko suggests that the experiences of racial oppression are deeply entangled with animal oppression as a fundamental component of domination of white privilege, culture, and beliefs. People of colour continue to struggle for fair consideration and inclusion, and disproportionately face injustices, including environmental racism. As noted earlier, environmental racism is the frequent pattern of establishing large factory farms away from predominantly white communities but nearer to people of colour, who then suffer the greatest adverse impacts from the air, water, and land pollution caused by the concentrated feed lots. Ko and FS advocate for the termination of all forms of oppression and speciesism that view humans as a superior and entitled species, driving the justification for animal exploitation (Ko, 2016).

Disparate views on farm sanctuaries

Sanctuaries, shelters, and humane societies have been established to prevent cruelty and provide safe places to care for animals removed from harm's way. Shelters may provide refuge for companion animals, rescued farmed animals, and wild animals. According to Animal Charity Evaluators (ACE) (2018), these types of interventions are relatively costly because of the small number of animals each organization can reach, especially in reference to larger farm animals. There is a developing discourse and critique of the efficacy of various animal protection efforts, but more empirical research is needed. Sanctuaries can only help a limited number of individuals and, "expending too many resources on direct rescue results in less money directed toward education and a lower overall impact in helping animals, and all advocates should give consideration to this concern when deciding how best to help animals" (Bockman, 2015). Impact limitations may stem from sanctuaries' remote locations and the inability to reach a large audience in person, and they can be costly to operate (Bockman, 2015).

However, when measuring the impact of sanctuary work, caution may need to be applied to anthropocentric measures of cost-effectiveness and mere numbers, as the gross figure of total animals in captivity for food continues to grow, and, consequently, the percentage that sanctuaries are able to rescue will continue to decline. Farmed animal rescues and sanctuaries can only care for an infinitesimal fraction of the animals exploited for food, so their biggest impact is from outreach efforts and programmes that educate and influence people about the lives of farmed animals and the benefits of veganism. Farm sanctuaries model relationships with farm animals as friends, not food, and challenge the cultural normative belief that cows, pigs, chickens, and other animals are sources of food rather than "subjects-of-a-life" (Regan, 1983). Consideration is needed regarding the value of saving each rescued animal, as well as the stories of people who become transformed in their beliefs and behaviours after engaging with individual animals, moving beyond their speciesism and examining the indoctrination within the food system and their roles in adding to unnecessary environmental destruction and violence to animals.

Recommendations to enhance efficacy of animal sanctuaries

Sebo (2016) advises that animal advocates pursue programmes in the emerging field of animal studies and include a wide variety of perspectives and areas of study. If learners become exposed to the many implications of the agri-industrial complex, apply a systems critique, and engage in full-cost accounting of the environmental, economic, social, political, spiritual, ethical, and health outcomes, learners may "gradually construct a holistic, comprehensive understanding of all of the forces that are shaping conditions that animals are in as well as all of the forces that are shaping the conditions in which we advocate for animals" (Sebo, 2016). He adds that advocates can systematically study the root causes of oppression and ways to liberate human and non-human animals, so they can engage in advocacy with a better understanding of the challenges they will face across disciplines. Another benefit arising from animal studies is that learners may appreciate, as noted in Chapter 9, the continuities and the discontinuities in liberation movements and how they may build solidarity across different, but connected, social movements.

ACE (2018) has practical advice for farm sanctuaries. They highlight the work of Farm Sanctuary by saying campaigns like their "someone, not something" effort (Farm Sanctuary, 2017) help personalize farmed animals and afford deeper understanding of where animal-based foods come from. Visits to animal sanctuaries enable citizens to meet and learn about rescued animals in friendly settings. Sharing animals' stories in person or through pictures and video, and observing and, when appropriate, interacting with rescued animals as they express themselves freely, enables people to better understand and appreciate the complexity and uniqueness of each animal. Animal rescue provides immediate relief for individuals but is not an economical way to help a significant number of animals, unless the rescued animals' stories can be leveraged to inspire people not to exploit and consume animals for food. Another way to extend the reach of sanctuaries is by adopting animals into good homes, freeing up sanctuary space, and allowing people to interact with animals in a greater number of locations.

Fundamentally, animal rights advocates and the farm sanctuary movement oppose speciesism, which has been defined as "prejudice or discrimination based on species especially discrimination against animals" (*Merriam-Webster*, 2019). Ryder (1970/2010), Singer (1975), Regan (1983), and Joy (2011) challenge the self-centred and narcissistic tendencies that value humans as separate from and above other life forms. These arguments suggest that treating members of one species as morally superior and more important than members of other species, even when their interests are similar, is faulty and, ultimately, destructive thinking. The term speciesism became officially embedded in the English language, and incorporated into the *Oxford Dictionary*, in 1985. Legal efforts continue to be pursued in animal law to move beyond animals being viewed as property. Despite the relative level of welfare or quality of life, animals' rights are denied when they are exploited, harmed, and, ultimately, killed (Be Fair Be Vegan, 2016). Terms developed by agribusiness marketers to increase sales of animal products, like free-range, cage-free, organic, grass-fed, local, or humanely raised, almost always sound better than they are, and even if animals were treated better, exploiting them in any way still undermines the goal of animal liberation. A focus on the fundamental issue of the right of sentient beings not to be exploited remains paramount (Wrenn, 2018a). Francione, a professor of law states,

> If we really believe animals have moral value, if we really believe that animals are not just things, we must fundamentally change our behavior and seriously look at the matter of animal use and not just the matter of animal treatment.
>
> (As cited by Livingston, 2013, n.p.)

In an effort to help the greatest number of animals, sanctuaries seek to inspire people to become vegans while also challenging neoliberal interests that influence government policy and investments (Wrenn, 2018a, 2018b). ACE and Wrenn propose that the animal rights movement formulate research grounded in the scientific method in order for farm sanctuaries to assess the optimal methods to achieve the greatest animal liberation. Financial and political support for sanctuaries should be channelled towards educational and advocacy impacts beyond individuals and families, to institutions with systemic influence. Such efforts could set in motion multiplier effects for greater advances.

Future research

While students of veterinary sciences are taught about routine factory farming procedures, such as castration, dehorning, branding, teeth clipping, tail docking, and beak trimming, they are also beginning to learn more about pain management, animal welfare, animal behaviour, and the human-animal bond (Hewson et al., 2005). Research on the sentience of non-human animals is evolving. While the research focus has revolved around negative aspects – pain, stress, distress, and suffering – animals also experience positive aspects of sentience, such as rewards and pleasures, as reflected through play, food, sex, and touch:

> Not just science but also ethics suffer [from] this, for when we see animals as only the products of a competitive struggle for survival, we risk overlooking the positive qualities of their lives. Pleasure has moral import for such practices as factory farming and laboratory research, for it amplifies the moral burden of depriving animals the opportunity to lead fulfilling, enjoyable lives.
>
> (Balcombe, 2009, p. 208)

As billions of animals remain viewed as and produced for food, and many others are used in experiments and for clothing, strategies for effectively transforming these systems and changing "hearts and minds" and behaviours are required. Further investigation is needed into new, or reclaimed, business models, as proposed in the chapter on integrity economics, that include compassionate values and that calculate broader societal interests and better align food system practices for desirable outcomes. Also, more attention is required around collaboration amongst researchers, social change leaders, governments, legal advocates, and academic institutions. Though many may be working on similar goals, they may remain separated according to fields of study or simply lack of coordination and interconnectivity.

Conclusion

Because humans are social animals who are influenced by observing the behaviours of others, farm sanctuaries play a role in reshaping how humans perceive and relate to farm animals. The farm sanctuary movement grew out of the desire to help end the suffering of farm animals and to ultimately help humans transform our relationships with animals. The movement now encompasses hundreds of shelters around the globe where animals rescued from slaughter are given lifelong care. Farm sanctuaries also provide space and opportunities for visitors to meet and connect with individual farm animals and model examples of people interacting with farm animals as friends, not food. The animals' stories and people's experiences with them can be shared and communicated directly, person to person or through media and online channels that reach wider audiences. Still, animal care and shelter operations require significant resources and can be further leveraged by using land and facilities to model vegan living, such as through plant-based agriculture. Sanctuaries started by rescuing animals from an abusive system and now play a larger role that goes beyond presenting new kinds of relationships with farm animals, to providing examples, support, and tools for compassionate vegan living. The sanctuaries can also begin to tap institutional resources, including agricultural subsidies and government and academic infrastructures that have traditionally benefitted animal agriculture, to support and better enable a plant-based food system. And as Baur writes in *Living the Farm Sanctuary Life*, more concerted efforts are needed to help us live and eat in alignment with our values, in mindful connection to animals, mindfully with our food, and, particularly, by eating plants for human and planetary health (2015). Our lives depend on our shared willingness to face truths we have been blind to. In addition to changing hearts and minds about animals and food, farm sanctuaries could align their efforts with other movements working to transform and shift food systems. The stakes are significantly higher now with agricultural, ecological, and climate crises fuelled predominantly by animal foods. We must not fail to advocate for the rights of animals, for in doing so, we also protect the well-being of humans and our life-supporting ecosystems.

References

Animal Charity Evaluators. (2018). *Causes we consider*. Retrieved from https://animalcharityevaluators.org/advocacy-interventions/prioritizing-causes/causes-we-consider/#fn1-11-4754

Alvaro, C., Jackson, L. A., Kirk, S., McHugh, T. L., Hughes, J., Chircop, A., . . . Lyons, R. F. (2010). Moving Canadian governmental policies beyond a focus on individual lifestyle: Some insights from complexity and critical theories. *Health Promotion International*, 26(1), 91–99.

Bai, Z., Ma, W., Ma, L., Velthof, G. L., Wei, Z., Havlík, P., . . . Zhang, F. (2018). China's livestock transition: Driving forces, impacts, and consequences. *Science Advances*, 4(7), eaar8534.

Balcombe, J. (2009). Animal pleasure and its moral significance. *Applied Animal Behaviour Science*, 118(3–4), 208–216.

Baur, G. (2008). *Farm Sanctuary: Changing hearts and minds about animals and food*. New York, NY: Simon & Schuster.

Baur, G., & Stone, G. (2015). *Living the Farm Sanctuary life: The ultimate guide to eating mindfully, living longer, and feeling better every day*. New York, NY: Rodale Press.

Be Fair Be Vegan. (2016). *Being vegan is easy*. Retrieved from www.befairbevegan. com/faq.html

Beverland, M. B. (2014). Sustainable eating: Mainstreaming plant-based diets in developed economies. *Journal of Macromarketing, 34*(3), 369–382. doi:10.117 7/0276146714526410.

Bockman, J. (2015). *The value of sanctuaries and how to maximize their impact*. Retrieved from https://animalcharityevaluators.org/blog/the-value-of-sanctuaries-and-how-to-maximize-their-impact/

Campbell, N. (2015). *PlantPure nation* [Documentary film]. Mebane, NC: Plant-Pure, Inc. Retrieved March 8, 2019, from www.plantpurenation.com

Campbell, T. C., & Jacobson, H. (2013). *Whole: Rethinking the science of nutrition*. Dallas, TX: BenBella Books.

Cherian, Z. (2016). Q&A with animal rights activist and author Gene Baur. *The Dartmouth*. Retrieved from www.thedartmouth.com/article/2017/02/qa-with-animal-rights-activist-and-author-gene-baur

Ellis, C., & Bochner, A. P. (2000). Autoethnography, personal narrative, reflexivity: Researcher as subject. In N. K. Denzin & Y. S. Lincoln (Eds), *Handbook of qualitative research* (2nd ed.) (pp. 733–768). Thousand Oaks, CA: Sage Publication.

Farm Sanctuary. (2017). *The someone project: Farm animal behavior, emotion, and intelligence*. Retrieved from www.farmsanctuary.org/learn/the-someone-project/

Forgrieve, J. (2018, November 2). The growing acceptance of veganism. *Forbes*. Retrieved from www.forbes.com/

Gelski, J. (2017, February 27). Three targets for plant protein. *Food Business News*. Retrieved from www.foodbusinessnews.net/

Greenebaum, J. (2012). Veganism, identity and the quest for authenticity. *Food, Culture & Society, 15*(1), 129–144.

Harris, T. (2017). "The problem is not the people, it's the system": The Canadian animal- industrial complex'. In D. Nibert (Ed.), *Animal oppression and capitalism: The oppression of nonhuman animals as sources of food* (pp. 57–75). Santa Barbara, CA: Praeger.

Hatkoff, A. (2009). *Inner world of farm animals*. New York, NY: Stewart, Tabori & Chang.

Heuer, O. E., Kruse, H., Grave, K., Collignon, P., Karunasagar, I., & Angulo, F. J. (2009). Human health consequences of use of antimicrobial agents in aquaculture. *Clinical Infectious Diseases, 49*(8), 1248–1253.

Hewson, C. J., Baranyiová, E., Broom, D. M., Cockram, M. S., Galindo, F., Hanlon, A. J., . . . Ödberg, F. O. (2005). Approaches to teaching animal welfare at 13 veterinary schools worldwide. *Journal of Veterinary Medical Education, 32*(4), 422–437.

Joy, M. (2011). *Why we love dogs, eat pigs, and wear cows: An introduction to carnism*. San Francisco, CA: Conari Press.

Kevany, K. M., Baur, G., & Wang, G. C. (2018). Shifting food systems: Increasing well-being through plant-based approaches. *Explore: Journal of Science and Healing, 14*(6), 435–442. https://doi.org/10.1016/j.explore.2018.04.012

Kevany, K. M., Baur, G., & Wang, G. C. (2019). Transitioning to sustainable food choices: A course design. In W. Leal Filho & A. Consorte McCrea (Eds.),

Sustainability and the humanities (pp. 173–187). Cham, Switzerland: Springer International. https://doi.org/10.1007/978-3-319-95336-6_10

Ko, Aph. (2016). *African American vegan starter guide*, p. 19. Retrieved from www.farmsanctuary.org/wp-content/uploads/2016/10/AA_VeganStarterGuide_Web Version.pdf

Landers, T. F., Cohen, B., Wittum, T. E., & Larson, E. L. (2012). A review of antibiotic use in food animals: Perspective, policy, and potential. *Public Health Reports*, *127*(1), 4–22.

Levkoe, C. (2011). Towards a transformative food politics. *Local Environment*, *16*(7), 687–705. doi:10.1080/13549839.2011.592182

Livingston, M. (2013, October 24). *Animals as food: Symposium explores ethics and regulations*. Retrieved from http://wdat.is.depaul.edu/newsroom/year_2013/2690.html

MacDonald, M. (2009). *China encounters factory farming*. China Dialogue – China and the World Discuss the Environment. Retrieved from www.chinadialogue.net/article/show/single/en/3155-China-encounters-factory-farming

Mallin, M. A. (2000). Impacts of industrial animal production on rivers and estuaries. *American Scientist*, *88*(1), 26.

Mehl, S. C. (2017). *Hailing seitan silently: Negotiating vegan identities in a non-vegan world* (Unpublished doctoral dissertation). Northern Arizona University, Flagstaff, AZ. (Thesis Archive).

Merriam-Webster. (2019). *Speciesism*. Retrieved from www.merriam-webster.com/dictionary/speciesism

Nibert, D. A. (2013). *Animal oppression and human violence: Domesecration, capitalism, and global conflict*. New York, NY: Columbia University Press.

Nicole, W. (2013). CAFOs and environmental justice: The case of North Carolina. *Environmental Health Perspectives*, *121*(6), A182–A189. https://doi.org/10.1289/ehp.121-a182

Now This News. (2018, November 26). *Farm Sanctuary president Gene Baur on going vegan*. Retrieved from https://nowthisnews.com/videos/food/farm-sanctuary-president-gene-baur-on-going-vegan

Oprah. (n.d.). *Super soul: Everybody has a soul story*. Retrieved from www.super-soul.tv/category/supersoul-100/the-complete-list

Plant Based News. (2016). *Interview with vegan activist, Gene Baur*. Retrieved from https://www.plantbasednews.org/post/interview-with-vegan-activist-gene-baur

Regan, T. (1983). *The case for animal rights*. Berkeley, CA: University of California Press.

Roll, R. (2015, April 5). *How to live more in alignment with your values with Gene Baur*. Retrieved from www.richroll.com/podcast/genebaur/

Rollin, B. E., & Duncan, I. J. H. (2012). Farm animal welfare in Canada: Major problems and prospects. In World Society for the Protection of Animals (WSPA), *What's on your plate? The hidden costs of industrial animal agriculture in Canada* (pp. 135–160). Toronto, Canada: WSPA.

Ryder, R. D. (1970/2010). Speciesism again: The original leaflet. *Critical Society Journal*, *2*. Retrieved from www.criticalsocietyjournal.org.uk/Archives_files/1. Speciesism Again.pdf

Scrinis, G. (2007). From techno-corporate food to alternative agri-food movements. *Local-Global: Identity, Security, Community*, *4*, 112–140.

Sebo, J. (2016). *"Advocacy through education" panel at the 2016 Symposium for Multidisciplinary Research in Effective Animal Advocacy* [Video file]. Retrieved from www.youtube.com/watch?v=ICKxhc5VOr8&feature=youtu. be&list=PL_zoUwnwRlDeCwJrYt2Pv06U8ziVH6SpR

Singer, P. (1975). *Animal liberation: A new ethics for our treatment of animals*. New York, NY: HarperCollins.

Stake, R. (2000). Qualitative case studies. In N. K. Denzin & Y. S. Lincoln (Eds.), *The Sage handbook of qualitative research* (2nd ed., pp. 443–466). Thousand Oaks, CA: Sage Publications.

Stephenson, A. (2019). As more Canadians cut out meat, a plant-based movement takes root in Cowtown. *Calgary Herald*. Retrieved from https:// calgaryherald.com/business/local-business/business-opportunities-abound-as-plant-based-movement-takes-off

Tuttle, W. M. (2005). *The world peace diet: Eating for spiritual health and social harmony*. New York, NY: Lantern Books.

VegSource. (2017, January 11). *Food animals are someone not something – Gene Baur* [Video file]. Retrieved from www.youtube.com/watch?v=ybsx7uyNJbI

Walsh, B. (2011, March 30). The morality of mealtime. *Time Magazine*, pp. 23–25.

Weis, T. (2015). Meatification and the madness of the doubling narrative. *Canadian Food Studies/La Revue canadienne des études sur l'alimentation, 2*(2), 296–303.

Westra, L. (1996). Environmental integrity, racism and health. *Science of the Total Environment, 184*(1–2), 57–66.

Wrenn, C. L. (2018a). *Are vegans too open to free-riders?* Retrieved November 30, 2018, from www.coreyleewrenn.com/tag/interviews/

Wrenn, C. L. (2018b). *Can flexitarianism facilitate a vegan world? Research suggests another agenda*. Retrieved November 30, 2018, from www.coreyleewrenn.com/ flexitarianism/

9 The vegan challenge is a democracy issue

Citizenship and the living world

Terry Gibbs and Tracey Harris

Introduction

We begin with the assumption that commonly accepted notions of citizenship that are rooted in concepts of bounded nation states and communities (with clear geographical, cultural, or religious parameters) are not tenable in a globalized, interdependent world. Climate change, ecological degradation, and the finite nature of fossil fuels on which our lifestyles rest, bring urgency to the question of re-evaluating the boundaries of citizenship. The ongoing exploitation of nature, humans, and non-human animals on which the current economic system of capitalism depends is not only ethically problematic but also may ultimately undermine the future of life on this planet. The increasingly polarized distribution of wealth within and between nations, the destruction of nature, and the wide-scale, pervasive exploitation of humans, other animals, and nature at a global level requires an ethical re-evaluation of the current system. We argue that these interlinking forms of exploitation are intimately connected to the structural violence at the root of a capitalist system that encompasses virtually every nation on the planet. And, given that the profit-driven logic at the heart of all forms of capitalism inevitably results in widespread inequality and exploitation (Leech, 2012; Picketty, 2014), any long-term solution would require not only shifting individual beliefs and behaviours but also require fundamental structural change.

Belief systems and organizational arrangements of citizenship and accountability are intimately linked. We argue here that under the current economic system, they have become delinked to the degree that suffering on one end of the system (e.g. where communities are displaced or face human rights violations due to "development" projects, where biodiversity is devastated, or where animals face systematic abuse in the process of becoming "food") is not acknowledged or compensated by the other end of the system (e.g. those who benefit economically through profits and/or through access to particular resources/goods, such as cheap oil, genetically modified foods, consumer products, animal "meat"). In this vein, and drawing on Johan Galtung's concept of structural violence, Garry Leech (2012) notes,

> If a social system creates and maintains inequality in both power and wealth that benefits certain social groups while preventing others from

meeting their fundamental needs, even if unintentionally, then structural violence exists. And if such inequality is inherent in a social system, then so is structural violence.

(p. 12)

Gibbs has elsewhere referred to the externalities of our structurally violent economic system as "bodies in the basement" (Gibbs, 2017). Sometimes the externalities literally involve deaths of people, non-human animals, and nature; other times, they imply human/animal rights violations, increasing inequalities, and disease. In this chapter, we will explore how and why this delinking occurs and why an interconnected concept of citizenship taking a structural approach to compassion could provide the key to creating forms of democracy more suitable to the 21st century. In other words, how could we think about building compassion into broader political and economic institutions and practices?

There are two claims commonly used to justify the existing concepts of democracy and citizenship. First, due to the high level of rights and living standards in the global North, some argue that, while flawed, our democratic system is generally working, and second, global or universal visions of citizenship cannot work because human communities are bounded by cultural, ethnic, and national identities. Citizenship concepts under capitalism have focused on individuals as holders of rights within the bounded territory of the nation-state. The Judeo-Christian legal order, within which the rights structure is framed, has reinforced and generally protected this view. Democratic citizenship theory has, in turn, emphasized the active agent who participates in processes calling for transparency and accountability, while placing less attention on broader economic systems, which in various ways hinders true accountability.

It soon becomes clear, however, that even with these commonly held notions, our current democracies fall far short in delivering accountability and equality, and we argue that the approach to citizenship tied to the nation-state is at the centre of this problem. So, while we may look at the contradictions of capitalism – which sit comfortably with Western liberal democracy – and simply despair, it is important not to throw the baby of citizenship out with the bathwater of our hollowed-out democracies. And by "hollowed out", we are not denying the fact that many citizens in the global North do enjoy privileged living standards and a high degree of rights. Rather, we are emphasizing that these privileges are enjoyed in large part due to the ongoing economic exploitation of humans, other animals, and nature at a global level.

It is interesting to note how those arguing for the inclusion of non-human animals and nature into citizenship debates have to jump through extensive interpersonal, political, and theoretical hoops to justify their efforts (Donaldson & Kymlicka, 2011; Joy, 2017). Meanwhile, those advocating for the extensive rights of economic actors, particularly corporations, to intervene in political processes and to benefit from the resources of communities and countries where they are not even citizens, are simply seen as part of the "common sense" of contemporary capitalism.

While we may be troubled enough about the exploitation that takes place within our national boundaries, how did we get to the point where economic actors – often with little or no transparency or accountability – can penetrate the most intimate and life-giving aspects (such as water and seeds) of communities where they do not have citizenship? It is this lack of transparency and accountability, reinforced by particular belief systems and institutional arrangements, that allow for the routine exploitation of non-human animals and nature because certain actors are given rights to exploit other animals and nature, and there are no effective systems in place to stop them. So even without going as far as to call for an end to capitalism (as the authors that follow convincingly do), we may simply protest on the basis of a belief in a genuine democracy – one that extends beyond political account-ability through representation to address the economic context in which political accountability takes place. In other words, democracy, to be truly meaningful, must extend to the economic sphere. Democratic systems doing this would by necessity address many, if not most, of the issues identified in this chapter and point to a vision of citizenship that would extend beyond national boundaries. With this vision of citizenship in mind, we are able to make visible the interconnected nature of various forms of exploitation in the contemporary era.

On the other side of the question of exploitation of non-human animals and nature, and directly related to the notion of accountability, is the con-cept of agency. While it is generally accepted that people should have rights and agency as citizens, we have yet to properly situate other animals and nature under our existing democratic traditions. But before discussing what this broader vision may entail, we first examine how the various exploita-tions are linked and why this is important. How, for example, does the exploitation of other animals produced as "food" lead to other forms of exploitation?

Interconnected exploitations

When it comes to non-human animals in food-producing industries, we continue to tell ourselves stories about them and their lives that have no real connection to their lived realities. We socialize our children to believe these stories as well. We pretend that animals used for food live in pretty red barns and roam rolling green hills (Harris, 2017). We pretend that dairy cows want to share their milk with us and not their babies (Canavan, 2017). We pretend that animals enlist and sacrifice themselves to us as food (Medoro, 2014), for research (Arluke, 1994), and for products, and that this is necessary and unavoidable. Through such ubiquitous storytelling, the connections between intensive agriculture and the exploitation of the land, human populations, and animals are distorted, falsely presented, and sometimes lost (Nibert, 2013).

On the other hand, with recent reports and articles from the UN's Inter-governmental Panel on Climate Change (IPCC), the US government and the academic community, the link between environment and animals is gaining increased attention (see, for example, IPCC, 2018; Goodland & Anhang, 2009). The focus for many may not be on the need to include non-human animals in the moral community per se. The definitive link between our dietary habits – particularly the other animals constructed as "food" – and climate change is now entering the mainstream and becoming part of a new, expanded narrative beyond the incomplete and false stories mentioned earlier (see, for example, the documentary *Cowspiracy*, 2014).

The intersections of oppression between human and non-human animals points to the connectedness between the treatments of marginalized "others", whether those others are human or other animals (Nibert, 2002). The exploitation of non-human animals is intrinsically linked to the destruction of our planet, the destruction of human cultures, and the expropriation of land and water, and addressing this reality is part and parcel of working towards a truly compassionate democracy (Gibbs, 2017; Nibert, 2002). How can we truly conceive of a more equitable world and move forward for environmental change without having concern for others, whether humans or other animals?

Many involved in democracy movements, environmental movements, and rights movements are accustomed to being the "good guys". But the animal question is very personal. It relates not only to larger power structures that are often perceived as residing outside of us and outside of our power of control, but is also intimately connected to how we live our daily lives: who and what we eat, who and what we wear, who we choose to love and call family (Joy, 2010). The consideration of non-human animals raises complicated and difficult questions. For people accustomed to being on the side of good, it can be a very difficult place to be asked to reside. It calls for personal change, and what is often perceived as personal sacrifice, in ways that may not be asked of us in other rights movements – and this can be unsettling. When we consider this oppression and work towards its elimination, we must change the way we live our everyday lives. But in fairness, it is unsettling because it asks us to consider relations of power in very personal ways, and it demands that we make deliberate decisions about our personal lives and day-to-day choices (Foer, 2009). Veganism, for example, could be a choice that allows us to respond by making individual choices in our own daily diet *and* working to have the institutions that we work in or with to make animal-friendly procurement decisions. Essentially, we need to work towards the creation of understandings and coalitions, which will require reaching out to those initially negative or ambivalent to animal protection and rights (Joy, 2017).

Our constructions of other animals as food is intimately connected to the suffering of billions of non-human animals each year worldwide and the deaths of approximately 700 million animals annually in Canada alone. But with the recognition of animal oppression comes the implications and disruptions that these changes may cause to our daily routines and lives. The social and cultural shifts and rifts that this may create cannot be underestimated. Our relationship with non-human animals is deeply embedded in our cultural lives and our societies (Smith-Harris, 2004), as well as our capitalist systems. What we consider food, for example, is personal, but more importantly, it is tied to culture and society in important ways that must be understood and recognized if we are to push for real change at both the individual and structural levels in realistic and sustainable ways.

What people socially construct as food has important ties to gender, class, family, religion, cultural traditions, community, and many other realms of social and cultural life (Greenebaum, 2017). Food is linked to societal norms about what is expected of us, and it is essential that this be recognized if lasting changes are to happen in human relationships with non-human animals constructed as food. Because food is intrinsically tied to important cultural symbols, significant life celebrations, norms related to masculinity and femininity, and familial expectations, such "cultural items take on tremendous meaning within a culture or subculture of a society" (Steckley & Letts, 2013, p. 72). This understanding can be significant in explaining the resistance to change involving our daily routines. Unfortunately, such resistance may facilitate the continued utilization of other animals and lead to their continued exploitation.

Recognizing the significance of these cultural and subcultural norms and symbols is important if we want to ensure other animals become firmly rooted in global debates about democracy and citizenship. We need to understand these power relations from the real places that people reside. If we fail to acknowledge the significance of non-human animals in people's lives (even as food or products), the inclusion of this important area of oppression in citizenship movements is bound to fail. It is not realistic to simply tell people that they should stop utilizing non-human animals and the products made from their bodies given the reasons for doing so are deeply embedded in culture and societal expectations. We need to bring the animal question to the forefront and demonstrate clearly its connections to other forms of oppression (Nibert, 2017). This discussion also needs to happen compassionately (Greenebaum, 2017; Joy, 2017). It is important to begin the discussion by acknowledging that others may not necessarily care about or recognize the significance of animal oppression. By clearly linking it to other forms of oppression that individuals or groups may find meaningful, we may begin to move forward the concern for animal equality.

According to David Nibert (2013), "Structural violence refers to physical and psychological harm experienced by humans and other animals that result from societal economic and political policies and practices" (p. 276). This concept brings to the forefront issues that are often hidden and made to seem accidental, such as "world" hunger and diseases of affluence, such as heart disease, when in actuality they are intrinsically linked to issues of power and exploitation. Other important social thinkers also demonstrate the connections between various forms of inequality. bell hooks (2013), for example, recognizes "interlocking systems of domination" and argues that "to name interlocking systems of domination is one way to disrupt our wrong-minded reliance on dualistic thinking" (p. 4). She claims that "[f]or me it's like a house, they share the same foundation, but the foundation is the ideological beliefs around which the notions of domination are constructed" (p. 79). And Carol Adams (1994) adds that we need to be cognizant of the intersections of oppression and how each of us may at times experience oppression, such as those based on gender or ethnicity, while at the same time maintaining or benefitting from another form of oppression that subjugates others, especially non-human animals as food or products. However, it is important to recognize that the exploitation of human groups or non-human animals does not occur in isolation.

The subjugation of marginalized humans and "meat" animals, demonstrates that capitalism has simply intensified, not created this inequality. Nibert argues that the "oppression of humans causes much of the mistreatment of other animals, and the awful treatment of other animals fuels human exploitation" (2002, p. 5). He highlights that one of the most significant "entanglements of oppression" occurs in the treatment of other animals as "*food* for humans" (p. 5). Demonstrating that the domestication of other animals allows for the exploitation of marginalized human groups throughout history and into current times, such as the expropriation of Native American lands and violent exploitation of their peoples in order to secure pastures for "cows and sheep" (2002, p. 44). His work examines the oppression of other animals, but also provides links to the marginalization of and violence against human groups as well. He demonstrates that unequal power relations are deeply rooted in the capitalist system of production and that ideologies of control ensure the maintenance of this unequal system for both humans and other animals. He offers an alternate and remarkable analysis of history that brings to the forefront connections that have not been made before, such as how the oppression of animals for food has helped facilitate, and in some cases outright caused, the oppression of many human groups. Nibert uses the example of the displacement of indigenous populations to allow for the expansion of cattle ranching as evidence of this point. Because of capitalist expansion of expropriated land for cattle ranching "hundreds of millions of humans around the world do not have access to land to produce plant-based food for themselves or their communities" (Nibert, 2013, p. 224). The oppression of animals and humans are intrinsically linked in these examples, and this clearly points to the "entanglements of oppression" (Nibert, 2002).

Given what we have just learned, how do we move forward and ensure that other animals are at the forefront of discussions on global citizenship? Singer and Mason (2006) argue that under industrial capitalism, "we don't usually think of what we eat as a matter of ethics" but we should (p. 3). Many humans fail to consider food choices as a politicized choice because they do not know how their food is produced. Simply put, transparency is the principle that "[w]e have a right to know how our food is produced" (p. 270). This knowledge would be a powerful transformation, as many food industries are not forthcoming about the treatment of other animals, workers, or the environment. It can also be difficult to gain information regarding genetically modified (GM) ingredients or growth hormones. Transparency would make knowledge about products easily accessible for those who want to make an informed decision about what they buy or consume or to agitate for real social and political change.

There are numerous ways to respond to structural violence. Our responses can be expressed individually with "small c compassion" – being kind to others, giving to local charities, helping our neighbours, putting solar panels on our houses, buying fair trade coffee, eating a plant-based diet, and so on. But in order to fully confront the violence of the current system and create new ways of doing things that contribute to new societal values, a systemic process is also needed, one that builds compassion into our institutions and into our political and economic processes. In other words, one that promotes "big C compassion" (Gibbs, 2017). Individually, we have the opportunity to challenge cruelty at every meal. But that individual challenge would certainly become easier, more affordable, and more widespread and culturally relevant if structural challenges, such as a more humane and local food procurement and economic system, helped reshape the meaning of citizenship with regard to "food" animals.

The meaning of citizenship

The challenge, therefore, is not to integrate ethics into the already existing paradigm, but to actually turn the current paradigm on its head. As noted earlier, the first step in this process is to make visible the interconnected nature of various forms of oppression. This is the first stage of transparency and social action where we confront entrenched beliefs and values. This acknowledgement allows us to see that "solutions" must reach for an inclusivity that cuts across race, class, gender, species, and nature frameworks, and that transcends the traditional boundaries of the state.

A number of scholars have highlighted the challenges inherent in liberal democratic approaches to citizenship when applied to 21st-century problems, particularly noting the roots in modernist concepts of national identity. These approaches fail to account for the reality of transborder cultures and communities, and the multicultural nature of many countries around the world. A further challenge is that liberal democracy has historically been associated with capitalism and thus is rooted in the de facto division of political and economic spheres, meaning that democracy exists to varying degrees in the political sphere but is generally very limited in the economic sphere (e.g. state regulation, welfare state policies).

Under neoliberal globalization, there has been a concerted push to further decrease the areas of economic activity under democratic control. A well-documented consequence of this plays out daily in the global South and increasingly in the global North. Unaccountable international institutions (i.e. the International Monetary Fund, the World Bank, and the World Trade Organization) endow multinational corporations with economic rights that allow them to operate in countries around the world while simultaneously disempowering labour and decision making at the community level. For example, many indigenous communities throughout the global North and South are forced to endure the externalities (i.e. destruction of culture and nature) that result from the operations of multinational corporations in the extractive industries, even though such actions are often in conflict with community values and belief systems that are intimately linked to nature. Meanwhile, corporate shareholders and consumers in the global North largely enjoy the benefits of such ecologically and culturally destructive activities.

Gibbs, Leech, and other scholars have utilized the concept of structural violence to analyze such activities. For example, Leech (2012) goes so far as to argue that capitalism – because of the sheer numbers of people who needlessly die annually under this system – constitutes "structural genocide". Given the systemic nature of the problem, it is clear that establishing meaningful citizenship requires taking a structural approach.

So what may the ethical principles be that could frame an interconnected and, therefore ethical, view of citizenship? A key issue related to interconnected citizenship is that of agency. While there is recognition that humans should have rights and agency as citizens, neither non-human animals nor nature are viewed as deserving rights or agency under our existing democratic traditions. We tend to associate citizenship and democratic control with the deliberative capacities of autonomous human individuals. However, Donaldson and Kymlicka (2011) note that we have sought to provide fundamental citizenship rights to people with severe mental disabilities and to children despite their inability to independently exercise their agency (p. 59). Therefore, a broader discourse around citizenship could provide similar rights to animals and nature, even though they also cannot independently exercise their rights. They (2011) argue for the recognition of the rights of "liminal animal denizens", laying out a complex approach that seeks to recognize the different categories of animals and suggesting that their relationship to the broader polity will vary.

While Donaldson and Kymlicka (2011) stress the importance of animal subjectivity to counteract theoretical attempts to lump non-human animals in with the category of nature, they also point to interwoven exploitations. This reality allows for a discourse that, while acknowledging the uniqueness of particular species, recognizes the interdependence that is fundamental to all living things. Along those lines, they note,

> In fact, one could argue that our addiction to animal exploitation is harming us, even killing us. Meat-centered diets are less healthy than vegetarian diets; moreover, the agricultural processes needed to produce that meat rival transportation as a leading cause of global warming. Human colonization of wild animal territory is destroying the lungs of the planet, the vitality of our soils, the stability of weather systems, and the supply of fresh water. The simple fact is that the human species cannot survive on this planet if we do not become less dependent on the exploitation of animals, and destruction of their habitat.
>
> (p. 253)

With a starting point of interdependence and transparency, chains of accountability begin to become evident. The true costs of particular activities become visible. How quickly might the system change, for example, if we had a way of restricting the negative externalities of the extractive industries or large-scale monoculture farming to those communities and individuals that are directly benefitting from the wealth generated? In mining, industrial agriculture and factory farming, capitalism has ensured that the benefits are privatized, and the harms are socialized, and this is a problem for citizenship theory and practice. As Donaldson and Kymicka (2011) note,

> Any plausible conception of citizenship must acknowledge the value of agency, but it must also acknowledge that capacities for agency expand and contract over time, and vary across persons, and that a central task of a theory of citizenship is to support and enable what is often a partial theory of citizenship.
>
> (p. 60)

We would add to this that a theory of agency, and thus of citizenship, that does not recognize power relationships within and between countries under globalization will fall short.

Towards a concept of interconnected citizenship

It is beyond the scope of this chapter to give an exhaustive account of the numerous examples of individuals and communities across the globe engaging in and/or theorizing about social justice movements and projects that speak to alternative views of citizenship. Rather, what we will do here is identify a few key examples of perspectives that could make a significant contribution to building a new theory of interconnected citizenship. We will highlight Vandana Shiva's concept of "earth democracy" and then touch on the potential contributions of eco-socialism to this debate. Finally, we will explore how contemporary social movements in Latin America may shed light on interconnected citizenship with particular focus on the legal entrenchment of nature's rights in Ecuador and Bolivia.

The notion of an interconnected citizenship is countercultural in the North to the degree that it requires a worldview that is in opposition to the logic and parameters of Western industrial capitalist societies. Interconnected citizenship contradicts the individualistic-, linear-, progress-, and growth-oriented ideology that drives the capitalist economy. But a number of perspectives have emerged in both the global North and the global South in recent years that point in this direction. Interesting links can be drawn between eco-socialist traditions in the North, for example, and indigenous movements in the South. In all of these examples, a focus is placed on the concept of the "commons". The exploitation of humans, other animals, and nature has occurred through the systematic enclosure and exploitation of once commonly held lands. Large-scale production for profit requires the systematic displacement of peoples from their lands and the commodification of non-human animals and resources goes hand in hand with this process. Historically, this was often referred to as part of the civilization process without which modern progress could not occur (Harvey, 2003).

Under neoliberal globalization, the process continues as communities struggle to form counter-narratives and movements. From the eco-socialist angle, and echoing indigenous philosophy, author Joel Kovel (2007) argues that the idea of property is central to the problem of exploitation:

> Taken all in all, the earth we inhabit should be regarded, not as our collective property but as a wondrous matrix from which we emerge and to which we return . . . Indeed, ownership of the planet is a pathetic illusion. It is plain hubris to think that the earth, or nature, can be owned – and stupid to boot, as though one can own that which gives us being, and whose becoming we express.
>
> (p. 271)

Kovel (2007) and others call for a new socialism that involves the emancipation of both humans and nature based on a usufructuary (property held in common and protected) relationship to nature under a participatory democracy and the social ownership of the means of production (p. 268; Leech, 2012). Similarly, David Nibert (2002) argues for a socialist system characterized by democratic decision making where "a reversal of environmental destruction and the reduction of oppression of humans and other animals could be realized" (p. 247).

Essentially, all three authors emphasize the importance of "recapturing the commons from capital" (Leech, 2012, p. 114). Vandana Shiva's (2005) concept of "earth democracy" similarly focuses on the reclaiming of the commons as crucial to ending corporate globalization and the "cultures of exclusion, dispossession, and scarcity" that it creates. She argues that the reduction of all beings and resources into commodities "robs diverse species and people of their rightful share of ecological, cultural and economic, and political space" (p. 2).

Shiva (2005) goes on to devise simple yet profound principles for earth democracy based on living economies and living cultures. For our purposes here, her second principle, "the earth community is a democracy of all life", is particularly relevant. As Shiva notes,

> We are all members of the earth family, interconnected through the planet's fragile web of life. We all have a duty to live in a manner that protects the earth's ecological processes, and the rights and welfare of all species and all people. No humans have the right to encroach on the ecological space of other species and other people, or to treat them with cruelty and violence.
>
> (p. 9)

Shiva (2005) pays particular attention to the primacy of food self-reliance, which, she argues, is at the root of community resilience. The Navdanya movement, which works across 17 states in India with a focus on seed and food sovereignty, is an example of the principles of protecting and strengthening indigenous knowledge and culture in action. With regard to non-human animals, it is a movement that, while not eliminating the use of other animals for food, calls for an end to systemic cruelty and factory farming. Navdanya describes itself as a "network of seed keepers and organic producers", and Shiva herself, as a leader in the movement, has emphasized the significance of the seed as the root of all life: human, animal, and plant. Patenting and ownership of plant seed under the current intellectual property rights regime, she argues, is painfully symbolic of the degree to which capitalist ownership has penetrated even the basis of life itself, thereby violating the very foundation of the commons (Shiva, 2005).

All of these perspectives, from eco-socialism to food sovereignty to earth democracy, emphasize the notion of inclusion and the maintenance of decision-making power as close to the community level as possible. But inclusion is a slippery concept that has been manipulated by powerful actors to ensure continuity of the status quo. Referring to the work of Fidel Tubino, Catherine Walsh (2010) notes that not all attempts at "inclusion" are equal. While Europe may have put a kinder and gentler face on contemporary capitalism than Anglo-America, it is still dependent on this exploitative global system. The multilateral institutions, in cooperation with the European Union, have been keen to integrate the language and practices of the indigenous as long as they do not challenge the overall paradigm of neoliberal economic policy. As Walsh (2010) points out,

> The application of these tools can be clearly witnessed in the emergent policies and programmes of public social institutions that recognize and include indigenous and afro-descendent peoples, their cultural practices,

and even their knowledges without changing the dominant nature or structure of these institutions, what can be understood as functional interculturality.

(p. 17)

"Functional interculturality" is an insidious and pervasive part of the process of "post-neoliberal" policymaking that extends into the language of the international financial institutions and even into debates around corporate social responsibility. We see this functional interculturality particularly in the mining sector where there is increased pressure to integrate "stakeholders" into dialogues around resource extraction on indigenous lands affecting humans, other species, and nature (Chomsky, Leech, & Striffler, 2007; Gibbs, 2017).

With an awareness of the dangers of co-optation and manipulation, indigenous peoples in Latin America have fought to defend their own vision of nature, their relationships with other species, and development not only through the actions of popular movements in the region but also by enshrining the "rights of Mother Earth" in Bolivian and Ecuadorian law. The principles of what is known as *Buen Vivir* have informed and structured this contribution. *Buen Vivir* refers to an alternative view of development that captures the "Good Life" in the broadest sense of the term. New laws do not necessarily create new societies, but they can certainly play an important role in reorienting political debate and processes of inclusion.

The concept of *Buen Vivir* emerged in the late 1990s as part of the critique of the neoliberal austerity programmes implemented by the International Monetary Fund and the World Bank in tandem with the rise of leftist movements and governments in the region at the time led by Hugo Chávez (Venezuela), Rafael Correa (Ecuador), and Evo Morales (Bolivia).

Gudynas (2011) explains how the inclusion of the rights of Mother Earth in the constitution of Ecuador in 2008 and legal framework of Bolivia in 2009 is an important step forward in terms of the formal codification of these rights and the potential legitimization of a new paradigm that these rights imply. Gudynas (2011) also notes that the approach in each country has been quite different. In Bolivia, *Buen Vivir* goes to the heart of the values of the state itself. In Ecuador, the emphasis is more on laying out a set of rights, many of which can be found in the Western tradition (freedom, participation, protection, etc.), with the innovation being the extension of these rights to nature. Speaking of Bolivia, Catherine Walsh explains,

> In a country that has long exalted its *mestizo* character, favoured whitening and whiteness, and looked to the North for its model of development, the incorporation of buen vivir as the guiding principle of the Constitution is historically significant. Its new conceptualization as public policy is a result largely of the social, political, and epistemic agency of the indigenous movement over the last two decades. It responds to

the urgency of a radically different social contract that presents alternatives to capitalism and the "culture of death" of its neo-liberal and development project.

(Walsh, 2010, p. 18)

The concept of Mother Earth, as now entrenched in Bolivian law, is based on a broad definition rooted in multicultural indigenous concepts, including "harmonious living", "the good life", "land without evil", and "the noble life" (Gudynas, 2011). It is a vision of nature that includes humans and other animals; it is about the interconnectedness of the entire web of life. This web of life is defined as,

> complex and dynamic communities of plants, animals, micro-organisms and other beings in their environment, in which human communities and the rest of nature interact as a functional unit, under the influence of climatic, physiographic and geologic factors, as well as the productive practices and cultural diversity of Bolivians of both genders, and the world views of Indigenous nations and peoples, intercultural communities and the Afro-Bolivians.

(La Asamblea Legislativa Plurinacional de Bolivia, 2010)

The law defines Mother Earth as "a collective subject of public interest" and as "the dynamic living system formed by the indivisible community of all life systems and living beings whom are interrelated, interdependent, and complementary, which share a common destiny" (La Asamblea Legislativa Plurinacional de Bolivia, 2010, Articles 3 and 4). Clearly, the potential implications of the law for the concept of interconnected citizenship are vast and, if enforced, could challenge the basis of the capitalist development model.

Meanwhile, in Ecuador, *Buen Vivir* is expressed in the Quechua concept of *sumak kawsay*, which refers to "a fullness in life in a community, together with other persons and nature" (Gudynas, 2011). Gudynas argues that the Ecuadorian text may ultimately be more powerful than its Bolivian counterpart because it openly declares that the development model of the state must be in line with *Buen Vivir* in order to fulfil the rights of Mother Earth, or *Pachamama*. In Chapter 7 of the constitution, titled "Rights of Nature", articles 71 to 74 define these rights. They include nature's right to regeneration and restoration, the use of precaution and restriction mechanisms to protect species from extinction, and the rights of individuals and groups to appear before public bodies to defend these rights. Also, significantly, Chapter 1, Article 10 of the constitution reads, "Nature shall be the subject of those rights that the Constitution recognizes for it" (Republic of Ecuador in 2008, as cited by Gudynas, 2011). These rights speak to our broader theme of agency and to the idea of the law as potentially providing increased opportunities to express compassion in our broader political processes.

By acknowledging the rights of nature and entrenching them in the legal frameworks of the state, Bolivia and Ecuador have created the possibility of turning the capitalist paradigm of development inside out by presupposing the interconnectedness of all living things and a new citizenship based on interdependence. As Schilling-Vacaflor notes, this new "constitutionalism", a variant of which we also find in Venezuela, is evidence of "the intent to overcome the deficiencies of previous democratic models, which were characterized by a wide gap between the state and civil society, high levels of social inequality, and deficient recognition of cultural diversity"(Schilling-Vacaflor, 2011, p. 16). We concur with Schilling-Vacaflor and others, however, that new laws do not necessarily create new societies, but they can certainly play an important role in reorienting political debate and processes of inclusion. Communities in the global North and South continue to grapple with the reality of trying to survive economically in the global capitalist system as they construct alternatives, while simultaneously resolving their own internal contradictions around issues of race, gender, animals, and nature. However, as recent developments in Latin America, such as the electoral victories in several countries of right-wing presidents, make evident, any democratic advances regarding notions of citizenship will need constant safeguarding.

Conclusion

Our objective has been to highlight the need to shift our political culture so that it emphasizes the respectful and ethical treatment of humans, other animals, and nature in order to establish the basis for a compassionate democracy. If such ethical principles were to guide our interactions with humans and other animals in all pursuits, it would create a significant shift in global equality, democracy, and citizenship. From a practical and ethical standpoint, it would make factory farming unacceptable given that alternatives exist, and it is still possible to revert to small-scale agriculture. It would place the onus on rich nations to look closely at the continued utilization of non-human animals and industrial agriculture for food when it is clear that nutritionally dense alternatives exist that may also provide healthier options for the millions suffering from the diseases of affluence, such as obesity and cardiovascular disease.

Almost all countries and communities are currently caught up in the logic of capitalism, which promotes conventional, large-scale development and agriculture as essential for putting food on the table while simultaneously feeding a seemingly insatiable consumerism that is destroying the planet. But there is a paradox in this approach because the very model that is presented as necessary to ensure our survival also threatens our survival. Challenging the capitalist model is not an easy sell, particularly in the global North, because it means that we have to change our lifestyles, consume less, and engage compassionately with the people and other animals that are impacted by our daily practices (Harris, 2018). Therefore, building a new ethic rooted in interconnected citizenship requires that we see ourselves and our future as inextricably bound up with the health and well-being of all humans, other animals, and nature.

References

Adams, C. J. (1994). *Neither man nor beast: Feminism and the defense of animals.* New York, NY: The Continuum Publishing Company.

Andersen, K., & Kuhn, K. (2014). *Cowspiracy: The sustainability secret* [Motion picture]. Santa Rose, CA: A.U.M. Films & Media/First Spark Media.

Arluke, A. (1994). "We build a better beagle": Fantastic creatures in lab animal ads. *Qualitative Sociology, 17*(2), 143–158.

Canavan, J. (2017). "Happy cow" welfarist ideology and the Swedish "milk crisis": A crisis of romanticized oppression. In D. Nibert (Ed.), *Animal oppression and capitalism: The oppression of nonhuman animals as sources of food* (pp. 34–55). Santa Barbara, CA: Praeger.

Chomsky, A, Leech, G., & Striffler, S. (Eds.). (2007). *The people behind Colombian coal: Mining, multinationals and human rights.* Bogotá, Colombia: Casa Editorial Pisando Callos.

Donaldson, S., & Kymlicka, W. (2011). *Zoopolis: A political theory of animal rights.* Oxford, UK: Oxford University Press.

Foer, J. S. (2009). *Eating animals.* New York, NY: Little, Brown and Company.

Gibbs, T. (2017). *Why the Dalai Lama is a socialist: Buddhism and the compassionate society.* London, UK: Zed Books.

Goodland, R., & Anhang, J. (2009). Livestock and climate change: What if the key actors are . . . cows, pigs, and chickens? *World Watch Magazine, 22*(6), 10–19.

Greenebaum, J. B. (2017). Questioning the concept of vegan privilege: A commentary. *Humanity & Society, 41*(3), 355–372.

Gudynas, E. (2011). Buen Vivir: Today's tomorrow. *Development, 54*(4), 441–447.

Harris, T. (2017). "The problem is not the people, it's the system": The Canadian animal- industrial complex. In D. Nibert. (Ed.), *Animal oppression and capitalism: The oppression of nonhuman animals as sources of food* (pp. 57–75). Santa Barbara, CA: Praeger.

Harris, T. (2018). *The tiny house movement: Challenging our consumer culture.* Lanham, MD: Lexington Books.

Harvey, D. (2003). *The new imperialism.* New York, NY: Oxford University Press.

hooks, b. (2013). *Writing beyond race: Living theory and practice.* New York, NY: Routledge.

Intergovernmental Panel on Climate Change. (2018). *Special report on global warming of 1.5C.* Retrieved January 25, 2019, from www.ipcc.ch/

Joy, M. (2010). *Why we love dogs, eat pigs and wear cows: An introduction to carnism.* San Francisco, CA: Conari Press.

Joy, M. (2017). *Beyond beliefs: A guide to improving relationships and communication for vegans, vegetarians, and meat eaters.* Petaluma, CA: Roundtree Press.

Kovel, J. (2007). *The enemy of nature: The end of capitalism or the end of the world?* London, UK: Zed Books.

La Asamblea Legislativa Plurinacional de Bolivia. (2010). Ley de Derechos de Madre Tierra. *Ley N° 071.*

Leech, G. (2012). *Capitalism: A structural genocide*. London, UK: Zed Books.
Medoro, D. (2014). Spinning the pig: The language of industrial pork production. In J. Sorenson (Ed.), *Critical animal studies: Thinking the unthinkable* (pp. 208–215). Toronto, ON: Canadian Scholars' Press Inc.
Nibert, D. A. (2002). *Animal rights/human rights: Entanglements of oppression and liberation*. Lanham, MD: Rowman & Littlefield.
Nibert, D. A. (2013). *Animal oppression and human violence: Domesecration, capitalism, and global conflict*. New York, NY: Columbia University Press.
Nibert, D. A. (2017). Introduction. In D. Nibert (Ed.), *Animal oppression and capitalism: The oppression of nonhuman animals as sources of food* (pp. xi–xxv). Santa Barbara, CA: Praeger.
Picketty, T. (2014). *Capital in the 21st century*. Cambridge, MA: The Belknap Press of Harvard University Press.
Republic of Ecuador. (2008). *Constitution of the Republic of Ecuador*. Accessed on June 24, 2019 from *The political database of the Americas* at http://pdba.georgetown.edu/Constitutions/Ecuador/english08.html
Schilling-Vacaflor, A. (2011). Bolivia's new constitution: Towards participatory democracy and political pluralism? *European Review of Latin American and Caribbean Studies*, *90*, 3–22.
Shiva, V. (2005). *Earth democracy: Justice, sustainability and peace*. Cambridge, MA: South End Press.
Singer, P., & Mason, J. (2006). *The ethics of what we eat: Why our food choices matter*. Emmaus, PA: Rodale.
Smith-Harris, T. (2004). There's not enough room to swing a cat and there's no use flogging a dead horse: Language usage and perceptions of other animals. *ReVision*, *27*, 12–15.
Steckley, J., & Letts, G. K. (2013). *Elements of sociology: A critical Canadian introduction* (3rd ed.). Don Mills, ON: Oxford University Press.
Walsh, C. (2010). Development as Buen Vivir: Institutional arrangements and (de)colonial entanglements. *Development*, *53*(1), 15–21.

10 Opportunities in food law for sustainability and succulence
Why the law has not caught up

Gabriela Steier

Introduction

It is over 20 years ago that the merit of plant based was made explicit. Nutrition studies had already corroborated the notion that plant-based diets are healthier and more sustainable than those including animal protein (Campbell & Campbell, 2004). As well, non-profit organizations started to publish about vegetarianism, and government watchdog groups gained traction (Center for Food Safety, 2019). Issues involving sustainable food production and plant-based diets were also being promoted by lobbyists in Washington, DC (Evich, 2015). Fast-forwarding a few decades later, sustainability and resilience are now terms that appear in nearly every course catalogue at universities in the USA. Nonetheless, the law is lagging behind most of the progress that the food movement and uncountable scholars in the interdisciplinary field of food law and policy have made over the past few decades (Nestle, 2013). It begs the question: why hasn't the law caught up?

This chapter provides a cursory overview of the global food law hindrances of a widespread plant-based diet and explores common treaties, legal issues, themes, and challenges that explain why the law has not caught up with the food movement and supporting science. A few success stories illustrate legal and political challenges and obstacles being overcome, giving hope that society will uproot the many misconceptions about sustainable plant-based diets. By way of examples only, this chapter contextualizes food law and plant-based diets with the role that sustainability considerations take in the current legal discourse.

Regulatory issues, themes, and challenges in establishing plant-based diets

Global food laws for free-market access under the World Trade Organization (WTO)

On a global level, only a few treaties constitute what could be construed as *food* law (Steier & Patel, 2017). The treaties under the purview of the

World Trade Organization (WTO) are multinational instruments that bind signatories to follow certain rules in the international playing field of trading in food, which is how food ultimately moves around the world from "farm to fork". Food trade accrues increasing *food miles*, an indicator of unsustainable practices. Nonetheless, food trade is a function of globalization. Individual countries have some autocracy, but must follow suit when seeking to engage in trade with the largest and most dominant economies (Steier, 2017b). As such, even countries with widespread plant-based diets, such as India (Wilson, 2013), succumb to pressures to import processed foods of the free market in an effort to compete. This competition, in the most general sense, is regulated by law. On the international level, these laws are treaties and agreements that countries enter into or adopt as signatories. Anti-dumping laws, for instance, should prevent countries from selling their surpluses of certain commodities to other countries at a lower price than local producers, thereby flooding the respective domestic market and impeding locals from selling their products. Laws, as the following paragraphs show, attach to all of these actions.

For instance, the WTO administers various agreements that should ensure free-market access within the parameters of certain rules, such as the agreements. The WTO's "main function is to ensure that trade flows as smoothly, predictably and freely as possible" (WTO, 2019c). One of the agreements – i.e. international laws – under the WTO's purview is the General Agreement on Tariffs and Trade (GATT). GATT was established in 1947 and revised in 1994. Other major agreements include the Technical Barriers to Trade (TBT), which according to the WTO "tries to ensure that regulations, standards, testing, and certification procedures do not create unnecessary obstacles", the foremost theme of all WTO agreements (WTO, 2019c). The TBT especially "recognizes countries' rights to adopt the standards they consider appropriate – for example, for human, animal or plant life or health, for the protection of the environment or to meet other consumer interests" (WTO, 2019c). Two specific agreements are explained in more detail next to illustrate the roles that such multinational agreements play in the global regulation of food.

The WTO's agreement on agriculture

The WTO's Agreement on Agriculture "outlin[es] its key principles, the work of the Agriculture Committee, and how disputes have interpreted WTO law on agriculture" (WTO, 2016). Specifically, it "provides a framework for the long-term reform of agricultural trade and domestic policies, with the aim of leading to fairer competition and a less distorted sector" (WTO, 2019a). The points targeted are as follows:

- *Market access* – the use of trade restrictions, such as tariffs on imports
- *Domestic support* – the use of subsidies and other support programmes that directly stimulate production and distort trade

- *Export competition* – the use of export subsidies and other government support programmes that subsidize exports (WTO, 2019a)

These distortions and subsidies that are tackled through the agreement are trade concerns, such as dumping, tariffs, and food safety. Most of the foods subject to this oversight are not the sustainable, plant-based ones of short supply chains, but rather the highly traded commodity crops and processed foods (Steier, 2017b). Underpinning these concerns are free-market access and capitalist ideals that seek to make food profitable rather than accessible and sustainable (Steier, 2017a). Non-trade concerns, on the other hand, "include food security and environmental protection" (Murphy, 2002). These non-trade goals are referred to as "multifunctional agriculture" and "include payments to farmers for good land stewardship practices and for humane treatment of animals"(Murphy, 2002). Agroecology and agroforestry, where agriculture and environmental integrity coexist, are examples of multifunctional agriculture (Leakey, 2017). Even though the negotiations under the Agriculture Agreement continue, obstacles persist within the countries benefitting the most from free-market access and food export. The USA and Australia, for instance, have rejected multifunctional agriculture during the 2003 negotiation rounds (Leakey, 2017), and this trend has continued.

The agreement on the application of sanitary and phytosanitary measures (SPS agreement)

The SPS Agreement, about "the application of food safety and animal and plant health regulations" (WTO, 1998), answers the important questions:

> How do you ensure that your country's consumers are being supplied with food that is safe to eat – "safe" by the standards you consider appropriate? And at the same time, how can you ensure that strict health and safety regulations are not being used as an excuse for protecting domestic producers?
>
> (WTO, 2019b)

In short, the SPS Agreement contains "basic rules for food safety and animal and plant health standards" (WTO, 1998), such as for the import and export of foods. Even though countries may set their own standards, the SPS Agreement requires scientific justification for those standards and encourages harmonization based on streamlined recommendations – where such recommendations exist (WTO, 1998). A hypothetical example of SPS measures may include a trade barrier on certain seeds that may threaten a specific ecosystem, such as Australia's, Hawaii's, or the Galapagos Islands'. Nonetheless, these standards "should be applied only to the extent necessary to protect human, animal or plant life or health. And they should not arbitrarily or unjustifiably discriminate between countries where identical or similar conditions prevail" (WTO, 2019a) to ensure free-market access as discussed as a WTO trend earlier.

Global food laws for non-trade goals under the World Health Organization (WHO) and the Food and Agriculture Organization (FAO) of the United Nations (UN)

As noted earlier in this chapter, there are trade and non-trade goals in international food law. Non-trade goals reach beyond multifunctional agriculture and include food safety and food security. Food safety is focused on the wholesomeness of food, such that it does not cause foodborne diseases. Food security revolves around the access to food so as to meet nutrition goals. Both prongs share the goal of meeting nutrition targets, which fall under the purview of the WHO and FAO. The following subsections briefly explain to which extent the WHO and FAO focus on plant-based nutrition.

The WHO and plant-based nutrition

The WHO is the "directing and coordinating authority on international health within the United Nations' system" with specific nutrition targets of, amongst others, "[eating] plenty of vegetables and fruit":

- Eat a wide variety of vegetables and fruit
- For snacks, choose raw vegetables and fresh fruit rather than foods that are high in sugars, fats, or salt
- Avoid overcooking vegetables and fruit, as this can lead to the loss of important vitamins
- When using canned or dried vegetables and fruit, choose varieties without added salt and sugars

Notably, the WHO gives a poignant reason in support of a diet rich in plant-based foods:

> Vegetables and fruit are important sources of vitamins, minerals, dietary fibre, plant protein and antioxidants. People whose diets are rich in vegetables and fruit have a significantly lower risk of obesity, heart disease, stroke, diabetes and certain types of cancer.
>
> (WHO, 2019)

As part of a healthy diet for adults, the WHO further recommends "[f]ruit, vegetables, legumes (e.g. lentils and beans), nuts and whole grains (e.g. unprocessed maize, millet, oats, wheat and brown rice)" and "[a]t least 400 g (i.e. five portions) of fruit and vegetables per day, excluding potatoes, sweet potatoes, cassava and other starchy roots" (WHO, 2018).

For many people, these recommendations are noble but largely unattainable. In the USA, for instance, the Centers for Disease Control and Prevention (CDC) reported that

> in 2015, just 9 percent of adults met the intake recommendations for vegetables, ranging from 6 percent in West Virginia to 12 percent in Alaska. Only 12 percent of adults met the recommendations for fruit, ranging from 7 percent in West Virginia to 16 percent in Washington, D.C. Results showed that consumption was lower among men, young adults, and adults living in poverty.
>
> (CDCP, 2017)

Reasons cited by the CDC are "high cost, limited availability and access, and perceived lack of cooking/preparation time can be barriers to fruit and vegetable consumption" (CDCP, 2017). Thus, a dissonance between the recommendations and real-life outcomes of fruit and vegetable consumption is evident. the market and pricing create obstacles; whether these obstacles created by the market and pricing are intentional or not is a question outside the scope of this chapter, but it invites further reflection.

Even though the USA remains a major economic power worldwide, yet has poor nutrition profiles, its consumers are highly aware of sustainability. It seems paradoxical that two-thirds of consumers utter strong preferences for sustainable brands, declarations, and products (Lein, 2018), but fail to achieve sustainability through plant-based diets. There are various obstacles that have not yet been overcome, including the overwhelming availability of processed and animal-based foods that appear cheap to vulnerable consumers due to externalized costs. Unfortunately, even the USDA's recommendations for a plant-based diet focus on processed and cooked meals that are in contravention of the WHO's recommendations in some respects (USDA, 2018b).

Sustainability and plant-based diets in international and US law

The Food and Agriculture Organization (FAO) of the UN offers ample recommendations for plant-based diets where "the sustainability of diets goes beyond nutrition and environment as to include economic and socio-cultural dimensions" (FAO, 2019). Showing a more progressive approach than the aforementioned USDA's, the FAO leaves no doubt in the links between plant-based diets and sustainability as "having a mostly plant-based diet, focus on seasonal and local foods, reduction of food waste, consumption of fish from sustainable stocks only and reduction of red and processed meat, highly processed foods and sugar-sweetened beverages" (FAO, 2019).

Germany, Brazil, Sweden, and Qatar are identified as having some of the only and foremost national dietary recommendations focusing on plant-based and sustainable diets, defined as

> those diets with low environmental impacts which contribute to food and nutrition security and to healthy life for present and future generations. Sustainable diets are protective and respectful of biodiversity and ecosystems, culturally acceptable, accessible, economically fair and affordable; nutritionally adequate, safe and healthy; while optimizing natural and human resources.
>
> (Fischer & Garnett, 2016)

Even though the recommendations of the FAO and WHO reflect national recommendations in many instances, including the rich debates of nutritionists, Big Food producers, and many other stakeholders, certain trends towards plant-based diets can be extracted. An in-depth discussion or comparison is beyond the scope of this chapter, but the following success stories and subsequent discussion further examine the role of food laws in establishing plant-based diets.

Success stories

Success story 1: Vegan mayonnaise

"This is the story of a socially conscious start-up that took on the forces of Big Food and won" (Kaplan, 2015), writes the *Washington Post* about this success story with,

> all the makings of an epic drama – lawsuits, lab experiments, accusations of a government conspiracy, secret emails, empty threats, allusions to the Brooklyn mob, a promise of a food revolution and an alleged attempt to mislead the public – with the fate of America's favorite condiment hanging in the balance.
>
> (Kaplan, 2015)

The whole case, alluded to as a David and Goliath fight, where Unilever's Hellmann's Mayonnaise went against the food start-up Hampton Creek, turned on the fact that "Just Mayo" contains no eggs but the FDA includes egg yolks in its definition of mayonnaise (Duran v. Creek, 2016).

In this dispute, a lawsuit was filed by one company against another. Considering the rippling effect of this seemingly straightforward case, however, reveals the power of food law. Here, a mislabelling claim was brought by a Big Food giant, Hellmann, one of the international stakeholders in the free market that the WTO oversees. Some reporters said that Hampton Creek had awoken a giant, but it could have been any other company threatening the oligarchy of the Big Food players in the global marketplace.

The packaging of Just Mayo jars feature an egg with a leaf or sprout growing in it, which can be interpreted to stand for an egg that is not from a chicken. This plant-based non-egg is the foundation for the mayo, whereas traditional mayo is a whipped egg and oil condiment of vast popularity. Whether this vegan alternative to store-bought mayonnaise was mislabelled was the subject matter of a lawsuit and a media storm. The resulting battle was one that the small food company, Hampton Creek, won. Prevailing in this time and age against a Big Food giant, Hellmann, is certainly a feat, but it also gives hope that alternatives to animal-based foods can become inexpensive commodities that shift the cost of profit to the environment, governments, or susceptible populations. The next example, non-dairy milk, supports the notion that commodity foods need not be unsustainable and animal-protein dependent, despite the macromarketing of the dairy and meat industries to the contrary, and their deeply rooted hold on US policy.

Success story 2: non-dairy milk

Although milk has lost its health halo, the dairy industry continues to push for milk and enjoy government support. This is the success story of dairy-alternative "milks" that have caused a media stir but have earned a place in grocery stores worldwide despite the classic dairy macromarketing.

An article published in the *British Journal of Nutrition* clearly linked the consumption of dairy and meat to obesity (Lin et al., 2011), which is known to cause a whole slew of other severe diet-related diseases from which even the WHO warns. Nonetheless, the US Department of Agriculture (USDA) reports that "the average person drinks 18 gallons a year. Back in the 1970s it was more like 30 gallons a year" (Evstatieva & Cornish, 2017). Notably, "[b]y the mid-20th century, Americans were told to drink two to three glasses of milk a day. . . . Dairy industry marketing? That was the stuff of legend" (Evstatieva & Cornish, 2017), reports the National Public Radio. And the USDA continues to include dairy on the myplate.gov recommendations (USDA, 2018a) despite the vast amount of science that corroborates the opposite recommendation (PCRM, 2019). The Physicians Committee for Responsible Medicine (PCRM) warns,

> Milk and other dairy products are the top source of saturated fat in the American diet, contributing to heart disease, type 2 diabetes, and Alzheimer's disease. Studies have also linked dairy to an increased risk of breast, ovarian, and prostate cancers.
>
> (PCRM, 2019)

Notably, the 2019 Canada Food Guide, based on the "best available evidence" and without apparent industry input, excluded dairy as a category

(Kirkey, 2019). It encourages more plant-based and less meat and dairy food choices. As an alternative to dairy milk, various plant-based options are taking the market by storm, such as soy, almond, and coconut milk: "Almond milk, for instance, has seen sales grow 250 percent over the past five years" (Kirkey, 2019). Nonetheless, soy, almond, and coconut milk, amongst the pleasingly vast array of dairy alternatives, are facing similar scrutiny as vegan mayonnaise because these beverages are not technically "milk".

The National Milk Producers Federation (NMPF), representatives of dairy farmers under the protection of the USDA (the US agency overseeing what is safe to grow), are macromarketing against dairy alternatives by using the same arguments that have been used repeatedly since the pharmaceutical industries and Big Tobacco started the "playbook" on it. NMPF representatives, for instance, claim that "other 'milk' products . . . are confusing consumers" (Kirkey, 2019). This is a friction point beyond the marketing, as it hints at the nutritional make-up of milk and its non-dairy competitors. Protein and calcium contents may vary, but so does cholesterol and vitamin content. The bioavailability of calcium from milk has been doubted for decades, but consumers still read the nutrition declarations and may think otherwise.

In December 2016, 32 Members of the US Congress, many representing the largest dairy producing states, urged the Food and Drug Administration (FDA) to change soy, almond, and coconut "milk" to another term, as milk was defined as originating from a mammary gland (Letter to FDA Commissioner, 2016). In fact, these congressmen signed on to an appeal to the FDA to "exercise its legal authority to investigate and take appropriate action against the manufacturers of those misbranded products" – namely, the dairy-alternative beverages (Letter to FDA Commissioner, 2016). Here, the legislative branch, Congress, has invoked the Federal Food, Drug, and Cosmetic Act's definitions of milk to appeal to the FDA (an executive agency) to take action against the 250-fold increase of non-dairy milk sales, while dairy milk sales have dropped by 7%. In a bar chart, these numbers would barely be visibly comparable, and yet the industry representatives had so much influence that all three branches of government were appealed to in this letter, one of many examples of the macromarketing power of the renowned dairy industry. The NMPF not only deployed macromarketing to the public but also intensive lobbying to government bodies. Price protection, stabilization, and continued federal support of the whopping market dominance of the dairy industry in the USA remains a strong indicator of the industry's power (CRS Report, 2011).

Recommendations and conclusion

Succulence and sustainability, as this book shows, combine compelling qualities in service of feeding more of the world with healthy foods. Considering the various legal obstacles that must be overcome as food is processed, transported, packaged, labelled, and traded, it appears that evading the situations where such complicated layers of international, national, regional, and local regulation applies only makes sense. Thus, those foods that are the least likely to be affected by such global regulation should be thriving the most – but the opposite is the case. Simply put, instead of surges in processed foods that are largely part of animal-protein rich and unhealthy diets, simple and plant-based options from short supply chains (think: local farmers' markets or cottage foods) should be the logical alternative. Better yet, locally and sustainably produced plant-based foods, given their fortunately diminished regulatory burdens worldwide, should be the staples of healthy diets around the world, unscathed by the toxic junk food industry. The shorter the supply chain of a food product, such as a piece of fruit or a vegetable sold at a farmers' market locally, the lower the regulatory burdens, the fewer laws apply, and the lower the hurdles of taxation. Processed foods with large environmental footprints accrue extensive food miles and are heavily regulated, taxed, and subject to price fluctuations of international market speculation. Reducing these obstacles would bring us closer to more sustainable models of local, short-supply-chain produce, aka the plant-based diet. As the data and examples cited in this chapter show, however, evading the legal obstacles is not always enough to promote a plant-based diet (see Figure 10.1).

Figure 10.1 represents a simplified schematic view of the influence exerted from *farm to fork*.

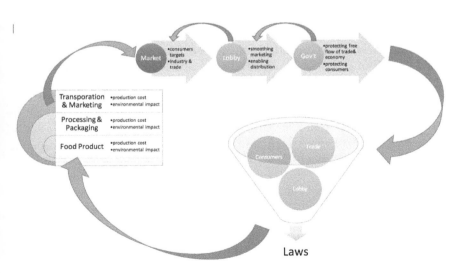

Figure 10.1 The feedback cycle of unsustainability

Source: Authors own work, created for this volume.

Beginning with the food product, a duplicity of interests exists: production cost and environmental impact. As this hypothetical food product is processed and packaged (which is minimal with fresh produce), further duplicity of interests complicates matters. The same is true with every layer added for transportation and marketing. When the food product enters into the market, more clashing interests arise, such as industry and trade or consumer targets. In order to open up distribution avenues, the food product becomes the subject matter of lobbying and an increasing amount of undue influence that may range from labelling to farm subsidies. The government is then tasked with permitting or prohibiting certain food products and must base its decisions on laws. However, the laws, until enacted, have gone through a funnel of conflicting interests and dilutions. As shown by the grey curved arrows in Figure 10.1, these laws then apply to the food production. Working through this cycle, with obscure and complicated clusters of interest, shows that the more processed and the further traded a food product, the less sustainable it becomes. Simple, fresh, and local produce seem to enable the clearest regulatory paths. Hypothetically speaking, a tax could weaken any step or erode the undue influence along this cycle and could be incentivizing more sustainable practices. For instance, governments may need to levy a tax that grows with the distance that food travels (food miles), or with the level of processing that the food has to undergo. Such a commodity tax could be a hypothetical legal disincentive to purchase those foods or to trade in them. Soda taxes for portion control have failed (Leonhardt, 2018), but the nature of the taxes here are more like the "polluter pays" environmental taxes.

Thus, the law should play a more active role in promoting a sustainable and plant-based diet that is culturally and regionally adequate, as proposed by the WHO and FAO recommendations.

Another possible regulatory intervention to promote plant-based diets could be the support to industrial macromarketers of mainstream plant-based foods of short supply chains through subsidies, tax cuts, or debt forgiveness programmes. To make needed changes, the existing US schemes of subsidies for the big-five crops in the Food Bill must be reversed. Therefore, "governments often support agriculture through direct economic assistance in the form of subsidies, provide funds for monopoly marketing organizations, and also protect their interests" (Leonhardt, 2018). For instance, researchers have aptly observed that

> [m]any developed economies remain significant exporters of meat and animal based products. Such industries are viewed by governments as vital to food security, economic wealth creation, job creation, and the identity of the nation.
>
> (Beverland, 2014)

Stopping this government support would immediately wreak havoc with the current food systems. But doing so also would create new opportunities to revise diets and establish more sustainable practices and develop different markets. Macromarketing is used by those companies profiting from unsustainable foods, so why has the law not put a halt to this vicious circle?

> In the U.S. complaints from livestock producers have resulted in governments moderating or withdrawing statements regarding the need to reduce meat consumption or switch to a plant-based diet. . . . More worryingly, despite being aware of the potential for harm the UK government failed to adequately warn consumers of the dangers associated with eating meat, such as Creutzfeldt-Jacob Disease, the human form of Bovine Spongiform Encephalopathy.
>
> (Beverland, 2014)

In fact, researchers investigating consumer perceptions of the match, or mismatch, between healthy and sustainable diets, and offering insight into consumers' motivation to eat healthily and sustainably, as noted in Chapters 8 and 9, found that a healthy diet, a sustainable diet, and a plant-based diet were closely associated by consumers in the UK, Germany, Belgium, and the Netherlands (Van Loo, Hoefkens, & Verbeke, 2017). In a stark contrast, US consumers rely more on meat, dairy, and eggs than ever before (Bloomberg, 2018). More action is needed for the law to catch up and institute requirements that foster more sustainable and civil societies.

References

Beverland, M. B. (2014). Sustainable eating: Mainstreaming plant-based diets in developed economies. *Journal of Macromarketing, 34*(3), 369–382.

Bloomberg. (2018, January 2). 'Beef will always be king.' Americans are set to eat more meat in 2018 than ever before. *Fortune.* Retrieved from http://fortune.com/

Campbell, C., & Campbell, T. (2004). *The China study: The most comprehensive study of nutrition ever conducted and the startling implications for diet, weight loss and long-term health.* Dallas, TX: BenBella Books.

Center for Food Safety. (2019). *Andrew Kimbrell.* Retrieved from www.centerfor-foodsafety.org/andrew-kimbrell

Centres for Disease Control and Prevention (CDCP). (2017, November 16). *Only 1 in 10 adults get enough fruits or vegetables.* Retrieved from www.cdc.gov/media/releases/2017/p1116-fruit-vegetable-consumption.html

Congressional Research Service (CRS). (2011). *Previewing dairy policy options for the next farm bill.* Retrieved from www.everycrsreport.com/reports/R41141.html

Duran v. Creek. (2016). *No. 3:15-CV-05497-LB, 2016 WL 1191685* (N.D. Cal. March 28, 2016).

Evstatieva, M., & Cornish, A. (2017, May 16). Why are Americans drinking less cow's milk? Its appeal has curdled. *NPR.* Retrieved from www.npr.org/sections/thesalt/2017/05/16/528460207/why-are-americans-drinking-less-cows-milk-its-appeal-has-curdled

FAO. (2019). *Food-based dietary guidelines.* Retrieved from www.fao.org/nutrition/education/food-dietary-guidelines/background/sustainable-dietary-guidelines/en/

Fischer, C. G., & Garnett, T. (2016). *Plates, pyramids, planet. Developments in national healthy and sustainable dietary guidelines: A state of play assessment.* Food and Agriculture Organization of the United Nations and the Food Climate Research Network at the University of Oxford. Retrieved from www.fao.org/3/a-i5640e.pdf

Kaplan, S. (2015, December 18). How little 'just mayo' took on big egg and won. *Washington Post.* Retrieved from www.washingtonpost.com

Kirkey, S. (2019, January 22). Got milk? Not so much. Health Canada's new food guide drops 'milk and alternatives' and favours plant-based protein. *National Post.* Retrieved from https://nationalpost.com/

Leakey, R. (2017). *Multifunctional agriculture.* Cambridge, MA: Academic Press.

Lein, S. (2018, August 18). Why sustainable branding matters. *Forbes.* Retrieved from www.forbes.com/sites/theyec/2018/08/20/why-sustainable-branding-matters/#24af90425b6e

Leonhardt, D. (2018, January 18). The case for the health taxes. *The New York Times.* Retrieved from www.nytimes.com/2018/01/18/opinion/soda-health-taxes.html

Letter to FDA Commissioner. (2016, December 16). Retrieved from www.nmpf.org/files/Welch-Simpson%20Letter.pdf

Lin, Y., Bolca, S., Vandevijvere, S., De Vriese, S., Mouratidou, T., De Neve, M., . . . Huybrechts, I. (2011). Plant and animal protein intake and its association with overweight and obesity among the Belgian population. *British Journal of Nutrition, 105*(7), 1106–1116.

Murphy, S. (2002). Structural distortions in world agricultural markets: Do WTO rules support sustainable agriculture? *Columbia Journal of Environmental Law, 27*, 605–606.

Nestle, M. (2013). *Food politics: How the food industry influences nutrition and health.* Berkeley, CA: University of California Press.

Physicians for Responsible Medicine (PCRM). (2019). *Health concerns about dairy: Avoid the dangers of dairy with a plant-based diet.* Retrieved from www.pcrm.org/good-nutrition/nutrition-information/health-concerns-about-dairy

Steier, G. (2017a). A window of opportunity for GMO regulation: Achieving food integrity through cap-and-trade models from climate policy for GMO regulation. *Pace Environmental Law Review, 34*(2), 1–32.

Steier, G. (2017b). *Advancing food integrity: GMO regulation, agroecology, and urban agriculture.* Boca Raton, FL: CRC Press.

Steier, G., & Patel, K. (Eds.). (2017). *International food law and policy.* New York, NY: Springer.

USDA. (2018a). *All about the dairy group.* Retrieved from www.choosemyplate.gov/dairy

USDA. (2018b). *Tips for vegetarians.* Retrieved from www.choosemyplate.gov/tips-vegetarians

Van Loo, E. J., Hoefkens, C., & Verbeke, W. (2017). Healthy, sustainable and plant-based eating: Perceived (mis)match and involvement-based consumer segments as targets for future policy. *Food Policy, 69*, 46–57.

Wilson, C. (2013, June 27). *Plant-based populations.* Food and Nutrition. Retrieved from https://foodandnutrition.org/july-august-2013/plant-based-populations/

WHO. (2018). *Healthy diet.* Retrieved from www.who.int/news-room/fact-sheets/detail/healthy-diet

WHO. (2019). *Nutrition*. Retrieved from www.who.int/nutrition/topics/5keys_healthydiet/en/

WTO. (1998). *Understanding the WTO agreement on sanitary and phytosanitary measures*. Retrieved from www.wto.org/english/tratop_e/sps_e/spsund_e.htm

WTO. (2016, October). *The WTO agreements series: Agriculture* (3rd ed.). Retrieved from www.wto.org/english/res_e/booksp_e/agric_agreement_series_3_e.pdf

WTO. (2019a). *Agriculture*. Retrieved from www.wto.org/english/tratop_e/agric_e/agric_e.htm

WTO. (2019b). *Sanitary and phytosanitary measures*. Retrieved from www.wto.org/english/tratop_e/sps_e/sps_e.htm

WTO. (2019c). *Standards and safety*. Retrieved from www.wto.org/english/thewto_e/whatis_e/tif_e/agrm4_e.htm#TRS

Part IV

Living consciously and compassionately

11 Integrity economics

Business supports for plant-based diets

Chaiti Seth, Sarah Pittoello,
Roberto Gueli, and Av Singh

Introduction

Sustainable food systems are as diverse, textured, and multi-flavoured as delicious, local food itself, with no one singular approach to sustainable diets (Ackerman-Leist, 2013). Food feeds our bodies, our minds, and our spirits, and is at the heart of social and cultural traditions. Food systems – the myriad ways in which our food is produced, processed, distributed, consumed, and disposed of – have significant social, cultural, health, ecological, and economic implications. Research is increasingly clear that plant-based diets have the potential to have the lightest ecological footprint and support human health (Garnett, 2011; McMichael, Powles, Butler, & Uauy, 2007; Poore & Nemecek, 2018). In our (the authors') collective experiences as agronomists, chefs, farmers, researchers, writers, and eaters, whole-food, plant-based meals can provide a solid foundation for the shift towards more healthy and sustainable food systems. A shift away from the typically meat-heavy North American diet to one that centres on and celebrates plant-based foods requires reimagining and recreating social and cultural norms, health perceptions, and economic structures to align with ecological realities. In this chapter, we focus on the role of business and economic opportunities on this path towards succulent sustainability. We take a nuanced and practical approach to sustainable diets, recognizing that food stands at the crossroads of these many spheres. We also propose that a widespread shift towards plant-based diets requires systems-level changes and highlight the complex questions that must be grappled with in this transition.

Integrity economics

Eating food is inextricably woven with its production, processing, and preparation. Feeding ourselves has been a primary human concern throughout history, and until recently, has occupied much of our time and energy (Pollan, 2007). However, the majority of food eaten in North America today is "processed, packaged and made ready to eat or to heat. . . [and] ultra-processed foods amount to virtually half the dietary energy consumed by

Canadians" (Moubarac, 2017, p. 4). These trends are exacerbated by the decline in the basic nutritional quality of staple cereals, fruits, and vegetables as a result of diminished soil health, breeding and selection of crops for yield rather than nutrition, loss of traditional crop varieties, and increased carbon dioxide in the atmosphere (Davis, Epp, & Riordan, 2004; Loladze, 2014). The industrialization of food production has outsourced many of the steps involved in feeding ourselves: food is increasingly an economic transaction (Fitch & Santo, 2016; Goggins & Rau, 2015). A shift towards food that is good for our bodies, souls, and planet must involve a redefinition of these economic relationships. In this chapter, we highlight businesses that take an alternative approach to economics, where financial and ecological sustainability go hand in hand, and there is a genuine effort to hold ethical values at the core of business (Daly & Farley, 2011; Schumacher, 1973; Shuman, 2015). Such an approach relies on direct, strong, and caring relationships. It involves asking difficult questions with integrity, recognizing, and nurturing *all* the relationships along the way, and collaborating to find solutions. We see this movement towards succulent sustainability as a process rather than an end, recognizing the importance of remaining curious, observant, and adaptive along this path, and honouring the complexity of interdependence by embracing and supporting the many paths we might take. We call this approach *integrity economics* and offer examples of businesses that demonstrate their vital role in building succulent, sustainable food systems.

A metaphorical plate

Each plate of food embodies many relationships, which stretch back through the people who prepared the food, past the processing facilities, and on to the lands and waters where it was grown or harvested. To explore business opportunities in plant-based diets, we use a metaphorical plate – a plant-rich feast of caraway sauerkraut, oat groats with roasted root vegetables, lettuce salad with a maple-sage dressing, tomato-lentil stew, and a wild mushroom ragout – all from the Annapolis Valley in Nova Scotia where we (the authors) live. We connect each of the foods on this plate back to businesses in this region that produce or supply them, showcasing the values and dilemmas of integrity economics in practice.

The stories on our plates

Conscious Catering: preparing a plant-rich feast!

This plant-rich feast of local, sustainable foods is prepared by our first business example, *Conscious Catering*. Conscious Catering is co-operated by Anke Kungl and Roberto Gueli (often with baby Maylah in tow) and serves local, organic, vegetarian, whole-food cuisine in New Brunswick and Nova Scotia. In addition to peeling, chopping, and cleaning, Kungl and Gueli also help harvest vegetables and source ecologically conscious ingredients. In their experience, any meal prepared from scratch with fresh, wholesome ingredients using traditional methods (or inspired experiments!) can be rich and enjoyed with conviviality. They are challenging prevalent cultural stories of healthy eating as expensive, boring, reserved for times of illness, or exclusive to food fads. They are rewriting the story of what it means to eat well by offering simple guidelines, such as eating a diversity and balance of whole, plant-based foods.

Kungl and Gueli – neither of whom are trained chefs – most often cater multi-meal or multi-day events, such as weekend retreats or conferences. They love surprising their satisfied clients with the revelation that they have eaten only vegetarian food for a whole weekend! As much as they enjoy cooking for others, Kungl and Gueli believe that part of their work is to encourage people to cook well for themselves. They co-authored a recipe book and offer classes that focus on self-care and connecting with food as enjoyable medicine, reminding eaters how rewarding, accessible, and delicious whole-food, plant-based cooking can be. They see truth in the old adage "health is wealth": a home cooked, plant-based meal can be more affordable than inexpensive takeout, even without including the savings on health care (Niebylski et al., 2014). To cut costs and reduce packaging waste, Kungl and Gueli source directly from farms and buy organic dry goods in bulk.

Conscious Catering is inspired by various cuisines, particularly ones rooted in systems of traditional natural medicine, such as Ayurveda, which value the presence of a diversity of tastes in every meal for nutritional balance and satisfaction (Kacera, 2006). Kungl and Gueli emphasize using unrefined non-GMO plant oils, quality whole salts, unpasteurized lacto-ferments, and copious amounts of fresh and dry culinary herbs, some of which are now grown on their own farm. The vegetarian menus they create are mindful of growing sensitivities to dairy, gluten, and sugar (Maren, 2018), and are designed to be lighter on eaters' digestive systems. Because both personal and cultural food habits have deep roots, Kungl and Gueli are sensitive in their approach, respecting boundaries and vulnerabilities: they recognize that most people look forward to an enjoyable meal rather than a headache from a sudden withdrawal of sugar or caffeine from their diet! They create dishes that are comforting, vibrant, and intriguing, and offer a variety of choices, finding that a diversity of options on the table brings a diversity of people to enjoy them.

Seven Acres Farm: caraway sauerkraut

The first bite on our metaphorical plate is a caraway sauerkraut – salty, tangy, effervescent, and full of life – made by Jocelyn Durston and Chris Kaza at **Seven Acres Farm** near Canning, Nova Scotia. Durston and Kaza produce heirloom vegetables, cut flowers, and vegetable ferments, including traditional krauts and inventive ones, such as juniper onion, and fermented drinks, including kombuchas and water kefirs. They sell their products at farmers' markets and local retailers in the Annapolis Valley. They are committed to veganic farming, which minimizes cruelty and uses no animal-based inputs, and delight in seeing the growth of ecological activity on their farm. They source ingredients from local farmers and prioritize supporting small-scale and young farmers who adhere to ecological farming practices.

Parallel to the way our consumptive patterns have led to the loss of bio-diversity in our natural environment, our internal biomes are also suffering. An onslaught of agricultural pesticides, insecticides, and herbicides (Horrigan, Lawrence, & Walker, 2002), as well as widespread use of antibiotics (Shallcross & Davies, 2014), is diminishing human biomes. Food writer and fermentation wizard Sandor Katz (2012) notes,

> The biological reality – that bacteria are our ancestors and the context for all life; that they perform many important physiological functions for us; and that they improve, preserve, and protect our food – contrasts sharply with the widespread perception of bacteria as our enemies.
>
> (p. 13)

In addition, the fast-food industry has created bacteria-deficient replicas of some of our favourite fermented foods, from bread to chocolate to pickles: what used to improve with age can now be mass produced with little need to wait. The consequence of these agricultural and food processing practices is a depletion of gut flora with a wide array of associated health issues, including depression, diabetes, obesity, and cancer (Singh et al., 2017). Fermentation is a traditional method of food preservation that invites and supports strains of beneficial bacteria that are symbiotic with the human body, especially our guts. As our awareness of the importance of our internal biodiversity grows (Orrhage & Nord, 2000; Singh et al., 2017; Xu & Knight, 2015), a demand for fermented foods provides an opportunity for value-added agricultural businesses.

Education and raising awareness about food choices in supporting health are key goals of Durston and Kaza's business. Relationships are central to their success: their customers enjoy coming to their farmers' market booth to support vendors with whom they have relationships. They see a growing demand and an unsaturated market for fermented foods in the Annapolis Valley. However, they grapple with how to grow their business to be modestly financially sustainable, while maintaining their values and connection to their work. Currently, Kaza works off farm, as does Durston in the off season. Increasing production would require staff, which would require sufficient increase in production to pay an employee and a shift for Durston and Kaza from hands-on production to include management. Time management to balance the ferment business and cultivating produce and flowers on their farm presents another challenge. Durston also finds it challenging to be aggressive in building their business, preferring to spend her time working on the land.

Longspell Point Farm: hearty oat groat and root vegetable salad and mixed greens

Next on our plate is a mound of hearty oat groats with bright root vegetables followed by a tender green salad, together adding texture, colour, and substance to our feast. There is growing awareness of the nutritional potential of whole grains, vegetables, and fruits (Health Canada, 2019; Slavin, 2004) as the building blocks of nutritious meals. Embracing the logic of diversity also builds resilience and makes good ecological and economic sense on the farm (Fortier, 2014; Shiva, 2015).

Longspell Point is a family farm located in Kingsport, Nova Scotia, that grows a wide variety of vegetables and grains. The McMahons have been farming for over 28 years. Two decades ago, they made the transition from conventional to organic methods, focusing on building their soil biology. Jeff McMahon speaks fondly of their growing ability to work soil that is "fluffier, loftier – where you can simply stick seeds in and watch them grow" (personal communication, 24 October 2018). He attributes this success to growing a balance of foods and "staying small enough that we don't do things we shouldn't be doing" (personal communication, 25 October 2018).

Longspell Point is a beautiful example of an ecologically sustainable farm, and its economic sustainability raises complex questions about the role of animals and meat consumption that are inherent to integrity economics. Animals play an integral role at Longspell Point, supplying fertility through manure, grazing marginal lands, contributing to farm income, and filling the niche of customers looking for sustainably and humanely raised meat. Financial sustainability for small-scale producers within economic structures and cultural norms that place higher value on products such as meat, wine, and chocolate than on staples such as vegetables and grains is a serious economic challenge. Complex questions surrounding the role of animals must be approached with integrity and a recognition of the broader economic and cultural shifts required to support a widespread move towards plant-based diets.

The McMahons value providing high-quality, safe, healthy food for themselves and their community, building strong relationships, and creating a place where their children and grandchildren love to return. Longspell Point Farm sells its produce through the farmers' market and provides grains and flours to local, independent bulk food stores, as well as artisanal bakeries. They have found a business model built on diversity, scale, strong relationships – with people and land – and hard work that is successful on their terms. Time, juggling all the different aspects of the farm, and a lack of appropriate funding programmes for small producers are ongoing challenges, but Jeff points out that experience and a sense of humour go a long way. He stresses the importance of integrity: staying true to your values and avoiding the temptation to take the easy route.

Hope Blooms: maple-sage salad dressing

The food on our plate is a feast for our noses as well as our eyes and taste buds. Wafting above the vibrant colours – deep orange carrots and ruby beets – a whiff of maple and sage rises from the translucent greens and reds of our Longspell Point salad. The salad dressing, handmade with local, organic herbs, comes from *Hope Blooms*. Salad dressing represents the magic of creating something delicious by combining things that don't easily mix well together: oil and vinegar. This metaphor is not lost on Hope Blooms. Now over a decade old, Hope Bloom's vision of bringing diverse communities together through engaging their youth in food entrepreneurship has never been more important.

Halifax's North End, an area marginalized by systemic racism, is home to Hope Blooms, a gathering place for members within the community to exchange stories, as well as seeds, and share cultures, as well as meals. It serves as both a community garden and an herb garden designed and managed by youth. Here they grow some of the ingredients in their premium salad dressings featured in various retail outlets and farmers' markets in Nova Scotia. The proceeds from the sale of salad dressings provide youth a source of employment and are also a future resource for post-secondary tuition. Youth empowerment and entrepreneurship may have been the primary goals of Hope Blooms, but the power of food as a connector, as a bridge between different worlds, is what shines through in their work. Families varying in ethnicity and socio-economic status come together in a multi-generational model to educate each other about the importance of what food they choose to purchase and put into their bodies. The role of a salad dressing, as something that pulls a salad together, highlights how Hope Blooms embodies the role of connector: connecting food to celebration, resistance, and resilience.

Eos Natural Foods: tomato-lentil stew

Next on our plate are protein-dense lentils in a rich and satisfying tomato-lentil stew. While some Nova Scotian farmers and gardeners grow their own dried beans and hazelnuts, most of the beans, lentils, nuts, seeds, and the butters and mylks they are made into, are sourced from distributors of bulk foods and supplies like *Eos Natural Foods* in Wolfville, Nova Scotia. Managed and staffed by a warm and knowledgeable team, Eos is stocked with consciously curated food, herbal medicine, natural body products, kitchenware, and linens. Eos opened its doors in 1973 and has been run by Amanda Vaz since 2013, with the goal of inspiring wellness in the community. Vaz and her staff take a gentle approach to encouraging better nourishment, which includes nutrition, cooking from scratch, rituals of sharing food with others, and exploring the relationships between nutrition, community, mental health, and the environment. Vaz hopes to inspire customers to take more responsibility for their own health and food choices.

Much thought is put into choosing the products Eos offers, as well as analyzing prices to ensure affordability. Plant-based medicines are seen as an essential part of health care. They do not carry products that contain genetically modified corn, soy, or sugar, artificial colours or flavours, glucose, or fructose. The few products that do not fit these criteria have been grandparented onto the shelves to accommodate the expectations of long-time customers. Vaz makes efforts to visit farms and processing plants, meet growers, and support local suppliers. During the growing season, there are local greens and ferments in the fridge, and the counters are covered with fresh cherry tomatoes, peppers, garlic, ginger, and berries.

Eos makes products available to a broad clientele who come for a wide variety of reasons: loyal customers in their 60s, 70s, and 80s who have been shopping at Eos for years; health-conscious women starting families; university students who are conscious, curious, or following trends; tourists; community members; and those referred by health practitioners to their large supplement section. Education is central to the business and being a small store with 12 employees offers plenty of opportunities for personal connections. Vaz believes that in addition to the products, customers come for social connection in a calming space.

In addition to high-quality food, Eos is committed to fairness to humans, other businesses that make-up the supply chain, and the environment. However, as natural foods become mainstream, large suppliers, such as Costco and Amazon, are able to provide these same products at reduced prices, and more customers are buying groceries online. Also, the mass of available health information is saturating and confusing: it is easy to take advantage of people when they are vulnerable, particularly around health. In such an environment, Vaz strives for Eos to be a thoughtful and sensitive place. She sees her customers consciously choosing to support Eos and making the best choices they can. She encourages her staff to honour these intentions and sees her business not as a political platform, but an opportunity to share knowledge and empower customers to make informed choices.

Grown and foraged: wild mushroom ragout

The last dish on our plate may be the most important in this shift towards succulent sustainability: something we've harvested ourselves. On this plate, it's a ragout of wild oyster mushrooms foraged from the woods, but it could also be swiss chard grown in a garden, dandelion greens harvested from a lawn, blackberries found on a walk, or fresh parsley grown in a planter on a windowsill. The defining characteristic of this portion of the meal is that it's the result of a relational transaction – a direct connection with the source of our food – rather than an economic one. Growing and foraging is an act of rebellion and empowerment. It is a positive action that can be taken in the midst of the enormity of the challenges in our food system. In Wendell Berry's (1971) words, "Better than any argument is to rise at dawn and pick dew-wet berries in a cup" (p. 49). Harvesting food creates space for growing care and commitment in the relationship with our bodies and the land and fosters an appreciation of efforts of growers and businesses in our local community. Increased support of local businesses as a result of this appreciation perpetuates the growth of an integrity economic system.

The current economic model pushes consumers to be removed from food, leaving knowledge in the hands of experts. Integrity economics involves a re-integration of food as a central issue and eaters as empowered actors, even producers, in food systems. Growing vegetables, harvesting wild berries or herbs, or foraging mushrooms are small and big acts that reignite connection to food and land, allowing eaters to reclaim from the transactional economic sphere some autonomy over what we put into our bodies. Harvesting food sharpens discernment around fluctuating food trends and health claims, moving "health benefits" from the world of calories and nutrient content to knowing the quality of food through lived experience. Harvesting and foraging draw attention to plants and their particular cycles, seasonality, and timing, allowing eaters to momentarily step out of human-centric perspectives and see these sources of nourishment as the gifts that they are (Kimmerer, 2013). Locally producing and preparing even one aspect of a meal offers an opportunity to counter the all-to-common waste – of food and packaging – grounded in an appreciation for the effort and resources required, and it brings accountability to taking more than needed or letting food rot in the fridge.

Acadia University: scaling out and deep

While individual decisions about what we put on our plates have a significant collective impact, larger players such as institutional food service providers wield substantial influence on food production, processing, and consumption patterns. In a market-driven economy, the combination of profit-oriented corporations and the commodification of food within an industrialized food system (Ackerman-Leist, 2013; Morgan & Sonnino, 2008) means that economic considerations largely overshadow social, health, and ecological costs. Shifting institutional menus to feature more plant-based options offers the potential for significant investment in local vegetable, fruit, legume, and grain production, leading to health benefits for eaters and environmental and economic benefits for the whole community.

Acadia University hosts approximately 3,500 students in the Annapolis Valley. Over the past six years, concerned faculty, staff, and students have been engaged in sustained efforts to shift towards more healthy, just, and sustainable food at Acadia. In this pursuit, one common, and unpalatable, response from food service providers is that such changes will result in increased cost of food services. Plant-based menus are one solution to this dilemma, as they can simultaneously lighten the load on our bodies, our wallets, and the planet. Plants are typically less expensive than even the cheapest meats and seafood, allowing providers the financial flexibility to invest in high-quality, sustainable produce. A plant-focus is also an opportunity to align menus with seasons and avoid the baggage of animal welfare concerns. Plants provide a much higher nutritional return for land, water, and energy used: for example, land produces two to ten times as much protein when planted in cereals than when it is devoted to beef production; for legumes, this ratio is between 10:1 and 20:1 (Horrigan et al., 2002).

In May 2017, the annual conference of the Canadian Network of Environmental Education and Communication took place at Acadia and change makers at the university used this opportunity to showcase what delicious, healthy, and sustainable institutional food could look like. Nine meals plus snacks were served for over 350 people using over 80% local ingredients, including organically grown vegetables, fresh and frozen fruit (it was, after all, May in Nova Scotia), grains, and flours. Plant-based, seasonal menus that prioritized quality over variety were critical to offering sustainable foods at lower prices than the average cost of regular catered meals. An increased plant focus in menus to meet multiple outcomes of health, sustainability, and affordability is now a key part of Acadia's Food Services Plan, which informs its residential, retail, and catering operations.

Conclusion: boundaries and relationships foster integrity

The basis for an integrity economic system is interdependence: recognizing, celebrating, supporting, and serving our relationships with ourselves, our families and close friends, our broader communities, and the more-than-human life that surrounds and sustains us. In the current economic model, growth is ostensibly boundless, and choice and independence are valued over celebrating interdependence and having fewer, value-driven options (Daly & Farley, 2011). In an interview with Snell (1992), Wendell Berry reflects,

> Today, local economies are being destroyed by the pluralistic, displaced, global economy, which has no respect for what works in a locality. The global economy is built on the principle that one place can be exploited, even destroyed for the sake of another.
>
> (p. 29)

In contrast, an economy that cares for all relationships is necessarily one that respects human, social, and ecological boundaries. In a consumerism-driven society, boundaries are seen as limitations; in integrity economics, boundaries define the container within which people can thrive, and living within these boundaries provides connection and direction – the antidote to the sense of lack that drives consumerism. In an economic system that largely ignores them, acknowledging these boundaries and the ecological, social, and personal consequences of crossing them is a conscious choice. Negative and positive feedback loops provide information about where these boundaries are: we might experience them internally, learn about them through feedback from another, observe changes in our environment, or learn about them through research. For example, a shift in behaviour towards eating little to no meat may come as a result of the experience of how your body feels when eating a higher proportion of plant-based foods or of hearing stories from friends about the treatment of animals in factory farms. This shift could also be inspired by the increasing variety of enticing, plant-based options available at local restaurants that fuel your imagination and confidence in cooking plant-centric meals or by reading an article about greenhouse gas emissions associated with meat production. Noticing and committing to being responsive to these various feedback loops is one way to navigate the complexity of food systems. This response is needed at both the personal level – finding and negotiating the boundaries that matter most in our personal, daily food choices, such as how it is produced or procured – and at a societal level – having laws and policies to ensure that food systems are cognizant and respectful of these boundaries, which may include public procurement policies with targets for local and plant-based procurement or governmental supports for small-scale, sustainable producers. Food, as both an intimately personal and universal experience, is an accessible gateway to experiencing interdependence.

We recognize that there are many challenges in achieving this vision. It will require a cultural shift in our relationship to food and the perceived cost barrier of internalizing social and ecological costs through sustainable production: there is an urgent need for systemic supports for producers and eaters. Yet we are fuelled by the conviction that food systems can be ecologically restorative, socially cohesive, and key to building vibrant and resilient local economies; these case studies are inspiring examples of doing so. Each business in this chapter demonstrates economic opportunities that exist within these geographical, ecological, and human boundaries. Geographical boundaries are reflected in working with the culture, land, and climatic conditions of the region in which they are based. Ecological boundaries are respected by celebrating simplicity and seasonality, and by keeping initiatives at a scale where humans, more-than-human beings, and local landscapes are not shrunk beyond recognition. Human boundaries are recognized in working to provide nourishment through minimally and thoughtfully processed foods that are affordable and accessible, support animal welfare, and provide decent living and working conditions for people. By building relationships of trust and transparency, these businesses engage in collaboration and community building, respecting social boundaries, and strengthening social bonds. These boundaries can serve as signposts on a road map for those creating business models with integrity and help pave the way towards succulent sustainability.

The people behind businesses that embody integrity economics all see the educational role of their work: they are providing not only products and services but also the opportunity to challenge conventional economic equations, to bring more of our relationships within the sphere of our transactions, and to imagine and live out other ways of feeding ourselves. For us, the complexity *and* cohesiveness of working towards sustainable food systems lies in embracing all of these relationships. In this conversation about the benefits of, and feasible paths towards, plant-based diets, it is imperative to address contexts, limitations, and contradictions. One of the defining characteristics of integrity economics is the willingness to ask difficult questions and diving into practical examples that highlight the economic structures and cultural changes needed to make a widespread, societal shift towards plant-based foods indeed raises many questions. Is there a place for small numbers of sustainably and humanely raised animals in small-scale, mixed farms? Can the roles animals traditionally play in providing fertility and grazing pastures be more sustainably fulfilled in other ways? How difficult is it for farms to be economically viable if they cut out income from higher value products such as meat? How must our economic landscape change to support producers to provide the plant-based foods we need to be eating? Is a shift towards a more plant-centric diet rather than one that completely eliminates animal products more palatable and imaginable for the majority of the population? Changes need to be humanly as well as environmentally, socially, and economically viable in order to be sustainable, and lasting changes must be motivated by joy and excitement, rather than guilt. Succulence must go hand in hand with sustainability.

These questions are complex and require ongoing engagement. This complexity is partly why this chapter offers, not answers, boundaries and values as starting points and guiding lights on this path towards succulent sustainability: a future where feeding the human population also sustains and enriches the planet and more-than-human beings, and supports local communities and economies while nurturing good health through delicious, nourishing food!

References

Ackerman-Leist, P. (2013). *Rebuilding the foodshed: How to create local, sustainable, and secure food systems*. White River Junction, VT: Chelsea Green Publishing.

Berry, W. (1971). *Farming: A handbook*. Berkeley, CA: Counterpoint LLC.

Daly, H. E., & Farley, J. (2011). *Ecological economics: Principles and applications*. Washington, DC: Island Press.

Davis, D. R., Epp, M. D., & Riordan, H. D. (2004). Changes in the USDA food composition data for 43 garden crops, 1950 to 1999. *Journal of the American College of Nutrition*, 23(6), 669–682.

182   *Chaiti Seth, et al.*

Fitch, C., & Santo, R. (2016). *Instituting change: An overview of institutional food procurement and recommendations for improvement.* Baltimore, MD: Johns Hopkins Centre for a Livable Future.

Fortier, J. (2014). *The market gardener: The successful growers handbook for small-scale organic farming.* Gabriola Island, Canada: New Society Publishers.

Garnett, T. (2011). What are the best opportunities for reducing greenhouse gas emissions in the food system (including the food chain?). *Food Policy, 36*(1), S23–S32. https://doi.org/10.1016/j.foodpol.2010.10.010

Goggins, G., & Rau, H. (2015). Beyond calorie counting: Assessing the sustainability of food provided for public consumption. *Journal of Cleaner Production, 112*(Pt. 1), 257–266. doi:10.1016/j.jclepro.2015.06.035

Health Canada. (2019). *Canada's food guide.* Retrieved from https://food-guide.canada.ca/en/

Horrigan, L., Lawrence, R., & Walker, P. (2002). How sustainable agriculture can address the environmental and human health harms of industrial agriculture. *Environmental Health Perspectives, 110*(5), 445–456.

Kacera, W. (2006). *Ayurvedic tongue diagnosis.* Twin Lakes, WI: Lotus Press.

Katz, S. (2012). *The art of fermentation.* White River Junction, VT: Chelsea Green Publishing.

Kimmerer, R. (2013). *Braiding sweetgrass.* Minneapolis, MN: Milkweed Editions.

Loladze, I. (2014). Hidden shift of the ionome of plants exposed to elevated CO_2 depletes minerals at the base of human nutrition. *eLife, 3*, e02245. doi:10.7554/eLife.02245

Maren, C. (2018, January 24). *The epidemic of food allergies and sensitivities.* Retrieved from https://drchristinemaren.com/food-allergies-and-sensitivities

McMichael, A. J., Powles, J. W., Butler, C. D., & Uauy, R. (2007). Food, livestock production, energy, climate change, and health. *Lancet: Energy and Health, 5*(370), 1253–1263.

Morgan, K., & Sonnino, R. (2008). *The school food revolution: Public food and the challenge of sustainable development.* London, UK: Earthscan.

Moubarac, J. C. (2017). *Ultra-processed foods in Canada: Consumption, impact on diet quality and policy implications.* Montréal, Canada: TRANSNUT, University of Montreal.

Niebylski, M., Lu, T., Campbell, N., Arcand, J., Schermel, A., Hua, D.,. . . ., & Liu, P. (2014). Healthy food procurement policies and their impact. *International Journal of Environmental Research and Public Health, 11*(3), 2608-2627.

Orrhage, K., & Nord, C. E. (2000). Bifidobacteria and lactobacilli in human health. *Drugs Under Experimental and Clinical Research, 26*(3), 95–111.

Pollan, M. (2007). *The omnivore's dilemma: A natural history of four meals.* New York, NY: Penguin Random House.

Poore, J., & Nemecek, T. (2018). Reducing food's environmental impact through producers and consumers. *Science, 360,* 987–992. doi:10.1016/j.foodpol.2010.10.010

Shucmacher, E. F. (1973). *Small is beautiful: Economics as if people mattered.* New York: Harper & Row.

Shallcross, L. J., & Davies, S. C. (2014). Antibiotic overuse: A key driver of antimicrobial resistance. *British Journal of General Practice, 64*(629), 604–605.

Shiva, V. (2015). *Earth democracy: Justice, sustainability and peace.* Berkeley, CA: North Atlantic Books.

Shuman, M. (2015). *The local economy solution.* White River Junction, VT: Chelsea Green Publishing.

Singh, R. K., Chang, H., Yan, D., Lee, K. M., Usmak, D., Wong, K., . . . Liao, W. (2017). Influence of diet on the gut microbiome and the implications for human health. *Journal of Translational Medicine, 15*(1), 73. doi:10.1186/s12967-017-1175-y

Slavin, J. (2004). Whole grains and human health. *The Nutrition Society, 17*(1), 99–110.

Snell, M. B. (1992). The art of place: An interview with Wendell Berry. *New Perspectives Quarterly, 9*(2), 29–34.

Xu, Z., & Knight, R. (2015). Dietary effects on human gut microbiome diversity. *British Journal of Nutrition, 113*, S1–S5.

12 Plant-based food movements designed to increase health of individuals and the nation

Sally Lipsky and Kathleen May Kevany

Introduction

Through the case study method, this chapter examines the leadership of health and environmental advocate Nelson Campbell, along with the roles played by interconnected organizations and networks seeking to improve public health by emphasizing health promotion and illness prevention. This is the story of a growing social movement. The need for social change is apparent: the growth in modern industrial agricultural and global corporatization is resulting in unprecedented public health and environmental outcomes. While still a scourge on humanity, the number of people dying worldwide from infectious diseases is declining. However, evidence shows that in greater numbers, morbidity and mortality are escalating due to non-communicable, lifestyle diseases. The World Health Organization recognizes that social determinants of health contribute to these debilitating lifestyle diseases (World Health Organization, 2011, 2014). Clinical medicine is equipped to deal with only some of the causes and solutions to non-communicable diseases. Social factors – including poverty, inequity, social justice, and marginalization – are combined with, and become compounded by, political and economic forces. These forces, which manifest as health policy focused on illness care and food environments driven by market control, result in unhealthy outcomes for communities, particularly for those most disadvantaged (Morland & Evenson, 2009). In a global context, more resources and researchers need to be dedicated to non-communicable diseases, as attention to these diseases is not currently prioritized in line with their contribution to the global burden of disease (McQueen, 2013). To effectively grapple with the range of health issues and their contributing factors requires collaboration amongst medical specialists, political and social scientists, economists, and environmentalists, amongst others, as part of systemic, integrated approaches. To avoid the continuous spread of preventable, unnecessary illnesses, health promotion activities should emphasize social action and social change focused on prevention.

Methods

Literature review

This research includes a review of the literature that shines light on problems arising from industrialized food systems, as well as alternative approaches that are seeking to avert greenhouse gas emissions (GHGE) and reductions in symptoms contributing to non-communicable diseases. We set out to answer two research questions: (1) What are some theories for social movements applicable to the emergence of the plant-based movements? (2) What might an in-depth review of a plant-based movement reveal about the process, partners, and possible outcomes? We conclude with recommendations that are supported by findings in the literature and the case study.

Case study and participant observation

We utilize an explanatory case study method, widely used in social sciences, as an effective approach for data collection and as a tool to illuminate contemporary real-life phenomenon. We include a single-case design and integrate findings from the literature review and participant observation to strengthen the validity of the data (Zainal, 2007). As a researcher on plant-based food movements, one of the authors (Kevany) attended, observed, and interviewed Nelson Campbell at a Healing America kick-off event in January 2018 and at the launch of the PlantPure Community Action Model for social change in November 2018. Kevany was able to document some of the elements of the campaign orchestrated by Campbell and his extended team, along with the veracity of the message and the degree of receptivity. Data gathered from these events and interviews also inform this analysis.

Scientific foundations

Meat-centric diets

As described in the previous chapters, human and environmental health have been under threat by highly processed meat-centric diets. Growing bodies of literature have revealed the adverse impacts of industrial animal agriculture and the connections of these food systems to debilitating climate change. Tolkien (1937/2002) reminds us that it does no good to leave a dragon out of your calculations, if you live near one. Goodland (2012) seems to adhere to this policy with a headline, "Food and Agriculture Organization (FAO) Yields to Meat Industry Pressure on Climate Change" (n.p.) challenging the minimization of the adverse impacts of animal agriculture by the FAO, which reported it was only 18% of global emissions (Steinfeld et al., 2006). Another assessment by Goodland and Anhang suggests a more pronounced impact from animal agriculture. These authors indicate that the life cycle and supply chain of domesticated animals raised for food have been vastly underestimated as a source of GHGs with at least 51% of human-caused greenhouse gas attributable to livestock (2009, p. 11). Without significant change, the detrimental environmental effects of our food system could increase by 50%–90% by 2050 (Springmann et al., 2018).

Food environments

In addition to the impacts of meat diets on global warming and climate change, links to disease, obesity, and food environments are widely known (Holsten, 2009; Morland & Evenson, 2009). Yet diets aimed at reducing harm have been challenging to achieve. At an ever-increasing level, corporations have taken control of food systems. By design, corporations are driven by profit and, all too often, maximize profit by selling products that trade health for increased sales. Liberalized trade agreements and greater access to global markets by multinational corporations facilitate broader distribution of food products low in nutrition and high in fat, oil, salt, and sugar (Nestle, 2013). Such forces are enabling a worldwide *nutrition transition* (Lang, 2009; Mason & Lang, 2017), where foods of lower nutrition are replacing foods with higher nutritional value as the common food produced and consumed. For example, the ubiquitous positioning of unhealthy foods and the distance to, and inaccessibility of, healthy food outlets – including supermarkets, fruit and vegetable markets, and natural food stores – adversely affect family food environments and individual diets (Morland, Wing, Roux, & Poole, 2002). Food environments arise from a composite of government policies, political and industry influences, and built environments, as well as consumer beliefs and behaviour around food. Colin Campbell (2018) explains how dietary guidelines have been politically compromised and informed by scientifically inaccurate advice, and consequently they misinform professionals and the public, particularly around the dietary amount of protein required. And unsurprisingly, nutritionists, dieticians, physicians, and other health professionals perpetuate this misunderstanding of what Colin Campbell describes as "the most disastrous policy in the past century with adverse consequences that are more significant than many people may realize" (personal communication, 2 November 2018). As he further describes, "No information on health is so profoundly important but so misunderstood. WFPB effects are broad and prevent and suspend or cure all types of ailments. The change is rapid and sustained, while animal proteins are correlated to all cancers" (T. C. Campbell, 2018).

Growing obesity

These conditions are producing obesogenic environments driven by dominant beliefs, practices, and norms that lead to places that breed less health, particularly for those most disadvantaged (Sandler, 2007). These conditions should be viewed as structural injustices that are systemic and social, rather than driven by biological or personal circumstances (Sandler, 2007). Prevalence of obesity and diabetes is increasing worldwide (Holsten, 2009; WHO, 2016). Annually, the majority of deaths are associated with modifiable lifestyle behaviours, such as dietary intake and physical activity (The Secretariat for the Intersectoral Healthy Living Network, 2005). Greger (2015) notes, "For most of our leading killers, nongenetic factors like diet can account for at least 80 or 90 percent of cases" (p. 12). As Western populations increase their rates of chronic diseases (obesity, coronary heart disease, hypertension, type 2 diabetes, autoimmune diseases, cancers), a growing body of research underscores the role plant-centred diets have in preventing, fighting, and even reversing these same diseases (Buettner, 2012; Schnabel et al., 2019). According to a recent EAT-Lancet report, dramatic change to our food systems is urgently needed to reverse perilous threats to human and planetary health (Willett et. al., 2019). To adequately address the critical challenges of planetary and human health, societies must tackle the issue central to both – unsustainable, global food systems (Swinburn et al., 2019).

Plant-centric diets

Goodland and Anhang (2009) note that replacing livestock products with healthier, plant-friendly food options could be our most direct strategy for reversing climate change. This strategy aligned with the suggestion made a decade ago by the then chairman of United Nations Intergovernmental Panel on Climate Change (IPCC) that selecting less meat could be a workable approach for immediate action in reducing GHGE and climate change (Walsh, 2008). Similarly, scientists studying targeted goals of the 2015 Paris Agreement conclude that shifts from animal to plant-based protein are necessary (Harwatt, 2018). In his book *Whole, Rethinking the Science of Nutrition*, Colin Campbell invites readers to imagine a story:

> Let's say Group B, the control group, still gets four to five [heart] attacks a week on average. Group A, the group getting the new treatment [WFPB], gets no more attacks at all. None. Zero. Hundreds of data points are no longer required when the effect is so large. The likelihood that such profound, consistent results are the result of chance is nearly zero.
>
> (2013, p. 23)

Such mounting evidence calls into question the lack of expeditious transformation of our food systems to prevent escalating lifestyle diseases, increase equity, and reduce and reverse environmental impact.

Whole-food, plant-based movement

These connections between diet, lifestyle, and disease are also detailed in the groundbreaking *China Study* (2004). In this book, renowned researcher of nutritional biochemistry, T. Colin Campbell, with his son Dr. Thomas Campbell, analyze 20 years of data collected from one of the largest and most comprehensive studies of human nutrition. The authors describe the strong relationship between food and disease and explain how a whole-food, plant-based (WFPB) diet optimizes long-term health and well-being. A WFPB diet consists of a wide variety of succulent fruits, vegetables, grains, legumes, nuts, and seeds. A plant-based diet contains no animal-based foods – beef, pork, poultry, seafood, eggs, or dairy – and has minimal added oils, sugar, salt, and processed foods. Colin Campbell, often referred to as the "science father" of the plant-based movement, states, "There are virtually no nutrients in animal-based foods that are not better provided by plants" (Campbell & Campbell, 2004, p. 230).

There is a distinction between vegan and WFPB diets. Like plant-based eaters, vegans do not eat animal-based foods. However, vegans may be consuming many foods of little nutritional value, such as processed meals and snack foods, and desserts made with added sugar, oil, and refined flour. WFPB eating can be equated with a health-promoting vegan diet. Table 12.1 summarizes some of the differences amongst dietary patterns.

An expanding body of research, along with more public attention to diets, have contributed to the social movements around plant-based, local foods, sustainable diets, and animal rights, amongst others. Particularly in Western countries, rapidly growing movements towards consuming less animal foods and more plant foods are becoming more evident (Shanker & Mulvany, 2019). This growth is breeding a significant expansion of the demand

Table 12.1 Descriptors for some dietary patterns

	Plant Foods	*Animal Foods*	*Processed Foods*	*Added Fats, Oils, and Sugar*
Whole Foods, Plant Based	Include	Exclude	Minimal	Minimal
Vegan	Include	Exclude	May include	May include
Vegetarian	Include	No meat, poultry, or seafood Include dairy and eggs	May include	May include
Omnivore	Include	Include	May include	May include

Source: Campbell, T. C., & Campbell, T. M. (2004). *The China study: The most comprehensive study of nutrition ever conducted and the startling implications for diet, weight loss and long-term health*. Dallas, TX: BenBella Books (used with permission).

for plant-based foods, consumer items, and lifestyle products. For example, between 2016 and 2017, sales in plant-based foods grew in excess of 8% (Cision, 2017). In the UK, those selecting plant-based foods rose by 360% between 2006 and 2016 (Quinn, 2018). In Germany, consumption of meat has declined steadily since 2011 (The Local.de, 2018). Walton suggests that 17% of Americans are eating a plant-based diet either exclusively or predominantly, while another 60% said they are cutting back on meat-based products (as cited by Gelski, 2017). A 2018 Canadian study showed that 63% of those living on largely plant-based diets were under 38 years of age (Charlebois, Somogyi, & Music, 2018). From average citizens to health-care professionals, scientists, and environmentalists, increasing numbers of people, particularly younger people, are promoting and adopting plant-based diets. Next, we look into such efforts that culminate into social movements.

A social movement model

Levi Strauss social change theory

Food movements are helping to create change by challenging how we understand, respect, and interact with food (Scrinis, 2007). Many food movements seek to inspire change by illuminating unexamined practices and assumptions that previously were impenetrable (Meyer & Land, 2005). A social movement, as defined by researchers, would need to demonstrate a series of strategic campaigns, where citizens make sustained, collective effort to transform an existing political, economic, or social system (Fuchs, 2006). Social movements emerge out of a perceived need for, and opportunity to bring about, desired change. The San Francisco-based Levi Strauss Foundation developed a contemporary theory for social change in its work with non-profit organizations (Grant, 2014). As opposed to the traditional top-down hierarchy, this approach contains four fluid, concentric circles – with leadership in the centre, followed by organizations, networks, and, in the outer circle, a larger social movement. To increase speed and scope of change, collaborative outreach and use of social media are instilled throughout as illustrated in Figure 12.1. The Levi Strauss theory is distinctive with its design to embrace grassroots action, shared leadership, collaborative partnerships, diverse and engaged constituents, and a vision where the whole is greater than the sum of its parts (Grant, 2014). This theory is applied to understand the objectives, structures, and intricacies of our case study, the primary subject of this chapter.

Case study of a social movement: PlantPure Nation

Leadership

In 2015, Nelson Campbell released his film, *PlantPure Nation* (Corry & Campbell, 2015), in theatres in over 100 communities across the US.

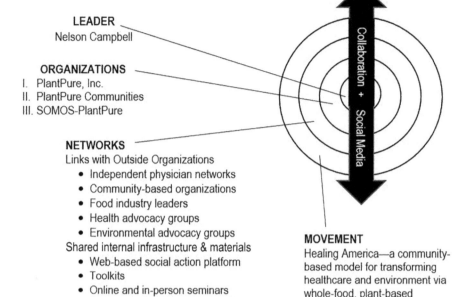

LEADER
Nelson Campbell

ORGANIZATIONS
I. PlantPure, Inc.
II. PlantPure Communities
III. SOMOS-PlantPure

NETWORKS
Links with Outside Organizations
  • Independent physician networks
  • Community-based organizations
  • Food industry leaders
  • Health advocacy groups
  • Environmental advocacy groups
Shared internal infrastructure & materials
  • Web-based social action platform
  • Toolkits
  • Online and in-person seminars
  • Frozen meals and other food products
  • Local Pods (plant-based support groups)
  • Ten-day immersion program
  • Film production assets and team

Collaboration + Social Media

MOVEMENT
Healing America—a community-based model for transforming healthcare and environment via whole-food, plant-based nutrition

Figure 12.1 Elements of the PlantPure Community Action Model. Adapted from
     Grant, 2014, Levi Strauss social change theory.
Source: Authors own work, created for this volume.

Touring with him was his father, T. Colin Campbell, who sought to stress the importance of people needing to know about their food, the corruption in politics driving ill-informed national nutrition guidelines, and the power of the agri-food industry in undermining public health. Nelson's commitment to developing his community action movement grew out of his knowledge of his father's renowned nutrition research and educational career. Nelson's advocacy work draws on his own background in political science and economics, and his insights and experiences as a socially conscious business entrepreneur.

In *PlantPure Nation*, Nelson explores a wide range of issues, including food sources and availability, limits of modern medicine, and corruption within the political process. The film documents result from a ten-day Jumpstart programme in a small town in rural North Carolina. Participants received ten days of prepared meals, along with plant-based education and cooking demonstrations. Results of biometric testing (height, weight, body mass index, blood pressure, cholesterol, LDL, HDL, and triglycerides) after only 10 days were remarkable. As a result, the plant-based immersion programme quickly gained momentum in the community, with five successive programmes, each one drawing larger crowds. This small sample offered promising evidence and provided the basis for a political showdown on the floor of the Kentucky House of Representatives. The film details Nelson's partnership with a Kentucky legislator and their unsuccessful bid to establish a pilot programme that would build upon the benefits of a plant-based diet. Given the influence of the animal agriculture industry on government and policy, it was unsurprising that this legislative approach did not succeed. The film concludes with a rousing, bottom-up call for viewers to form local support and advocacy groups to align resources around these methods to improve the health of communities and their members.

Organizations

PlantPure, Inc

Following the documentary, Nelson and his team launched the for-profit PlantPure, Inc. organization as a vehicle to develop and deliver plant-based foods, along with transformational education materials for in-person and web-based learning. Under the PlantPure brand, delicious, nutritious entrees are produced, frozen, and marketed to those transitioning to plant-based living. PlantPure also fills a significant gap with programmes for employers and physicians. The PlantPure Rx programme enables physicians to prescribe patients a food-based, ten-day immersion programme, modelled after the successful Jumpstarts demonstrated in *PlantPure Nation*. PlantPure also developed a seminar programme that can be delivered in-person or online on its web-based platform.

PlantPure Communities

In 2016, Nelson founded the non-profit PlantPure Communities organization (PPC) with the purpose of "building stronger, healthier, more sustainable neighborhoods" (PlantPure Communities, 2019). PlantPure Communities provides tools and information to support groups and organizations to work creatively to increase reach and impact. The organization employs a professional staff, with Jodi Kass as the executive director and Nelson as chairman of the board of directors. Also, an advocacy council offers guidance on public policy, programme activities, and recommendations for collaboration with other groups and organizations. For example, PPC works with the Physicians Committee for Responsible Medicine (PCRM) to advocate for the provision of healthful foods through the national Supplemental Nutrition Assistance Program for low-income households.

Local pods

A key component of PPC is its support of the rapidly growing network of Pods. Pods are independent, yet interconnected, local groups that focus on promoting the whole-food, plant-based culinary philosophy and educating the community through programming and exposure to the succulence of plant-based foods. Each Pod has a local leader who volunteers to organize meetings and programmes, prepare communications, welcome new members, and reach out to potential partners. To guide and support local leaders, the PPC organization provides online toolkits containing resources, recipes, handouts, and templates for organizing and engaging people in community events. Toolkits include Transitioning to WFPB, Dining Out, College Campuses, Restaurant Campaign, Gardening, School Lunch, and VegFests. Also, new Pod leaders are encouraged to participate in a mentorship programme that connects them with more experienced leaders. Furthermore, PPC provides leaders with access to online office hours, seminars, and an interactive Facebook community. There are over 500 Pods worldwide, with growing numbers daily, totalling over 200,000 participants as of March 2019.

Local Pods play an important role in the plant-based movement by providing comradery and reinforcement – key to sustaining WFPB habits. As an illustration, approximately 10% of adults are lapsed vegans or vegetarians who have reverted to eating animal foods primarily because of isolation and lack of involvement with like-minded people, and most would like to resume a healthy plant-centred diet (Humane Research Council, 2014). By building on the principles of self-directedness, local leadership, inclusion, and broad engagement, local Pods can be significant catalysts for community change as they mobilize resources and citizens to transition towards plant-based living.

Moving medicine forward

PPC has also developed targeted campaigns with other leaders and partners. The Moving Medicine Forward Collaboration, led by Dr. Michael Klaper, works to incorporate whole-food, plant-based nutrition into physician training. Educating physicians about how food choices impact disease is crucial to integrate WFPB nutrition into patient care and preventative approaches. Increasing medical professionals' knowledge of healthy eating and active living is also discussed in Chapters 6 and 7.

Food-climate coalition

Another PPC project is its Food-Climate Coalition Building Initiative. PPC is working with other health and environmental leaders to build a coalition to heighten public awareness of the environmental impact of food choices, especially the impact of these choices on our climate. This network works across fields and organizations to create much-needed social and environmental change (N. Campbell, 2018).

Oasis Jumpstart Program

In keeping with Nelson's vision of serving people in food deserts and low-income communities, PPC offers the Oasis Jumpstart Program to bring the plant-based nutrition message into underserved communities. Private donations provide monies for biometric testing and a supply of frozen meals for 10-day immersions, which typically involve 30–35 participants. Local Pod members provide educational materials, cooking demonstrations, and support throughout the ten days and beyond. Eleven Oasis Jumpstarts were completed in 2017 and 2018 in underserved neighbourhoods in Arizona, California, Georgia, Rhode Island, and Tennessee. More are planned for 2019.

PPC's restaurant campaign

Pod members also are instrumental in advancing another initiative, PPC's Restaurant Campaign. This is a coordinated, proactive partnership with local restaurants to encourage them to offer at least one plant-based, oil-free meal on their menu. This campaign is gaining traction: as of March 2019, 106 restaurants have earned Certificates of Participation in the Restaurant Campaign. Though the majority are in the US, restaurants engaged in this effort are also in Australia, Bulgaria, Canada, Denmark, India, Israel, and Italy.

Networks of organizations

PlantPure Community Action Model

The aforementioned organizational and community programmes are being integrated into a holistic, community-based model called the PlantPure Community Action Model. Developed and supported by PlantPure, Inc., PlantPure Communities, and other partners, this model is positioned to aid health-care providers, Pods, and other local groups to bring the message of plant-based nutrition to every sector of a local community.

Key to the PlantPure Community Action Model is the engagement of physicians. More physicians are showing interest in the results arising from WFPB diets, and this has led to a pioneering collaboration with SOMOS Community Care. SOMOS Community Care is a network of over 2,500 independent primary care physicians working in underserved neighbourhoods in four of the five boroughs of New York City. These physicians serve a population of mainly Medicaid patients of Latino culture who face many day-to-day challenges with health, employment, and finances. SOMOS is unique in that it is a community-based primary care provider with a mission of proactive outreach, especially to medically high-risk individuals. SOMOS is committed to understanding local cultures and families, and working to help them enjoy preventative health care and quality of life.

PlantPure Rx

Dr. Diego Ponieman, SOMOS chief medical officer, is leading the charge for this collaboration that includes physicians, nurses, dietitians, staff, patients, community leaders, and community resources. The collaboration is focused on the PlantPure Rx programme. As noted previously, this programme is a ten-day, physician-supervised immersion that supports patients in learning about and experiencing the health benefits from eating a plant-based diet. The PlantPure Rx programme provides daily plant-based meals that are frozen and ready to heat and eat during their immersion programme. Patients also benefit from education, initially in the form of a one-day seminar at the outset of the ten-day immersion, as well as a cooking class on the seventh day. They obtain biometric testing and meet with their physician before and after the programme. After patients complete the ten-day immersion, they also are introduced to the local Pod, where they can obtain ongoing education and much-needed peer support. Though SOMOS extends into the four boroughs of New York City, this plan initially focuses on the Washington Heights community with the goal of studying and then replicating the Plant-Pure Rx programme in other communities served by SOMOS.

Built into the design of the SOMOS strategy are strong external partnerships:

- Community Partners: An anchoring community group agrees to provide space for seminars, Pod meetings, and health screenings, and helps with outreach into the local area.
- PlantPure Communities: The local Pods hold regular neighbourhood-based meetings that include peer support – crucial for sustaining plant-based lifestyles – along with sharing learning materials, recipes, success stories, and plant-based potlucks.
- PlantPure Food Support: PlantPure provides frozen meal entrees without any profit markup for use in the ten-day immersion program. In addition, PlantPure is developing a new line of meal starter products that are affordable for low-income consumers.
- PlantPure Seminar: The seminar consists of five, hour-long instructional modules that introduce participants to the science and succulence of a plant-centred diet, to be delivered in English and Spanish, and presented in person by an instructor or online.

The SOMOS strategy is focused primarily on demonstrating how physicians can help to heal their patients through plant-based nutrition, using a ten-day immersion programme, supported by the education and food of PlantPure and the Pod programme of PlantPure Communities. After this physician-driven programme is demonstrated and evaluated in New York, additional elements are scheduled to be added. A key component to expanding this movement is the web-based social action platform that enables Pods and other local groups to launch outreach campaigns in a community and target the public, employers, health-care providers, faith-based groups, schools, and other local sectors.

Additional plans include working with independent physicians to form a network, and if such a network exists, these physicians would be invited to deliver the ten-day immersion programme. As well, important support will be provided to enable these networks to negotiate capitated contracts with health insurers. These contracts will provide upfront payments to health-care providers to deliver care to a defined patient population over a defined time period. If providers of services can reduce the types and range of care needed through reductions in illnesses and medications, cost savings can be realized and become a bonus for the physician network. These capitated contracts, therefore, are a mechanism to support physicians who are committed to healing their patients through plant-based nutrition with a financial complement to the community-based PlantPure programme. Reductions in health-care costs and savings to government and insurance funders can be found in the literature – for example, a 2017 study from the UK and Belgium as countries enjoying improvements in health and reductions in the burden on the health-care system (Schepers & Annemans, 2018).

Disrupting medicine

Yet within the broader context, the health-care industry offers no financial incentive for large health-care systems to embrace plant-based eating to prevent or heal disease. These systems rely on a steady stream of insured sick patients seeking treatment in the form of drugs, surgeries, testing, and other expensive procedures. Perhaps ironically or tragically, as Nelson stated, there is a symbiotic relationship between sick patients and the profitability of the industries delivering health care in the US (personal communication, 2 November 2018). To substantially reduce demand and subsequent costs for health care, Nelson says we must get people and the environment healthy: both are more effectively achieved through a whole-food, plant-based diet (personal communication, 2 November 2018). As a result, Nelson's PlantPure Community Action Model, with its innovative approaches, cross-sectoral collaboration, patient empowerment, and financial incentives through capitated insurance contracts has the potential to disrupt and transform the practice of medicine.

This model returns the focus to the primacy and power of the person, who, with support for developing new habits and his or her self-determination, can dramatically improve his or her health status. Independent physicians who carry less of a burden of capital-intensive investments in clinical infrastructure and technology, compared to the larger health systems, are freer to innovate and employ preventative care with lower costs. Physicians could then focus more on helping patients with their healing and well-being, and in the process enjoy some financial and professional rewards through keeping patients healthy. In this model, physicians and medical teams work together to educate and help heal and prevent, rather than to simply treat or manage lifestyle diseases. The design includes connecting patients with plant-based communities that provide social support, practical assistance with dietary changes, and exposure to the preparation and taste of succulent plant foods. This combination of ingredients contributes to sustaining lifestyles changes. Action can be driven by a compelling vision of prescient leaders that ignites the participation of motivated individuals and networks of organizations dedicated to improving individual and community well-being. Such a model does not need to rely on governments or businesses to drive change; leaders are all the people taking action to improve their health and that of the environment. Building on their signs of progress, the expansion of this PlantPure Community Action Model is planned for launch across the USA through the Healing America Campaign.

Healing America Campaign

Nelson and Colin Campbell kicked off the introductory leg of the Healing America Campaign in 2018 through travelling to cities and towns across the US to share their vision and framework for community mobilization. Based on the scientific foundations for a plant-based diet (Campbell & Campbell, 2004), Nelson articulated a message seeking to transcend political and socio-economic differences by focusing on the desire citizens share around attaining more health and happiness, and his vision for a new paradigm of community empowerment. This new social movement provides structures, symbols, and motivating messaging to enable communities to improve the lives of their members. With the level of engagement that has been aroused across the country, Nelson Campbell is uniting citizens around reclaiming their health, empowering local communities, and healing the environment.

The Healing America Campaign will scale a strategy across the US that can be succinctly summarized in three steps:

1 Organize independent physicians into networks and recruit existing networks
2 Help these physician networks negotiate capitated insurance contracts
3 Leverage the PlantPure Community Action Model with the Pod infrastructure to support plant-based nutrition in communities nationwide, and aid physician networks in their quest to heal patients through plant-based nutrition (N. Campbell, private communication, 2 November 2018)

In early 2020, Nelson expects to undertake a second national tour to launch the PlantPure Community Action Model in cities across the US, with initial focus on communities with a strong Pod presence. Additionally, this campaign will leverage the aforementioned web-based social action platform, not only to empower Pods to undertake outreach initiatives in their local communities but also to share information amongst Pods regarding best practices.

Forging a movement

Some indicators thus far suggest the strategies are working. In just over three years, more than 200,000 people have engaged with this movement. These numbers suggest that participants are benefitting from the plant-based lifestyle, recruiting others to the movement, and remaining active in the Pod network of PlantPure Communities.

Nelson and his team intend to grow this movement through the creative use of media. As the Healing America Campaign progresses, in addition, Nelson and his team are planning to produce short educational, provocative, and inspiring videos based on stories and themes from the campaign and may extend their reach further through hosting a Healing America online show that includes special guests and updates from the campaign, as well as a companion culinary education show. See Table 12.2 for further listings of organizational and network components fuelling this movement.

As with *PlantPure Nation*, the feature film *Healing America* will end with a "call to action" to inspire community leadership to work together to heal the environment, advance social justice, and significantly enhance the physical and emotional health of individuals and communities. Key messages of *Healing America* (2019) include the following:

- Whole-food, plant-based eating can heal people and our planet, and it is imperative that we collectively and immediately address this pressing problem of climate change.
- Armed with information, resources, and organizational structure, citizens can work together within local communities to collectively address health, environmental, and social problems.
- A new social and political paradigm of community empowerment can help heal the partisan divide that characterizes political debate, not only in the US but also around the world.

Conclusion

This case study examined the multiple elements involved in a social movement. We applied the Levi Strauss social change theory to analyze the Plant-Pure Community Action Model. The role of the visionary leader appears paramount to develop and activate interconnected networks of people

Table 12.2 Interconnected organizations and networks within a movement

PlantPure, Inc. +	PlantPure Communities + Communities	SOMOS and Other Early → Adopters	Healing America Movement Movement
1 Film production *PlantPure Nation* 2 Ongoing media productions 3 Plant-based food products 4 Educational programming 5 *PlantPure Rx*: ten-day immersion programme • Frozen meals/meal kits • Instructional seminar 6 Web-based social action platform to support community campaigns 7 Outside partnerships: • Food industry • Health-care providers • Corporate wellness providers	8 Pod network 9 *Oasis*: 10-day immersion programme for low-income groups • Frozen meals/meal kits supplied without profit markup • Local Pods • Educational modules and online toolkits for Pods 10 Restaurant Campaign 11 Food/Climate Coalition Building Initiative 12 Outside partnerships: • Moving Medicine Forward Collaboration • Food/Climate Coalition Advocacy Partners	13 Physician-supervised 10-day immersion programme • Frozen meals/meal kits • Local Pods • Instructional seminar and educational modules for Pods 14 Web-based social action platform to support community campaigns, including food-climate advocacy 15 External Partners: • Community organizations • PlantPure, Inc. • PlantPure Communities	16 PlantPure Community Model-Components 17 National & international network of pods 18 Film production Healing America feature film 19 Other media productions 20 External Partners: • Healthcare and other partners • Pod network • Other local community organizations

Source: Authors own work, created for this volume.

willing to take action for human and environmental health. The formation and presence of substantial organizational infrastructure also seem essential to the pace of progress made in the span of four years. Additionally, the networks of partners and like-minded agents of change contribute to the outreach and inclusion of many more becoming involved with this movement. The evidence suggests this is a movement that is not about to fade, as it has many more initiatives underway. Given that the public appetite is growing for succulent and sustainable food choices, we anticipate further growth in this and other food movements that enable citizens to engage collectively in transforming their food systems. Further assessments are required to determine the continued efficacy of the campaign, the programmes, and their impact on human and environmental health. For example, while short-term results show improvements in biometric indicators through the ten-day immersion programmes, longer term studies would be of value, especially regarding sustaining changed behaviours and lifestyle.

Nelson Campbell and his team are creating the architecture for a grassroots movement for social, political, and environmental change. The components required for success are many, including vision, risk-taking leadership, willingness to partner with key organizations, and a focus on empowering and engaging local communities and cross-sectoral networks. With greater numbers of people taking action together, the impact of this movement may become even more pronounced and noticeable. As choosing plant-based options enables more foods to be produced and distributed more ethically, effectively, and efficiently, it makes sense that more people might be willing to make this their default option. As Campbell and Jacobson (2013) note,

> At this point, any scientist, doctor, journalist, or policy maker who denies or minimizes the importance of a whole food, plant-based diet for individual and societal well-being simply isn't looking clearly at the facts. There's just too much good evidence to ignore anymore.
>
> (pp. xiii–xiv)

References

Buettner, D. (2012). *The blue zones: 9 lessons for living longer from the people who've lived the longest*. Washington, DC: National Geographic.

Campbell, N. (2018). *Food climate campaign*. Retrieved December 7, 2018, from https://plantpurecommunities.org/foodclimatecampaign

Campbell, T. C. (2018). *Nutrition: The missing medical science* [Video file]. Retrieved from www.youtube.com/watch?v=iR0HH4Zd0_Y

Campbell, T. C., & Campbell, T. M. (2004). *The China study: The most comprehensive study of nutrition ever conducted and the startling implications for diet, weight loss and long-term health*. Dallas, TX: BenBella Books.

Campbell, T. C., & Jacobson, H. (2013). *Whole: Rethinking the science of nutrition*. Dallas, TX: BenBella Books.

Charlebois, S., Somogyi, S., & Music, J. (2018, October 30). *Release: New Dalhousie study finds that 6.4 million Canadians limit the amount of meat they eat, and number will likely grow.* Retrieved from www.dal.ca/faculty/management/news-events/news/2018/10/30/release__new_dalhousie_study_finds_that_6_4_million_canadians_limit_the_amount_of_meat_they_eat__and_number_will_likely_grow.html

Cision. (2017, September 13). *Plant based foods sales experience 8.1 percent growth over past year.* Retrieved from www.prweb.com/releases/2017/09/prweb14683840.htm

Corry, J., & Campbell, N. (2015). *PlantPure nation* [Documentary film]. Mebane, NC: PlantPure, Inc. Retrieved from www.plantpurenation.com

Fuchs, C. (2006). The self-organization of social movements. *Systemic Practice and Action Research, 19*(1), 101–137. doi:10.1007/s11213-005-9006-0

Gelski, J. (2017, July 5). A broader market for plant protein. *Food Business News.* Retrieved from www.foodbusinessnews.net/articles/9571-a-broader-market-for-plant-protein

Goodland, R. (2012, July 11). FAO yields to meat industry pressure on climate change. *The New York Times.* Retrieved from https://bittman.blogs.nytimes.com/

Goodland, R., & Anhang, J. (2009). Livestock and climate change: What if the key actors in climate change are . . . cows, pigs, and chickens? *World Watch Magazine, 22*(6), 10–19.

Grant, H. M. (2014). *Pioneers in justice: Building networks and movements for social change.* San Francisco, CA: Levi Strauss Foundation. Retrieved from http://levistrauss.com/wp-content/uploads/2014/05/Levi-Strauss-Foundation-Pioneers-in-Justice.pdf

Greger, M. (2015). *How not to die: Discover the foods scientifically proven to prevent and reverse disease.* New York, NY: Flatiron Books.

Harwatt, H. (2018). Including animal to plant protein shifts in climate change mitigation policy: A proposed three-step strategy. *Climate Policy, 19*(5), 533–541. doi:10.1080/14693062.2018.1528965

Healing America. (2019). *Join the movement to heal America!* Retrieved from http://healingamericatogether.com

Holsten, J. E. (2009). Obesity and the community food environment: A systematic review. *Public Health Nutrition, 12*(3), 397–405.

Humane Research Council. (2014). *Study of current and former vegetarians and vegans.* Retrieved from spot.humaneresearch.org/2014vegstudy

Lang, T. (2009). Reshaping the food system for ecological public health. *Journal of Hunger & Environmental Nutrition, 4*(3–4), 315–335. doi:10.1080/19320240903321227

Mason, P., & Lang, T. (2017). *Sustainable diets: How ecological nutrition can transform consumption and the food system.* London, UK: Taylor & Francis.

McQueen, D. (2013). Commentary: NCDs, health promotion and public health. *Global Health Promotion, 20*(4 Suppl.), 90–92.

Meyer, J. H., & Land, R. (2005). Threshold concepts and troublesome knowledge (2): Epistemological considerations and a conceptual framework for teaching and learning. *Higher Education, 49*(3), 373–388.

Morland, K., Wing, S., Roux, A. D., & Poole, C. (2002). Neighborhood characteristics associated with the location of food stores and food service places. *American Journal of Preventive Medicine, 22*(1), 23–29. doi:10.1016/S0749-3797(01)00403-2

Morland, K. B., & Evenson, K. R. (2009). Obesity prevalence and the local food environment. *Health & Place, 15*(2), 491–495.

Nestle, M. (2013). *Food politics: How the food industry influences nutrition and health* (3rd ed.). Berkeley, CA: University of California Press.

PlantPure Communities. (2019). *About PlantPure communities*. Retrieved from https://plantpurecommunities.org/about-plantpure-communities/

Quinn, S. (2018, May 18). Number of vegans in Britain rises by 360% in 10 years. *The Telegraph*. Retrieved from www.telegraph.co.uk/

Sandler, J. (2007). Community-based practices: Integrating dissemination theory with critical theories of power and justice. *American Journal of Community Psychology, 40*(3–4), 272–289.

Schepers, J., & Annemans, L. (2018). The potential health and economic effects of plant-based food patterns in Belgium and the United Kingdom. *Nutrition, 48,* 24–32.

Schnabel, L., Kesse-Guyot, E., Allès, B., Touvier, M., Srour, B., Hercberg, S., . . . Julia, C. (2019). Association between ultraprocessed food consumption and risk of mortality among middle-aged adults in France. *JAMA Internal Medicine, 179*(4), 490–498. doi:10.1001/jamainternmed.2018.7289

Scrinis, G. (2007). From techno-corporate food to alternative agri-food movements. *Local-Global: Identity, Security, Community, 4,* 112–140.

Shanker, D., & Mulvany, L. (2019, January 25). We'll always eat meat: But more of it will be 'meat'. *Bloomberg Business Week*. Retrieved from www.bloomberg.com/

Springmann, M., Clark, M., Mason-D'Croz, D., Wiebe, K., Bodirsky, B. L., Lassaletta, L., . . . Rami Zurayk, P. (2018). Options for keeping the food system within environmental limits. *Nature, 562,* 519–525.

Steinfeld, H., Gerber, P., Wassenaar, T. D., Castel, V., Rosales, M., & de Haan, C. (2006). *Livestock's long shadow: Environmental issues and options*. Food & Agriculture Organization.

Swinburn, B., Kraak, V. I., Allender, S., Atkins, V. J., Baker, P. I., Bogard, J. R., . . . Dietz, W. H. (2019, February 23). The global epidemic of obesity, undernutrition, and climate change: The Lancet Commission report. *The Lancet Commissions, 393*(10173), 791–846. doi:10.1016/S0140-6736(18)32822-8

The Local.de. (2018, February 7). *Meat production drops 'significantly' as Germans spurn the sausage*. Retrieved from www.thelocal.de/20180207/consumption-and-production-of-meat-in-germany-on-the-decline

The Secretariat for the Intersectoral Healthy Living Network. (2005). *The integrated pan-Canadian healthy living strategy*. Retrieved from http://publications.gc.ca/pub?id=9.666741&sl=0

Tolkien, J. R. R. (1937/2002). *The hobbit*. New York, NY: Houghton Mills.

Walsh, B. (2008, September 10). Meat: Making global warming worse. *Time Magazine*. Retrieved from http://content.time.com/

Willett, W., Rockström, J., Loken, B., Springmann, M., Lang, T., & Vermeulen, S., . . . Jonell, M. L. (2019). Food in the Anthropocene: The EAT – Lancet Commission on healthy diets from sustainable food systems. *The Lancet Commissions, 393*(10170), 447–492. doi:10.1016/S0140-6736(18)31788-4

World Health Organization (WHO). (2011). *Rio political declaration on social determinants of health*. Rio de Janeiro, Brazil: World Health Organization.

World Health Organization. (2014). *Global status report on noncommunicable diseases 2014*. Retrieved October 13, 2016, from www.who.int/nmh/publications/ncd-status-report-2014/en/

World Health Organization. (2016). *Global report on diabetes*. Retrieved October 13, 2016, from http://apps.who.int/iris/bitstream/10665/204871/1/9789241565257_eng.pdf

Zainal, Z. (2007). Case study as a research method. *Journal Kemanusiaan, 5*(1), 1–6.

13 What's on the menu? Succulent sustainability goes to school

Mary McKenna, Jessica Wall, and Suchitra Roy

Introduction

"Next week we get to eat the radishes", an elementary school student announces proudly as we tour the school's garden. Would she be so excited about eating radishes if she were not participating in growing them? Would she even know where radishes come from? An increasing number of school students are reaping the many benefits of plant-based diets, including gardening and post-harvest activities, diverse educational experiences, and preparing and eating plant-based foods.

Succulent sustainability focuses on tasty, enriching, nourishing plant-based food grown and eaten within equitable and just food systems that support environmental, economic, and social health. Schools are an excellent setting for these initiatives because they reach young people who are still developing their knowledge, skills, and values pertaining to food and the environment. Succulent sustainability provides multiple avenues for students to learn academic subjects and life and vocational skills and experience positive role modelling. Through succulent sustainability, students can improve their food literacy, especially their literacy related to plant-based diets, within a framework of sustainability education. Food literacy "involves broad sets of skills and knowledge about food origins and systems; individual and collective food experiences; food identification; physical, emotional and mental effects of food; as well as basic abilities related to food" (Truman et al., 2017, p. e213). It may also include a critical component: "A foundation of knowledge, understanding and awareness that allows people to perform actions related to food and think critically about their relationship to the broader food system" (Truman et al., 2017, p. e213).

Sustainability education addresses social and ecological aspects of the food system and food choices, as well as strategies for improving environmental impacts of food production, processing, transport, preparation, consumption, and waste (Rojas et al., 2011), and includes food topics, such as local, seasonal, organic, and fair trade foods, animal welfare, and plant-based diets. Table 13.1 provides examples of potential components and outcomes,

Table 13.1 Succulent sustainability: examples of components and outcomes

Sample Components	Sample Outcomes
Grow food sustainably from seed selection/propagation to post-harvest; through outdoor gardens, garden towers, greenhouses, or windowsill gardens; from short-term projects, such as micro-greens, to long-term projects, such as apple trees. Implement projects that are traditionally, historically, and culturally relevant; promote acceptance of new foods; and celebrate diverse food cultures. Teaching a number of academic subjects through hands-on experiences.	Increased hands-on knowledge and skills regarding gardening, harvesting, and post-harvesting that connect to classroom teaching. Increased moderate physical activity. Increased life skills through socializing, teambuilding, and planning, and increased connections to the natural environment. Increased knowledge about careers in agriculture. Increased pride by students in their school environments and increased school engagement by parents.
Buy food sustainably through local food procurement from direct contact with primary producers and processors or regional food hubs, and from sources that are sustainable, seasonal, and fresh (when possible), based on fair trade practices and safe handling practices and waste minimization.	Increased support for those who use sustainable production practices, such as local farmers. Increased community resilience. Decreased carbon footprint due to sustainable food production and distribution practices and decreased long-haul transportation.
Prepare food sustainably in plant-based and seasonal cooking classes for students and through school food service outlets and entrepreneurial food labs. Preserving food, composting food, and minimizing waste. Teaching academic subjects through hands-on experiences, including entrepreneurship.	Increased life skills, such as food preparation, budgeting, and waste reduction. Increased appreciation and willingness to try new foods and increased knowledge about food tastes and textures, seasonal foods, and food costs. Increased skills and knowledge regarding vocational cooking and entrepreneurship. Increased skills and knowledge of mathematics, science, social studies, and other academic subjects.
Offer food sustainably and support positive role modelling by capitalizing on seasonal, affordable, and plant-based foods and dishes in all food outlets and at all events (plus school fundraisers), and offering them within food environments that make the healthy choice the easy choice, minimize waste, and enable composting and recycling.	Improved dietary intakes by students and better health of students. Increased connection to local communities. Increased traditional and cultural food knowledge. Improved tastiness of food and school-wide modelling of normative healthy eating of sustainable plant-based food. Decreased food waste.

Sample Components	*Sample Outcomes*
Educate about food sustainability through curricular and extracurricular opportunities to grow, buy, prepare, offer, and eat food sustainably, and explore multi-sensory properties of food within succulent sustainability. Using food education to address larger issues of food systems, such as policies, ethics, food security, growing food, food processing and distribution, food consumption and food cultures, food waste, food and the environment, and policies, programmes, and practices by individuals and society that influence the food system. Visits or tours with farmers, gardeners, chefs, or other community food leaders and advocates about food and sustainability. Awareness building by students about food and sustainable eating within the school and community.	Improved knowledge and skills pertaining to food and food systems, inter-relationships amongst individuals, communities, producers, policies, and society, and knowledge of actions to improve food systems. Increased understanding of connections between academic learning (e.g. science, health, history, culture, language, mathematics, ecology, and social studies) and experiential learning with food.
Implement sustainable food policies to support land use for growing food; local food procurement; food safety, transportation, distribution, availability, culture, and heritage; facilities; education and training; waste reduction; and food systems integration.	Enhanced food systems that are interconnected through policies and programmes, and support plant-based, sustainable food. Improved physical, societal, social, economic, and environmental health.

Source: Authors own work, created for this volume.

and although each is presented individually, they are interconnected and collectively encompass a systems approach to food sustainability.

Succulent sustainability in Canadian schools

Although all schools in Canada have the potential to implement succulent sustainability initiatives, an examination of the current school food landscape indicates that more work is needed to improve students' food intakes and school environments:

- Canada's young people need to eat more plants! A survey of 13,749 young people between the ages of 2 and 18 found the average consumption of vegetables and fruit was less than five servings per day, well short of recommendations, especially for older youth. Food quality also needs improvement: only 13% of the calories consumed from grains were whole grains, 46% of the calories from fruit were from fruit juice, and 21% of the calories from vegetables were from potatoes (Jessri, Nishi, & L'Abbe, 2016).

- Fruit and vegetable availability in schools is increasing but needs improvement. Although no national data exist, British Columbia researchers found that between 2007–2008 and 2011–2012, elementary schools increased the availability of fruits and vegetables while middle and high schools did not, however, baseline levels at elementary schools were much lower (Watts, Mâsse, & Naylor, 2014).

- Currently, school food programme and policy lack national coordination, and there is no easy channel by which to support plant-based eating in schools. This situation may improve, as the 2019 federal budget announced their intention to create a national food programme (although attached no funds in the budget) (Department of Finance Canada, 2019), and the 2019 Canada's Food Guide promotes the consumption of plant-based foods (Health Canada, 2019).

- Few provinces recommend that schools procure provincially grown food: exceptions include Ontario and Nova Scotia (Nova Scotia Department of Education and Department of Health Promotion, 2006; Ontario Ministry of Education, 2010).

- Provincial curricula focus on food and health and individual choice, and seldom address critical food literacy (Anderson & Falkenberg, 2016; Robertson & Scheidler-Benns, 2016). Only 10% of science, health, physical education, and home economics courses that addressed food included critical food literacy (e.g. students learn about the local and global environmental impact of food choices) (Anderson & Falkenberg, 2016).

- Teacher training on school food sustainability needs attention. Research from Manitoba (Falkenberg & Babiuk, 2013) found that teacher education programmes addressed sustainability education in individual courses, not systematically. Potential reasons included a lack of leadership and a lower priority of sustainability education within education faculties (Falkenberg & Babiuk, 2013).

- Monitoring of school and student participation is limited. Only Farm to Cafeteria Canada (F2CC), a national organization that promotes farm-to-school activities, attempts to collect data. Results from 2018 indicated that 1,159 Canadian schools (pre-school through university; fewer than 10% of all schools) in every province and territory reached 809,827 students with some form of farm-to-school (F2S) programming. F2CC reported 559 schools have gardens or greenhouses; 572 offer classes on cooking/preserving local healthy foods; 423 purchase local healthy foods; 407 schools serve local, healthy meals; and 233 schools compost/ address food waste (Farm to Cafeteria Canada, 2018). Students may or may not participate in food activities. A 2011–2012 survey of 937 Vancouver students in grades 6–8 found that 51% of students participated or learned about recycling, 45% Canada's Food Guide, 36% food preparation, 35% foods grown in British Columbia, 32% composting, 27% choosing and/or tasting healthy foods, 21% gardening (although approximately 75% of schools had a garden), and 20% of students reported no food-related activity (Stephens, Black, Chapman, Velazquez, & Rojas, 2016).

Nevertheless, succulent sustainability is taking root across Canada in diverse forms, often grafting on to existing food-related activities. While most initiatives do not identify plant-based eating as a specific goal and none use the term succulent sustainability, their goals are complementary: to increase students' fruit and vegetable consumption, establish school food or farm-to-school programmes, promote food sustainability education, and/ or foster food literacy and leadership. Provincial, territorial, and municipal governments, non-governmental organizations, schools, and communities are leading school-based efforts, supported by students, families, elders, gardeners, farmers, educators, chefs, environmentalists, health professionals, community members, business leaders, and others.

Succulent sustainability in action: research and programmes

A number of research initiatives highlight the types of programmes, partnerships, and outcomes in different parts of the country, including a review of F2S, food and sustainability education, a food leadership programme for youth, a greenhouse project, and a garden project.

Research examples

Researchers in British Columbia highlighted a number of positive examples as part of a provincial review of F2S programmes (Powell & Wittman, 2018). F2S programmes aim to increase the amount of healthy local foods available in schools, promote hands-on experiential learning to improve food literacy, and strengthen connections between schools and communities. School gardens were the most common activity, with one school growing over 35 edible plants, offered in the school and sold to the community. In a school in an Indigenous community with a garden and greenhouse, elders helped students learn to use traditional plants. Another school developed a food literacy curriculum and organized outings for students to local farms. Improved food literacy was a key outcome of F2S programmes, which was fostered

not only through individual skills development and opportunities for healthy eating, but also increased understanding of the structural and

political context of food systems, environmental impacts of food production, community food security, and cultural significance of traditional and wild foods.

(Powell & Wittman, 2018, p. 203)

Think&EatGreen@School (TEGS) was a Vancouver-based project (2010–
2016) that promoted a food system that addresses food sustainability, security, and sovereignty (Rojas et al., 2011). The project aimed to create *food
citizens* who are well informed and practice food-related behaviours that
support a food system that is socially, economically, and environmentally
sound. The university/community/schools project engaged students, teachers, community partners, chefs, and others in food literacy, food growing,
harvesting, preparing, and cooking and waste management, integrating
school cafeterias, school curricula, and policy changes. The project provided small grants to support school projects (57 schools received a total
of $110,000), and organized professional development events for teachers
(over 360 participants) (Rojas, Black, Orregoa, Chapman, & Valley, 2017).
The results were that the number of gardens and the availability of healthy
food in schools increased but not the availability of sustainable food. At
the policy level, TEGS provided input into decisions at local and provincial
levels and helped establish the School Food Procurement Learning Lab in
Vancouver. The researchers concluded that the systems-based approach and
experiential learning activities were valuable; however, they believe it will
take longer and require additional actions to achieve large-scale food systems change (Rojas et al., 2017).

The Food Leadership for Youth Program in Toronto aimed to promote
food literacy, along with health, confidence, and empowerment amongst
high school girls who were new to Canada and/or from low-income
backgrounds (Goldstein, 2016). The no-cost programme operated after
school at the Stop Community Food Centre, which is an important
reminder of the roles community partners can play in supporting succulent sustainability. Participants prepared foods such as salads, pizzas,
or banh mi (Vietnamese sandwiches) and then ate together; organizers
incorporated questions and discussions about the food system into the
programme (Goldstein, 2014). Programme outcomes included improved
cooking skills and increased meals made from scratch, increased interest
in buying healthy foods, higher consumption of fruits and vegetables,
and more openness to trying new foods; greater influence on food-
related decisions by family and friends; increased interest in improving
the food system; and improved self-confidence (Goldstein, 2016). Goldstein (2014) concluded that while the programme enhanced some aspects
of food literacy, potential existed for the girls to participate more fully in
disrupting the existing food system. A visit to the Stop's website indicates
that two programmes provide "opportunities for young people 14+ to
grow, cook, and share healthy food, and to understand sustainable food

systems and the root causes of hunger and poverty from a social justice perspective" (The Stop, 2019).

Action on sustainable foods is not limited to warmer regions of Canada. In Fort Albany, a remote, sub-arctic community in Ontario, a greenhouse serves the community and school. Not only did they use the greenhouse to grow a variety of foods, but it inspired other activities, such as berry harvesting, composting, re-using/recycling, canning/preserving, "green" technology, home gardening, and seed saving. Two students who used the greenhouse commented, "I picked tomatoes in there and I washed them. Then I ate them. Some were sour and some were sweet", and "I got to go into the greenhouse with my science teacher. He talked about the greenhouse effect and how the plants absorb heat" (Skinner, Hanning, Metatawabin, & Tsuji, 2014, p. 9).

A garden project in a Nova Scotia elementary school provided multiple opportunities for student and community engagement. The garden began with a school planting party in the spring and was supported by students' families during the summer. Fall harvesting occurred as part of organized classes and a garden club, which was open to all. Food from the garden was used in the school's snack and lunch programme. Students gained knowledge and skills about growing, preparing, and eating foods, including kale and nasturtiums; valued food systems more highly; and the project contributed to student pride and ownership of their healthy school food environment (Carlsson, Williams, Hayes-Conroy, Lordly, & Callaghan, 2016).

Programme examples

Non-governmental organizations at all levels are working with schools to promote healthier eating that emphasizes plant-based foods and sustainability education. While some organizations focus solely on schools, others target multiple settings that include schools. Likewise, their primary mandate may be food and sustainability or another aspect of food, such as food security. Most organizations offer multi-component programmes, as shown in Table 13.2.

Benefits

As the previous examples highlight, food and sustainability programmes offer many opportunities for student learning and development that address and go beyond traditional academic subjects. Learning can be tailored to the needs of diverse learner groups, including Indigenous populations, new Canadians, students with special needs, and students from vulnerable groups. With purposeful design, all students can benefit in multiple ways.

Colley, Myer, Seabrook, and Gilliland (2018) summarized the benefits of nine Canadian school nutrition programmes, four of which were in Indigenous communities. Most programmes were multi-component, including

Table 13.2 Examples of organizations compatible with succulent sustainability

Organization and Jurisdiction	Mandate	Sample Activities
Farm to Cafeteria Canada, National	To educate and increase capacity to bring local, healthy, and sustainable foods into all public institutions	1 Grants and support to schools across Canada for farm-to-school (F2S) initiatives, such as gardens, local procurement, and salad bars 2 Interactive map of F2S activities 3 National F2S month 4 National F2S conference 5 Educational resources and research (Farm to Cafeteria Canada, 2018)
Agriculture in the Classroom Foundation, British Columbia	To bring local agriculture to students and teach them about food in BC	1 Bi-weekly free fresh fruit and vegetable snack programmes in classrooms 2 Teaching kitchens in schools where students prepare local dishes that are incorporated in the cafeterias 3 Training for school educators on how to integrate food, agriculture, and environmental sustainability in the classroom 4 Local fruit and vegetable fundraisers 5 School gardens (BC Agriculture in the Classroom Foundation, 2019)
Ontario Edible Education Network, Ontario	To get children and youth eating, growing, cooking, celebrating, and learning about healthy, local, and sustainably produced food	1 Advocacy on food literacy, school gardens, and food skills programmes 2 Coordination of local food action hubs that deliver to schools 3 Directory of resources for student nutrition programmes in Ontario for schools, parents, community members, and organizations (Ontario Edible Education Network, 2014)

Organization and Jurisdiction	Mandate	Sample Activities
Équiterre, Quebec	To facilitate the procurement of healthy, local, and sustainable food in public facilities and organizations in Quebec	1 Local and organic fruit and vegetable fundraisers 2 Local food procurement in schools 3 Educational kit on the agri-food system for elementary and secondary school students 4 Healthy snack services, school kitchen gardens, and culinary workshops 5 Healthy, sustainable, and locally grown foods in salad bars (Équiterre, 2019)
Réseau des Cafétérias Communautaires, New Brunswick	To provide nutritious and healthy meals, encourage the purchase of local products, and develop an entrepreneurial culture in communities and schools	1 Healthy local food services to Francophone schools 2 Visits to farms by food service staff to learn about foods they prepare for students 3 Educational materials about local foods 4 Student involvement in school cafeterias to increase entrepreneurial and leadership skills (Theriault, 2014)
FoodShare, Toronto	To ensure that all children and youth have access to healthy food at school through Student Nutrition Programmes	1 Healthy breakfast, snack, and lunch programmes in schools 2 Workshops and training for educators on best practices 3 Schoolyard farming that grows food on school grounds to create employment for students 4 Fresh, affordable, and diverse vegetable and fruit delivery (Bowser, 2019)

Source: Authors own work, created for this volume.

food, education, and/or policy, and/or involving families, peers, and/or community members. Results were not consistent across all programmes, however, benefits involved increased nutrition knowledge, including cooking; increased willingness to try new foods; improved self-efficacy; and positive perceptions of healthy eating. All programmes influenced food intake positively, including an increase in vegetable and fruit intake and a decreased intake of calories.

The BC School Fruit and Vegetable Nutritional Program increases the availability of BC-grown vegetables and fruits in schools. Organizers credit the programme with helping students try new fruits and vegetables, eating more of them, and learning safe food handling – providing a base for lifelong healthy and sustainable eating (BC Agriculture in the Classroom Foundation, 2019).

Garden projects may help older students gain vocational skills. Fresh Roots (2019) in Vancouver uses market gardens to grow food on school properties to help students prepare for potential careers, as well as offering mentoring opportunities while supporting student development and empowerment.

Some benefits are more difficult to assess. A survey of 45 Toronto schools with green school grounds, which may include gardens, reported on the contribution to student and community inclusion, irrespective of gender, class, race, or ability (Dyment & Bell, 2008). As indicated by one parent, "Everyone can join us in the garden. What a great place for a disenfranchised child to meet new people, dig and plant. Our garden is colour blind, inclusive, and warm. Anyone can help us, and they do" (Dyment & Bell, 2008, p. 178). Moreover, the social skills acquired in gardens extended into other aspects of school life, including improvements in students' tolerance, politeness, sharing, and kindness (Dyment & Bell, 2008).

Considerations

Research and programmes to date provide insights when establishing, expanding, and strengthening initiatives to help school students capitalize on the opportunities of succulent sustainability. Considerations include the following:

Build on existing partnerships

Multiple programmes and policies influence food environments and educational opportunities within schools. Even within a single school, different groups may operate different food outlets, food programmes, or other projects. Dyment and Bell (2008), for example, found that while many administrators, teachers, and parents were involved and interested in the Toronto green schools project, support was not universal. Where feasible, collaborating with active and interested individuals and groups will help achieve an environment that provides positive reinforcement for student learning about succulent sustainability and facilitates a systems approach to change.

Plan initiatives strategically

Planning needs to address the different education priorities within provinces, territories, and districts. Fortunately, because succulent sustainability encompasses so many diverse activities, it is very adaptable. For example, British Columbia emphasizes experiential, inquiry-based, and project-based learning. School gardening activities, composting, and food preparation activities address this priority fully. In New Brunswick, entrepreneurship education is encouraged and students in some schools prepare food for sale, with profits donated to charity.

Groups working with schools may find it helpful to consider a staged approach as they set goals and plan change within food systems. They may begin with shorter-term strategies to initiate change, such as classroom education and school gardens. With time, these initiatives may transition to expansion and increased reach, including F2S programmes and partnerships between local food growers and/or school gardens and school food outlets. Lastly, a longer-term aim to work toward throughout the process is to achieve stronger food systems that focus on sustainability, including policies that require sustainable procurement of foods at school (Carlsson & Williams, 2008).

Use and tailor existing educational resources

Many resources exist to help establish succulent sustainability, including information from F2CC, Sustain Ontario, and provincial governments. Alberta Food Matters (Atkey, 2013) developed a Universal School Food Strategy that supports healthy meals and snacks sourced by local producers, student involvement in the cultivation and preparation of food, education on the food system, and relationships with local producers and the development of local food procurement policies when feasible. Nova Scotia published a guide to promote local fruit and vegetables in schools (Annapolis Valley Health Promoting Schools Program, 2010), and New Brunswick published a F2S guide that helps groups establish, implement, and monitor programmes (Atkinson, 2017).

Ensure adequate funding and training

Because plant-based sustainability initiatives are often grafted onto existing activities, obtaining the necessary funds to achieve full implementation can be challenging. Current funding needs to increase to achieve full implementation of succulent sustainability, including the need for facilities to prepare, grow, and offer food in comfortable surroundings. One national advocacy group, the Coalition for Healthy School Food (2019), seeks federal funding for school food programmes and supports procurement of local food where feasible. Professional development for teachers and school staff is also needed, especially to enable a systems approach to sustainable food education. For example, farm visits by food service staff and adding plant-based foods with regional significance to cafeteria menus may increase their ownership and pride in school food.

Monitor process and outcomes

Much of the information in this chapter was drawn from monitoring and assessment activities by researchers and organizations. As Stephens et al. (2016) concluded, more work is needed to assess engagement by students on food sustainability topics and the short- and long-term impact of programmes. In turn, these results can help inform future programmes and policies.

Address policy gaps

Those who champion succulent sustainability must work together to obtain the support needed for robust, flourishing programmes that reach all students. Policy can support the physical infrastructure required, such as gardens and food preparation and serving facilities, funding and training needs, food safety, comprehensive food literacy and sustainability education programmes, and help schools connect with the larger food system to support systems change.

Conclusion (or the end of a new beginning)

This chapter opened with a true story of a student, proud of the radishes she grew in the school garden. It posed a couple of questions, but there are more questions to ask, such as what kind of growing practices did the school use, and how much did they discuss these with the students? Did the programme leaders help the students make connections between the radishes in the garden and the larger food system? What happened to the food from the garden? How many students were able to participate in the garden, how was it managed and by whom, and what was their training? What policy and programmatic support ensures that this plant-based programme will flourish?

Succulent sustainability cuts across traditional curricula and requires physical changes to school environments, additional funds and training, new approaches, collaboration, and bold thinking. These potential changes can be daunting to schools that already face multiple pressures from many sources. The fact that plant-based sustainability has made considerable progress is testimony to its many benefits. For Canada to continue to advance, schools must be supported to maintain and expand current momentum, and encompass all components of food literacy and sustainability, and society must strengthen system-wide changes for plant-based food sustainability. This way, all Canadian students will be able to enjoy radishes grown at their school for many years to come!

References

Anderson, H., & Falkenberg, T. (2016). The role and status of food and nutrition literacy in Canadian school curricula. *Alberta Journal of Educational Research*, 62(1), 87–109.

Annapolis Valley Health Promoting Schools Program. (2010). *Strive for five at school: A guide to promoting fruit and vegetables.* Retrieved from https://novascotia.ca/dhw/healthy-communities/documents/Strive-for-Five-at-School-A-Guide-to-Promoting-Fruit-and-Vegetables.pdf

Atkey, K. (2013). *A universal school food strategy for Alberta.* Retrieved from www.foodsecurityalberta.org/universal-school-food-strategy-alberta

Atkinson, R. (2017). *New Brunswick farm to school guide.* Retrieved from www.farmtocafeteriacanada.ca/wp-content/uploads/2018/03/NB-F2S-Storybook_EN_print_nocrop.pdf

BC Agriculture in the Classroom Foundation. (2019). *BC school fruit & vegetable nutritional program.* Retrieved from www.bcaitc.ca/bc-school-fruit-vegetable-nutritional-program

Bowser, F. (2019). *Healthy kids, healthy future.* Retrieved from https://foodshare.net/program/snt/

Carlsson, L., Williams, P., Hayes-Conroy, J., Lordly, D., & Callaghan, E. (2016). School gardens: Cultivating food security in Nova Scotia public schools? *Canadian Journal of Dietetic Practice and Research, 77,* 119–124. doi:10.3148/cjdpr-2015-051

Carlsson, L., & Williams, P. L. (2008). New approaches to the health promoting school: Participation in sustainable food systems. *Journal of Hunger & Environmental Nutrition, 3*(4), 400–417. doi:10.1080/19320240802529243

Coalition for Healthy School Food. (2019). *Who we are.* Retrieved from https://www.healthyschoolfood.ca/who-we-are.

Colley, P., Myer, B., Seabrook, J., & Gilliland, J. (2018). The impact of Canadian school food programs on children's nutrition and health: A systematic review. *Canadian Journal of Dietetic Practice and Research, 11,* 1–8. doi:10.3148/cjdpr-2018-037

Department of Finance Canada. (2019). *Investing in the middle class: Budget 2019.* Retrieved from https://budget.gc.ca/2019/docs/plan/budget-2019-en.pdf

Dyment, J. E., & Bell, A. C. (2008). 'Our garden is colour blind, inclusive and warm': Reflections on green school grounds and social inclusion. *International Journal of Inclusive Education, 12*(2), 169–183. doi:10.1080/13603110600855671

Équiterre. (2019). *Local food procurement.* Retrieved from https://equiterre.org/en/project/local-food-procurement

Falkenberg, T., & Babiuk, G. (2013). The status of education for sustainability in initial teacher education programmes: A Canadian case study. *International Journal of Sustainability in Higher Education, 15*(4), 418–430. doi:10.1108/IJSHE-10-2012-0088

Farm to Cafeteria Canada. (2018). *Benefits of farm to school: Evidence from Canada.* Retrieved from www.farmtocafeteriacanada.ca/wp-content/uploads/Impact Benefits-Sheet-2018_online_EN.pdf

Fresh Roots. (2019). *Good food for all.* Retrieved from https://freshroots.ca/about/our-vision/

Goldstein, S. (2014). *Advancing youth education on food and food systems to increase food literacy.* Retrieved from https://yorkspace.library.yorku.ca/xmlui/bitstream/handle/10315/30215/MESMP00088.pdf?sequence=1&isAllowed=y

Goldstein, S. (2016). Youth and food literacy: A case study of food education at The Stop Community Food Centre. In J. Sumner (Ed.), *Learning, food, and sustainability* (pp. 181–200). New York, NY: Palgrave Macmillan.

Health Canada. (2019). *Canada's dietary guidelines for health professionals and policy makers.* Retrieved from https://food-guide.canada.ca/static/assets/pdf/CDG-EN-2018.pdf

Jessri, M., Nishi, S. K., & L'Abbe, M. R. (2016). Assessing the nutritional quality of diets of Canadian children and adolescents using the 2014 Health Canada surveillance tool tier system. *BMC Public Health*, *16*, 381–395. doi:10.1186/s12889-016-3038-5

Nova Scotia Department of Education and Department of Health. (2006). *Promotion, food and nutrition policy for Nova Scotia public schools*. Retrieved from https://www.ednet.ns.ca/docs/foodnutritionpolicyguidelines.pdf.

Ontario Edible Education Network. (2014). *Ontario edible education network action plan*. Retrieved from https://sustainontario.com/custom/uploads/2013/06/EdibleEducationActionPlan_Jan2014.pdf

Ontario Ministry of Education. (2010). *P/PM 150: School food and beverage policy*. Retrieved from www.edu.gov.on.ca/extra/eng/ppm/ppm150.pdf

Powell, L. J., & Wittman, H. (2018). Farm to school in British Columbia: Mobilizing food literacy for food sovereignty. *Agriculture and Human Values*, *35*(1), 193–206. doi:10.1007/s10460-017-9815-7

Robertson, L., & Scheidler-Benns, J. (2016). Using a wider lens to shift the discourse on food in Canadian curriculum policies. *Cambridge Journal of Education*, *46*(2), 157–175. doi:10.1080/0305764X.2015.1091440

Rojas, A., Black, J. L., Orregoa, E., Chapman, G., & Valley, W. (2017). Insights from the Think&EatGreen@School Project: How a community-based action research project contributed to healthy and sustainable school food systems in Vancouver. *Canadian Food Studies*, *4*(2), 25–46.

Rojas, A., Valley, W., Mansfield, B., Orrego, E., Chapman, G. E., & Harlap, Y. (2011). Toward food system sustainability through school food system change: Think&EatGreen@School and the making of a community-university research alliance. *Sustainability*, *3*, 763–788.

Skinner, K., Hanning, R. M., Metatawabin, J., & Tsuji, L. J. S. (2014). Implementation of a community greenhouse in a remote, sub-Arctic First Nations community in Ontario, Canada: A descriptive case study. *Rural and Remote Health*, *14*(2545), 1–18.

Stephens, T. A., Black, J. L., Chapman, G. E., Velazquez, C. E., & Rojas, A. (2016). Participation in school food and nutrition activities among grade 6–8 students in Vancouver. *Canadian Journal of Dietetic Practice and Research*, *77*(3), 148–153. https://doi.org/10.3148/cjdpr-2016-003

Stewart, M. (2016). *Nourish your roots: Pilot evaluation 2015*. Bedford, NS, Canada: Nourish Nova Scotia.

The Stop. (2019). *Programs*. Retrieved from www.thestop.org/programs

Theriault, J. (2014). *Public health nutrition framework for action 2012–2016: Improving the food environment in schools in New Brunswick's francophone sud school district case study*. Retrieved from https://www2.gnb.ca/content/dam/gnb/Departments/h-s/pdf/en/Publications/Case-Study_2014_Vitalite_improving-the-food-environment_EN.pdf

Truman, E., Raine, K., Mrklas, K., Prowse, R., Carruthers Den Hoed, R., Watson-Jarvis, K., . . . Elliott, C. (2017). Promoting children's health: Toward a consensus statement on food literacy. *Canadian Journal of Public Health*, *108*(2), e211–e213. doi:10.17269/CJPH.108.5909

Watts, A. W., Mâsse, L. C., & Naylor, P. J. (2014). Changes to the school food and physical activity environment after guideline implementation in British Columbia, Canada. *International Journal of Behavioral Nutrition and Physical Activity*, *11*(50). doi:10.1186/1479-5868-11-50

14 Succulence and sustainability for life

Kathleen May Kevany

Introduction

In this closing chapter, we reflect on the journey we have taken across the landscape of food systems. The way we produce our food, the kind of food we consume, the way we eat, and the places in which we eat can help increase human, animal, and planetary health, and well-being, or, as has been more typical, they can contribute to our decline. Climate change is the biggest social justice, health, and environmental issue of our time. Through this multidisciplinary collection, we have provided systems analyses that substantiate the rationale for our recommending plant-based diets. Plant-based diets, undertaken on a larger scale, are a promising pathway, not just to mitigate but also to aid in reversing global warming and disrupting the prevalence of cancers, diabetes, obesity, and other ailments. In the pages ahead, we invite you to think about how you might share the key messages from these critical findings and how we might embark together on urgent action. We also encourage gathering together in an online community to share ideas and signs of success, and become further inspired by the bold progress of others. Adopting such diets could afford integral and interconnected solutions needed to restore succulence, sustainability, health, food security, and reverse environmental degradation, soil depletion, environmental racism, and speciesism.

Problems demanding responsible action

Food fuels us. Yet served up with our food are multiple forms of energy and most of them are non-renewable. To varying degrees, we all contribute to global food production with its heavy footprint that is threatening local ecosystems, social and political stability, and future capacity to feed ourselves. The palaeontologist Ungar (2018) reminds us that there has been no single ancestral human diet; diets have varied over time and place to enable us to be adaptive eaters, informed and influenced by changing climates, habitats, and knowledge of food. We are well informed now of climate change, biodiversity and habitat loss, contamination, and eutrophication of water systems, coupled with the epidemics of poor health fuelled largely by diets heavy in meat, dairy, and processed foods. The health-care system cannot endure the financial burden associated with diet-related chronic disease. In Canada, for example, three in five Canadians over 20 are suffering from chronic disease and 4 in 5 are at risk (PHAC, 2013), and 60% of Canadians are not consuming sufficient fruits and vegetables daily (Statistics Canada, 2011). Substantial shifts are needed to not only make Canadians healthier but also to address the financial and emotional strains suffered in countries around the world due to growing lifestyle diseases and eco-anxiety and distress.

The conditions in Canada are not unique. Challenges faced in Canada are also playing out around the world; our challenges are global as well as local. Can we see the writing on the wall or the rising sea levels at the doorstep? A 2019 headline reads, "Florida is Drowning. Condos Are Still Being Built. Can't Humans See the Writing on the Wall?" (Bergman, 2019). Climate change is increasingly affecting urban life, rural livelihoods, and agricultural yields. Yet agriculture continues to emit excessive greenhouse gases. Animal agricultural production is constrained by the increasing scarcity and diminishing quality of land and water resources. Channelling feed, food, and fuel through animals to feed the world is not a cost-effective or plausible solution. Devastation to crop production and harvests are contributing to social unrest and the greatest human migration ever seen. And greater volatility in weather patterns is expected to continue and to undermine harvests and food security. Inequitable global food systems and unemployment constraints prohibit access to food and contribute to persistent poverty, with 821 million undernourished in the world in 2017 (FAO, 2018). Inefficient use of significant global resources to produce meat and dairy are hampering the achievement of food security and making nutrition goals less attainable. Without strategies to reduce this inequality and, ideally, to reverse climate change (Hawken, 2016), these and other political and social problems are set to increase.

Many of our societies are facing unrelenting complexity-energy traps, as Qualman (2019) calls them, and these come at great costs. According to Statistics Canada, from 2000 to 2017, farmers grossed $47 billion per year from the markets, but after paying expenses, they were left with $1.6 billion per year in net farm income. If this amount was divided equally amongst the 193,492 farms in Canada, each would be left with $8,300. To support farmers, Canadian taxpayers transferred $3.1 billion per year, but farmers also borrowed $2.7 billion per year additionally (Statistics Canada, 2018 as cited by Qualman, 2018). Based on these figures, the system is not sustaining itself economically very well either. Although some producers prosper with the industrial agricultural model, many more do not.

At the same time, many climate policies affecting agriculture rely on voluntary efforts by individual farmers. Many farmers are adopting stewardship and management practices to reduce adverse impacts in atmospheric emissions and water quality (Greiner, Patterson, & Miller, 2009). Farmers around the world are striving to mitigate or adapt to climate change by adopting new methods and technologies, and advancing productivity largely with modifications to current systems (Haden, Niles, Lubell, Perlman, & Jackson, 2012). However, "investing further in complexity and higher energy costs begins to yield declining marginal returns" (Qualman, 2019, p. 162). As we have suggested in Chapter 2, we are calling for more full-cost or true cost accounting of our food system, the fuller environmental impact, as well as the health and ethical consequences. The euphemism of "externalities" understates the hardships created by our food systems and the burdens they place on people, animals, and ecosystems. The status quo is not affordable, justifiable, nor desirable.

Why plant-based diets and plant-rich living?

The previous chapters have revealed how plant-based diets, along with active living, offer the best preventative approach to illness, health-care costs, global warming, and unethical treatment for humans and animals. The justification for the ubiquitous meat-centric diet is more tenuous and unconvincing. While not a panacea, plant-based approaches do offer the most protective effects for individual and population health; they can not only help mitigate but also reverse global warming, stem the injustice of food insecurity, as well as add to greater global stability. Plant-rich living can help prevent marginalized communities from suffering as a consequence of industrialized agriculture and non-human animals from being subjugated to unnecessary harm, as discussed in Chapters 8 and 9. As Gibbs and Harris argue in Chapter 9, we are working to "make visible the interconnected nature of various forms of oppression", and this collection is increasing our preparedness to challenge assumptions and unquestioned practices that previously were impenetrable. With what we know, should plant-based not become our default diet and widely adopted? The overwhelming evidence reveals multiple benefits from becoming adaptable eaters and advocating for plant-based foods.

While the appetite for plant-rich living is growing, many universities – particularly agriculture, law, medicine, business, and environment programs – are not adequately teaching about these issues, or preparing graduates to harvest the emerging opportunities in plant-based proteins and product development, or replacing animal testing or use in experimental practices (Cleveland, 2014). Research groups can be found in many areas of dietetics and nutrition and food studies societies. We have research around plant production and horticulture. We have environmental studies as well as public health research, but plant-rich living and plant-based diets have not been given prominence in universities. In searching for programmes in Canada, interdisciplinary bodies addressing compounding issues arising from industrial food systems through plant-rich approaches could not be found. As noted in Chapter 7, medical professions are also ill-served when not educated about the importance of nutrition and particularly the merits of plant-based diets. The ideologies of disconnection (Latham, 2016) and the practice of reductionism (Campbell & Jacobson, 2013) still dominate scientific thinking and orientation. While it may be a long way to go to master integration (Watkins & Wilber, 2015), we must appreciate the whole picture with a holistic approach. The optimal food for the majority of the planet appears to be plant-based whole foods (Campbell & Campbell, 2004; Campbell & Jacobson, 2013; Esselstyn, Gendy, Doyle, Golubic, & Roizen, 2014). After all, the "purpose of life is health and that *the optimal and most just way to attain human health is to maximise the health of all organisms* (italics in original) with the most effective way to do that being through food" (Latham, 2016).

Consumer behaviour studies show an array of rationale for choosing to be more plant based. Citizen-consumers may locate themselves along a continuum of selecting plant-based and avoiding animal-based foods. A range of drivers are at play for those who identify as vegetarian, vegan, or plant based. Recent market studies by Waitrose and Partners (2018) indicate that of their respondents, roughly 60% of vegans and 40% of vegetarians were motivated over the recent five years to adopt this new diet and lifestyle for a variety of reasons. The majority were driven by animal welfare concerns at 55%; health reasons prompted 45% to make the change; helping the environment was the inspiration for 38% (Waitrose & Partners, 2018). From a Canadian study in 2018, 63% of those living on largely plant-based diets were under 35 (Charlebois, Somogyi, & Music, 2018). In the UK, the number is climbing for those abstaining from or reducing meat: the proportion of those eliminating all animal products has grown fourfold in the past four years from 150,000 to 600,000 (Vegan Society as cited by Smithers, 2018). Like the findings in Canada, the younger demographic, ages 18 to 34, is significantly driving growth in plant-based diets and plant-rich living. Some high school and college females were found to be motivated by weight control, thus restricting their diets (Forestell, Spaeth, & Kane, 2012). Lea and colleagues (2006) studied consumer readiness to follow a plant-based diet. The study found that the stage of change correlated to a perception of the health benefit of following, and the ease of adopting, a plant-based diet: "This year, we've seen vegan food go mainstream. Whether cooking at home, buying prepared food or trying the newly vegan-friendly restaurants, people are discovering that it tastes amazing" (Waitrose & Partners, 2018). As we learned in Chapter 13, now more frequently, children and youth are learning culinary skills and food literacy through school food programmes. They can test out and experiment with succulence and sustainability of food systems while also improving their tolerance, politeness, sharing, and kindness through respect for food (Bell & Dyment, 2008).

We can all appreciate that food is essential not only for human survival, but it is integral to holidays, celebrations, hospitality, and our evolving sense of ourselves. In her 1979 book, *You Eat What You Are*, Barer-Stein examined and profiled food people choose to eat, how they prepared it, served it, and ate it – fingers or knife and fork? Food choices are heavily influenced by cultural inheritance and personal beliefs. As noted by our authors, it also would be unwise to neglect to factor in the influences of neoliberalism, capitalism, and global corporatization, including how food environments become established and the role of mass media. For too many, food is associated with pain: we can have too much food, or we may suffer from having too little of it.

Plant protein dominants

While the majority in the world include some animal foods in their diets, human diets consist largely of plant-based foods. We know humans can thrive on plant-rich diets. Already the largest portion of the global protein supply is derived from vegetable sources. Henchion, Hayes, Mullen, Fenelon, and Tiwari (2017) assessed the global food supply for protein sources: 57% of our protein comes from plants, 18% from meat, 10% from dairy, 6% from fish, and 9% from other products. So we are well positioned to build on this global foundation of reliance on plant-protein plant foods. Additionally, producing more plants through agro-ecological principles restores soil fertility and helps sequester carbon.

Reversing global warming

Several research initiatives have identified plant-rich diets as one of the world's best strategies to draw down carbon (Project Drawdown, 2014–2019) along with offering healthy diets and sustainable food production (FAO, 2018; Searchinger et al., 2018; Willett et al., 2019)

These interdisciplinary studies developed scientific targets for global food systems that are good for people and the planet. They conclude that diets rich in plant-based foods and with fewer animal source foods confer both improved health and environmental benefits (Willett et al., 2019). Given the dysfunctions emanating from systemic issues, our solutions too must be systemic. In addition to a focus on dietary changes by consumers, emphasis must be placed on addressing political accountability, regulatory environments, and industry influence. Achieving agreement around healthy diets and sustainable food production, and consumption will advance our capacity to feed a global population of ten billion people by 2050. This is a task of enormous magnitude.

Farmers as leaders in sustainability

Over history, nations have developed through expanding their agriculture, including fisheries and forestry, and the infrastructure to support them (Albert & Isife, 2009). Agriculture has helped build civilizations. As argued in these chapters, our civilization is at a critical turning point. Changing course is critical – "business as usual" is no longer an option. In recent communications with Darrin Qualman, the author of *Civilization Critical* (2019), I shared an article about the race to build the next burger (Grunwald, 2019). Darrin shared he appreciated the line from the article, "globally, pastures occupy about one-fourth of the ice-free land on Earth. So changes in how meat is produced and consumed really could have outsize effects" (Grunwald, 2019). Darrin wrote,

> It reminds me of a conversation I had with a wise older cattle producer – a person sympathetic to the project of dramatically reducing emissions from all sources. He said something to the effect of . . . okay, but once the cattle herd is reduced then what? What happens to the land? On much of it, some farmer will probably rip it up for crops (and out will come CO_2) and then that farmer will pour on the fertilizer (and out will come nitrous oxide). His point is a good one. Everything is connected. When you pull at one strand of our food supply tapestry all sorts of things can unravel.
>
> (Personal communication, 6 April 2019)

Rockström suggests that greening the food sectors or eating up our planet is what is on the menu today (as cited in Carrington, 2018). We are faced with serious choices to be made.

If food and agricultural systems remain on their current path, the evidence points to a future characterized by persistent food insecurity and destabilized economies. Many countries have committed to increasing the sustainability of their food and agricultural systems and to the Sustainable Development Goals (SDGs). These goals require coherent and integral approaches to overcome growing inequalities and gender imbalances, to sustain peace, reduce GHG emissions, reverse the demand for resource-intensive animal food products, and prevent food loss and waste, amongst other challenges (FAO, 2018). As noted in Chapter 10, sustainable agriculture is needed to protect and improve upon the civil societies and equitable international trade. To progress at the pace and scale that is needed, farmers need high-quality and accessible information, financial incentives for updating practices, and opportunities to engage with others who also are shifting to sustainable strategies (Greiner et al., 2009).

Business opportunities

Leaders in the creative production and delivery of delectable, nutritious, energy-efficient, and low-carbon foods, "sustainable diets" in short, will help address the growing call for such products and thereby assist in contributing employment and income opportunities in the emerging greener-food economy (Seyfang, 2006). Dietary change and technological innovations on and off farms have become essential, along with strategies along the food value chain to reduce or eliminate food waste (Carrington, 2018). "The health of the planet, and keeping people healthy through better food choices are macro trends that are going to increasingly shape the future of food and agriculture in Canada" (Pulse Canada, 2015, p. 2). As people are living longer and more concerned about their health, addressing the needs of growing numbers of health-conscious consumers and organizations is good for business: "New product launches with plant-based claims have gone up almost seven times since 2011. Plant milks and alternatives for meat are all showing strong growth" (Schug, 2016). With more consumers choosing to avoid meat consumption in modern times and selecting foods that promote health, protect the environment, and do no harm to animals, significant business opportunities are emerging with increasing national and global demand for value-added, high-quality protein foods, as discussed in Chapters 2 and 4. Food and beverage companies are creatively adapting foods and ingredients to optimize particular "functions" and appeal to the consumer, younger and older. Yet more than pharmaceuticals and functional foods, diets largely based on plant-based whole foods are a priority to provide the greatest protective effects in health, equity, and the environment.

Systems of systems thinking

How shall we bring about these changes? Many have offered substantial frameworks or theories for change. Arnold and Wade (2015) state that systems thinking involves synergistic analytic skills, the capability of identifying and understanding systems, predicting behaviours, and devising interventions to produce desired effects. Wilber's integral theories (2001) are instructive for considering multicultural worldviews and the complexity of our problems and interconnectedness of our solutions. Meadows (2008) has written widely on networks of networks and systems thinking. Hosting open hearts and minds become essential in enabling us to wrestle with the magnitude of our challenges and to seize the opportunities disguised as intractable problems. We also borrow from the work of Martynenko (2019), as we embark upon strategies that incorporate intelligent observers, intelligent mechanisms, and intelligent information.

Intelligent and collaborative observers

The magnitude of our challenges is not for the government to solve or for which one sector is responsible; we are all in this together. We all are called on to be intelligent and collaborative observers and agents of change. While our wicked problems may seem big, complex, intertwined, and difficult to tease apart (Watkins & Wilber, 2015), these cannot be reasons for inaction. While we may be at different points in our awareness about climate change, animal rights, food insecurity, and epidemics of ill health, all who are able to help co-create collaborative, integrated solutions are urged to take action. As Watkins and Wilber (2015) write, wicked problems require some forms of behaviour change. Meadows (2008) encourages us to do this work of societal, political, and cultural transformation with humility and an openness for further evolution. As argued in the previous chapters, collaborative strategies are needed in reorienting institutions, politics, economics, and law, as well as our households and our own beliefs and practices.

Intelligent mechanisms

Etzioni (2006) suggests new technologies and disruptive approaches could be leveraged to replenish our debts to nature and help market segments build their green identities from more sustainable, greener products. While not without their critics, technologies, and tools, like biotechnology, may help reduce inputs commonly used in conventional agriculture. Agricultural adaptations that encourage no-till practices are reducing erosion and carbon dioxide emissions and improving soil health while using fewer fossil fuels. Controlled environment agriculture can also be advantageous in supplying plant foods year-round where natural climates may not support this. Examples of intelligent mechanisms may include urban farming and vertical farming, greenhouse technologies, LED lighting, hydroponics, aquaponics, and robotics, along with many other practical solutions.

Intelligent information informing humane responses

We must gather the best available evidence to guide sound policies and practical strategies. To do so, we must have sophisticated approaches to measuring impact through full-cost accounting, investing in prevention, and monitoring economic, social, and environmental outcomes. Our multiple and interconnected issues are demanding plausible solutions and coherence amongst various policies. Nilsson and colleagues (2012) define policy coherence as "an attribute of policy that systematically reduces conflicts and promotes synergies between and within different policy areas to achieve the outcomes associated with jointly agreed policy objectives" (p. 396). While wicked problems are complex, and complexity can be overwhelming, we must apply wise and humane solutions that do not themselves impose new problems (Qualman, 2019). We must acknowledge complexity while also seeking doable and sensible interventions: "More energy makes possible and supports more complexity; but more complexity *requires* more energy" (Qualman, 2019, p. 161). Exposure to intelligence information, like nutritional information on social media, can help citizens to more frequently adopt desired behaviours, such as consuming recommended servings of vegetables or fruit per day. With the information before us now, will we proceed with wisdom and integrity? We turn next to solutions and soul-utions.

Solutions and soul-utions

We envision a world where all are fed, nurtured, and love. Based on the evidence, we have been able to amass in this collection, we call for actions supporting healthy eating and active living across society. Without being prescriptive, we urge the design of *value-based*, not merely value-added, supply chains that offer inspiring options for producers and consumers to live according to their values. We must reclaim more respect for the sacred, pleasurable, and life-giving qualities of food.

Society

We all are called to fulfil our roles in building a fair, affordable, sustainable, and healthy food system. We must systematically identify and uproot causes of oppression and liberate human and non-human animals from it in all of its forms. Our adopting the new ethic of interconnected citizenship should provoke us to challenge the paradox of insatiable consumerism that is destroying the planet. These urgent times call for all of us to become conscious and compassionate citizen-consumers. Before us remains the prospects of reclaiming food as a basic human right, restoring food as a common good, and using intelligent information and mechanisms to enable us to reconnect with where our food comes from and how it is produced; together we can rebuild resilient food systems in every community. We strongly hope that our societies wisely heed any narcissistic tendencies or inclinations towards hubris that place humans as separate from and above other life forms. Echoing Meadows's wise words, we highly advise that wisdom and humility be combined with compassion to reshape humans' perceptions and relationships with all life forms. We particularly ought to undertake healthy questioning of the practices of confining and slaughtering animals for food.

Government

We encourage policymakers, particularly those in agriculture, health, economics, social, and environmental policy, to ensure policy coherence and coordination over the long term to achieve the food-related SDGs and to implement the Paris Agreement. Through monitoring intelligent information, governments can recalibrate towards desired outcomes. It is imperative that governments demonstrate leadership to replace obesogenic food environments. We call for increasing the availability of natural spaces, including parks, public green infrastructure, and active transportation networks. Governments, along with partners in the private and civil society sectors, should be collaborating on strategies to eliminate poverty and marginalization. Federal and state agencies should also exercise regulatory authority to ensure fair wages for all workers, ethical sourcing of food production inputs, fair and accurate labelling, and the safety of food production and processing techniques.

Governments also fill central roles in countering the negative consequences of the mainstream food industry. The effective use of taxes on soda and other sugar-sweetened beverages show the potential for taxing animal foods to decrease production and consumption. International law and trade agreements should promote sustainable and plant-based diets with cultural and regional relevance. Governments may need to levy *polluter pays* environmental taxes that grow with the distance that food travels or with the level of processing it undergoes.

Health

We advocate for integral thinking and preventative approaches across the life course through multidisciplinary/cross-disciplinary health-care professional teams. As having access to even one vegetarian family member, friend, or support person can make a significant difference in helping people shift thinking and habits around plant-based living, it would be prudent for health professionals to become familiar with resources and community groups that support plant-based diets. Health professionals also should be prepared to discuss meat consumption, as inclusion of meat is grounded in common cultural beliefs, family traditions, and self-identity, and it is very easy to access. We also suggest strategizing ways to decrease meat consumption frequency by increasing the availability of vegetarian foods wherever feasible, like becoming a champion for healthy food in hospitals, public cafeterias, and school canteens. More and more succulent, non-meat food choices are helping to change perceptions around the enjoyment and satiability of whole plant foods. Guidance on active living and healthy eating should become the gold standard.

Education

Given the gravity of the consequences, educational institutes at all levels should increase learners' food and media literacy, and their awareness of implications of the agri-industrial-complex. As our authors revealed, well beyond the point of purchase, we pay for our food in utility bills and taxes, and in costs to our personal health, quality of life, and a declining environment. To replace reductionism, higher education is mandated to undertake systems critiques and engage in full-cost accounting. We stress the importance of interdisciplinary studies and research with intelligent data collection for the best decision making for society. Universities ought to replace animal testing and experiments. Graduates should be prepared to harvest emerging opportunities in plant-based foods and product development, as well as the range of services in preventative health and well-being. We need better decision making across society through monitoring and gathering intelligent information and integrating true cost accounting. We anticipate studies of plant-rich living and plant-based diets will achieve greater prominence in universities. We endorse school food programmes that use existing educational resources, build on existing partnerships, wisely monitor process and outcomes, and obtain adequate funding and training, and thereby prepare educators and learners to advocate for policies and orchestrate desired outcomes where all can be fed, nurtured, and loved.

Citizen-consumers and citizen groups

While citizen-consumers may transition gradually to the most protective diet – whole-food, plant-based – it should be an enjoyable and fun time of exploration and experimentation with family and friends. We urge everyone to try new menus and relish dishes from a worldwide cuisine of succulent foods. We reiterate the importance of finding tantalizing ways to incorporate the range of delectable beans and lentils into regular meal planning. With time, taste buds will be reinvigorated for the sweet and sensuous flavours of whole, plant foods. We echo the advice from the Canada Food Guide that we relish every opportunity to eat mindfully and joyfully with others. We encourage more meals made at home that include a wide variety from all the food groups. We encourage citizen-consumers to explore interesting restaurants with friends and family, and the Internet for many varieties of succulent dishes. We advise becoming more adept at preparing staple meals that are efficient, nutritious, and delicious.

Also, we support food movements designed for spreading the power of succulence and sustainability. We applaud visionary leaders, like those highlighted in these chapters, who ignite the imagination and mobilize individuals and communities. Citizens should be encouraged to become active in organizations to reclaim our food systems, question any product's apparent halo, and push for policy changes to ensure producers are held to appropriate standards. For meat alternatives, readers are reminded that they are not cruelty-free if they are produced in ways that harm human health, animals, or the environment. Instead of processed foods or animal-protein-rich diets, citizens can select plant-based options from short supply chains (think: local farmers' markets and local foods, community supported agriculture, and "ugly" food boxes). Eating processed foods with large environmental footprints indirectly entwines our purchases with higher regulations, taxes, and international market speculation. When consumers purchase from shorter supply chains, such as vegetables sold at a farmers' market, we are, in effect, endorsing lower regulatory burdens, requiring fewer laws, and helping to lower the hurdles of taxation. Readers are encouraged to engage in further learning and leading as *Vibrant Eaters & Leaders* in an online community of practice. In this space, we can share tools and techniques to promote, adopt, and enjoy the benefits of plant-rich living. We welcome you to engage with us at eatingavibrantlife.com and www.facebook.com/eatingavibrantlife/

Business/industry

Opportunities for keeping people healthy through better food choices are not passing fads. An economy based on integrity recognizes, respects, and celebrates interdependence in our relationships, particularly exhibiting tremendous humility around planetary capacities and boundaries (O'Neill, Fanning, Lamb, & Steinberger, 2018). For us, our food and the complexity and cohesiveness of our food systems are simultaneously personal and universal, and a visceral opening for deeply appreciating our interdependence. When we commit to respectful and ethical treatment of humans, other animals, and nature, factory farming becomes obsolete and resources can be reinvested into an array of small-scale agricultural businesses that could adopt principles of regenerative, organic, or agro-ecology. The opportunities in this realm are immense, as are the range of emerging *protective diet* businesses. Meat alternative companies and large-scale agribusiness must demonstrate commitments to transparency, food system equity, and public health as central goals of business. We also join with others in advocating for transforming food waste and environmental pollution through innovations in the bio-economy and devising approaches to eliminate food waste.

Further work

Further investigations could be illuminating around strategies that increase adoption of more plant-based living and show indications of greater sustainability. We also wish to inquire into how schools of agriculture could take a leadership role in addressing the challenges in sustainable food systems. We also want to know more about success stories of local and regional strategies that advance food security and the SDGs while living within our planetary boundaries.

Conclusion

Shifting food systems is humanity's biggest challenge and greatest opportunity. With this collection, we wanted to underscore the sensuality of food and the sacredness around the production, consumption, and respect for the full life cycle of food. Transformation towards global sustainable diets is required. In this multidisciplinary collection, with its authoritative insights, we seek to mobilize actors from all sectors to recognize the urgency for coordinated, coherent, and compassionate actions. We are calling on governments foremost to leverage their assets and authority, along with industry leaders, academia, civil society, and decision makers, all interested citizens really, to work with us for policy changes and behavioural shifts that ensure more succulent and sustainable plant-based foods are produced and consumed. We trust you have richly consumed, digested, and now are well fuelled to take needed action. The stakes have never been higher, and our capacity for resolution must exceed our challenges. If we do, as the

EAT-Lancet commission suggests, "get it right on food" and make plant-based food our default, we will be securing our common future and improving lives everywhere. We ask for your ideas and collaboration. We know we can do this, and we trust we will not fail to take immediate and strategic actions together.

References

Albert, C. O., & Isife, B. I. (2009). Issues in developing a national policy on agricultural extension service in Nigeria: The perception of extension professionals. *Agricultural Journal, 4*(1), 22–26.

Arnold, R. D., & Wade, J. P. (2015). A definition of systems thinking: A systems approach. *Procedia Computer Science, 44,* 669–678.

Barer-Stein, T. (1979). *You eat what you are: A study of Canadian ethnic food traditions.* Toronto, Canada: McClelland and Stewart.

Bell, A. C., & Dyment, J. E. (2008). Grounds for health: The intersection of green school grounds and health-promoting schools. *Environmental Education Research, 14*(1), 77–90.

Bergman, M. M. (2019, February 15). Florida is drowning. Condos are still being built. Can't humans see the writing on the wall? *The Guardian.* Retrieved from www.theguardian.com/

Campbell, T. C., & Campbell, T. M. (2004/2006). *The China study: The most comprehensive study of nutrition ever conducted and the startling implications for diet, weight loss and long-term health.* Dallas, TX: BenBella Books.

Campbell, T. C., & Jacobson, H. (2013/2014). *Whole: Rethinking the science of nutrition.* Dallas, TX: BenBella Books.

Carrington, D. (2018, October 10). Huge reduction in meat-eating 'essential' to avoid climate breakdown. *The Guardian.* Retrieved from www.theguardian.com/

Charlebois, S., Somogyi, S., & Music, J. (2018). *Release: New Dalhousie study finds that 6.4 million Canadians limit the amount of meat they eat, and number will likely grow.* Retrieved from www.dal.ca/faculty/management/news-events/news/2018/10/30/release__new_dalhousie_study_finds_that_6_4_million_canadians_limit_the_amount_of_meat_they_eat__and_number_will_likely_grow.html

Cleveland, D. A. (2014). *Balancing on a planet: The future of food and agriculture.* Berkeley, CA: University of California Press.

Esselstyn, C. B., Jr., Gendy, G., Doyle, J., Golubic, M., & Roizen, M. F. (2014). A way to reverse CAD? *Journal of Family Practice, 63*(7), 356–364.

Etzioni, A. (2006). Voluntary simplicity: Characterization, select psychological implications and societal consequences. In T. Jackson (Ed.), *The Earthscan reader in sustainable consumption* (pp. 159–178). London, UK: Earthscan.

Food and Agriculture Organization of the United Nations (FAO). (2018). *The future of food and agriculture – Alternative pathways to 2050* [Summary version]. Rome, Italy: FAO.

Forestell, C. A., Spaeth, A. M., & Kane, S. A. (2012). To eat or not to eat red meat. A closer look at the relationship between restrained eating and vegetarianism in college females. *Appetite, 58*(1), 319–325.

Greiner, R., Patterson, L., & Miller, O. (2009). Motivations, risk perceptions and adoption of conservation practices by farmers. *Agricultural Systems, 99*(2–3), 86–104.

Grunwald, M. (2019). Inside the race to build the burger of the future. *Politico Magazine*. Retrieved from www.politico.com/magazine/

Haden, V. R., Niles, M. T., Lubell, M., Perlman, J., & Jackson, L. E. (2012). Global and local concerns: What attitudes and beliefs motivate farmers to mitigate and adapt to climate change? *PLoS One*, 7(12), e52882.

Hawken, P. (Ed.). (2016). *Drawdown: The most comprehensive plan ever proposed to reverse global warming*. New York, NY: Penguin Books.

Henchion, M., Hayes, M., Mullen, A., Fenelon, M., & Tiwari, B. (2017). Future protein supply and demand: Strategies and factors influencing a sustainable equilibrium. *Foods*, 6(7), 53.

Latham, J. (2016). *Food liberation: Why the food movement is unstoppable*. Retrieved from www.independentsciencenews.org/health/why-the-food-movement-is-unstoppable/

Lea, E. J., Crawford, D., & Worsley, A. (2006). Public views of the benefits and barriers to the consumption of a plant-based diet. *European Journal of Clinical Nutrition*, 60(7), 828–837. doi:10.1038/sj.ejcn.1602387

Martynenko, A. (2019). What is the future of intelligent systems in drying? In A. Martynenko & A. Bück (Eds.), *Intelligent control in drying* (1st ed., pp. 441–443). Boca Raton, FL: CRC Press.

Meadows, D. H. (2008). *Thinking in systems: A primer*. White River Junction, VT: Chelsea Green Publishing.

Nilsson, M., Zamparutti, T., Petersen, J. E., Nykvist, B., Rudberg, P., & McGuinn, J. (2012). Understanding policy coherence: Analytical framework and examples of sector-environmental policy interactions in the EU. *Environmental Policy and Governance*, 22, 395–423.

O'Neill, D. W., Fanning, A. L., Lamb, W. F., & Steinberger, J. K. (2018). A good life for all within planetary boundaries. *Nature Sustainability*, 1(2), 88.

Project Drawdown. (2014–2019). *Summary of solutions by overall rank*. Retrieved from www.drawdown.org/solutions-summary-by-rank

Public Health Agency of Canada (PHAC). (2013). *Preventing chronic disease strategic plan 2013–2016*. Retrieved from http://publications.gc.ca/collections/collection_2014/aspc-phac/HP35-39-2013-eng.pdf

Pulse Canada. (2015). *Measuring what matters, shifting focus from practice-based to outcome-based*. Internal document, Pulse Canada.

Qualman, D. (2018). *$100 billion and rising: Canadian farm debt*. Retrieved from www.darrinqualman.com/canadian-farm-debt/

Qualman, D. (2019). *Civilization critical: Energy, food, nature and the future*. Halifax, Canada: Fernwood Publishing.

Schug, D. (2016, November 30). The top 10 food trends for 2017 from Innova Market Insights. *Food Engineering*. Retrieved from www.foodengineeringmag.com/articles/96332-the-top-10-food-trends-for-2017-from-innova-market-insights

Searchinger, T., Waite, R., Hanson, C., Ranganathan, J., Dumas, P., & Matthews, E. (2018). *World resources report: Creating a sustainable food future*. Washington, DC: World Resource Institute.

Seyfang, G. (2006). Ecological citizenship and sustainable consumption: Examining local organic food networks. *Journal of Rural Studies*, 22(4), 383–395.

Smithers, R. (2018, November 1). Third of Britons have stopped or reduced eating meat – Report. *The Guardian*. Retrieved from www.theguardian.com/

Statistics Canada. (2011). *Fruit and vegetable consumption, 2011*. Retrieved from https://www150.statcan.gc.ca/n1/pub/82-625-x/2012001/article/11661-eng.htm

Ungar, P. S. (2018). The real paleo diet. *Scientific American, 22*(Suppl. 5), 44–49.

Waitrose & Partners. (2018). *Food and drink report 2018–19*. Retrieved from www.waitrose.com/content/dam/waitrose/Inspiration/Waitrose%20&%20Partners%20Food%20and%20Drink%20Report%202018.pdf

Watkins, A., & Wilber, K. (2015). *Wicked & wise: How to solve the world's toughest problems*. Croydon, UK: Urbane Publications.

Wilber, K. (2001). *A theory of everything: An integral vision for business, politics, science and spirituality*. Boulder, CO: Shambhala Publications.

Willett, W., Rockström, J., Loken, B., Springmann, M., Lang, T., Vermeulen, S., . . . Jonell, M. (2019). Food in the Anthropocene: The EAT – Lancet Commission on healthy diets from sustainable food systems. *The Lancet, 393*(10170), 447–492.

Index

Note: page numbers in *italics* indicate figures and those in **bold** indicate tables.

For Product Safety Concerns and Information please contact our EU
representative GPSR@taylorandfrancis.com
Taylor & Francis Verlag GmbH, Kaufingerstraße 24, 80331 München, Germany

www.ingramcontent.com/pod-product-compliance
Ingram Content Group UK Ltd.
Pitfield, Milton Keynes, MK11 3LW, UK
UKHW021005180425
457613UK00019B/818